Growth Through Governance

What Every Jewish Nonprofit Leader Needs To Know

Rabbi Jeremy Sher

Mazo Publishers

11/3/17 Dear Tammy! Thanks you for visiting us at Ha-Emek this evening! It was wonderful to have you with us.

Growth Through Governance:
What Every Jewish Nonprofit Leader Needs To Know

ISBN 978-1-936778-07-2

Published by

Mazo Publishers
P.O. Box 10474
Jacksonville, FL 32247 USA

www.mazopublishers.com
Email: mazopublishers@gmail.com
Tel: 1-815-301-3559

DEDICATION

This book is dedicated to people who took risks in order to give me a chance to do something of value.

It is dedicated first to Rabbi Natan Margalit, without whom I could never have found my way to rabbinical study. After four years seeking a path to the rabbinate, I made a sincere prayer that I might dwell in God's house, as in Psalm 27:4. I focused singly on that goal, whatever it might mean, until I was introduced to Natan and worked up the courage to talk to him. I found in him a kind teacher and a friend of intellectual integrity and spiritual depth, one who nurtures my fortitude and demands my decency.

It is dedicated, too, to Rabbi Debra Kolodny and Rabbi Mira Raz, who joined with Natan to form the *bet din* (committee) to witness my rabbinic ordination. They are my teachers and my friends.

It is also dedicated to Paul Berendt and the Hon. Larry Gossett, two men who each hired me when I must have seemed the least logical candidate, both at times when I happened to be in need of a chance. I hope I proved the wisdom of the risks they took on me. I still have the copy of my résumé on which someone crossed out the word "NO" and wrote "MAYBE."

It is dedicated to Rabbi Liza Stern, who, despite the irregularity of the request, the lack of precedent, the lack of budget, and countless other reasons it would have been perfectly normal to say no to me, nevertheless brought me on as Rabbinic Intern at Congregation Eitz Chayim in Cambridge, Mass., in order to give me the chance to have that internship as part of my rabbinic training.

It is particularly dedicated to my family, my parents Gerson and Margery, my brother Adam and my sister-in-law Meg, whose confidence in me has never wavered despite my ambitions and ideas probably often seeming all over the map, and who, despite their many risks on my behalf over the years, kept signing up for more. It is dedicated especially to my little nephew Eli Abraham: may this be the least interesting book of many he shall be privileged to love.

This book is further dedicated to the brave leaders who take risks on mentoring people who need a chance and seem worth developing. To them and to those who learn from them, may all your dreams gush into reality like torrents of lifegiving rain.

TABLE OF CONTENTS

ACKNOWLEDGMENTS

I crowdsourced advice on this book using a Facebook group. I wish to thank Rabbi Meir Azari, Barbara Ballinger, Aaron Chandler, Rabbi Getzel Davis, Ashwini Deshpande, Eran Dror, Jonathan Fields, Deborah Elizabeth Finn, Eric Flamm, Brian Gale, Rabbi Jordie Gerson, Rabbi Jeffrey Greenberg, Mary Higdon, Jonathan Karp, Anita Latch, Dorie Lee, Jessica Leuchter, Nicky McCatty, Mohamed Mansoor, Wanda Moats, Lior Nagar, Gary Pickholz, Rabbi Mira Raz, Lex Rofes, Jonathan Daniel Roger, Dana Schweppe, Zhelinrentice Levels Scott, Galit Sher, Rabbi Oren Steinitz, and Serena Waxworth for being part of the group and participating in the conversation as we read the drafts together.

I'm especially grateful to Lior Aryeora, Randy Carlton, Ilona Gerbakher, Leigh Ann Hildebrand, Martin Rawlings-Fein, Rabbi Haim Shalom, Adam Sher, and Jackie Frankel Yaakov for their insights and advice.

To Stacey Minott Hardy, John Hollywood, Rabbi Natan Margalit, Gerson Sher, Margery Sher, Mark Stought, and especially Penina Weinberg, I owe a special debt of gratitude. They read significant portions of the book and provided detailed comments that were invaluable to me as I tried to get all of this right.

Finally, I'd like to thank Alex Lee, who in addition to participating in the Facebook group, salvaged this project in his kindness by sending me a surprise refurbished laptop, after the laptop I bought in Israel had an unfortunate encounter with the Mediterranean Sea just a month before this manuscript was due to the publisher. That's the last time I get the clever idea to work on a beach: not the best decision, even if it did happen to be in beautiful Yafo, where long ago Jonah made a bad decision of his own.[1]

In this book, we'll talk about making better decisions.

---

[1] Jonah 1:3.

FOREWORD

After 20 years leading organizations as a professional and as a volunteer, I reflected how nice it would have been if, starting out, I'd known some of the skills, rules of thumb, tricks of the trade and opportunities for growth and joy that I've since learned. I'd have liked to write a letter to my former self, to share experience, save myself a lot of trouble, and highlight opportunities to learn. This book is an even better idea: a letter to you.

I write with over thirty years' combined experience on eight nonprofit boards, including four fiduciary boards, one government agency (the Seattle Human Rights Commission) and three non-fiduciary boards. I also bring the lessons of seven years as a political technology executive, partially overlapping with seven years in software entrepreneurship. I've been a leader of Jewish and secular organizations, synagogues on two continents, advocacy groups and civic organizations. My experiences in software and big data have led me to consider how best practices from those cutting-edge fields might apply to fiduciary and professional work in nonprofits.

I received ordination after a unique program with my longtime teacher, Rabbi Natan Margalit, and I'm honored to be a Jewish Renewal rabbi. As part of my studies, I earned my Master of Divinity degree from Harvard Divinity School, where I was honored with the prestigious Ministry Fellowship and a Sheldon Traveling Fellowship to fund a year in Israel. While in Israel, I became involved with a Reform synagogue in Yafo; the strategic-planning workshop and report I did for them were my first in Hebrew. May there be more!

For the volunteer leader or team manager, this book is worth buying just for the entirely original essays "How to Run a Good Meeting" and "Managing the Unplanned Project—and Why You'd Rather Not." Anyone concerned about insufficient volunteer power will find challenge and food for thought in Chapter 5, "Board and Committee Leadership," and Chapter 7, "People Management," while strategists in all walks of nonprofit life will appreciate the selection of "Strategic Issues Most Synagogues Face." Jewish text lovers will find the *shiurim* (lessons from Jewish text) to offer serious, fresh scholarship while specifically introducing the governance subject matter of each chapter. I believe my "Ethics" essay positions this book among the strictest and most careful approaches to ethics on the scene.

This book is also a one-stop shop for learning about professional project management, contemporary productivity practices like Scrum and Pomodoro, and high-level metrics of organizational capability or capacity, newly and originally applied to nonprofit and specifically Jewish organizations, all explained in plain English and put in the context of spiritual nonprofit leadership.

I hope the book will be entertaining, too. Filled with stories from the trenches, illustrative characters like worker bees, Dominators and Uncle Moe, and concepts like legitimacy, stagnation, working boards, the rejection-rework cycle, inspiration points and smiley-face messaging, I hope this book will be both useful and fun to read.

The book is intended for a general audience, but the footnotes are intended to appeal to a scholarly audience. I have not footnoted statements which stem from common experience or which are my opinion. Footnotes offer information, support my interpretations, or highlight disagreements and areas of continuing research. At times the footnotes take excursions from the main topic, in the interest of thoroughly investigating questions of scholarship.

Translations are mine, except as noted. The Jewish Publication Society 1917 translation of the Bible,[2] available at *mechon-mamre.org*, is referred to simply as the JPS. The Soncino Press translation of the Talmud,[3] available at *halakhah.com*, is referred to as the Soncino. Other translators are cited as their work appears.

Mishnaic sources are cited using M. *(Masechet) x:y* for chapter *x*, *mishnah y*, in the cited *masechet*/tractate. Sources in Gemara are cited using b. *Masechet* 2a style, where the "b." indicates the Bavli or a "j." indicates the Yerushalmi, and the *daf* (number) and *amud* (a/b) replace the "2a."

Let's learn together. Join me on my website, *npgovernance.org*, where we can discuss any aspect of the book, and where I hope conversation among readers will emerge. You and I are colleagues in the holy work of leading mission-driven organizations. May God establish the work of our hands.

Rabbi Jeremy D. Sher, M.Div.
Cambridge, Massachusetts

---

[2] Margolis et al. (1917).

[3] Epstein et al. (1935–1952).

Chapter 1
INTRODUCTION

1.1 SHIUR

> *Ben Bag Bag used to say: Turn it and turn it again, for everything is in it. Look into it, get gray and old over it. Stir not from it, for you can have no better rule than it.*
> *Ben Heh Heh used to say: According to the effort is the reward.*
>
> M. *Pirkei Avot* 5:22–23[4]

These words end the section of Talmud called Mishnah *Pirkei Avot*,[5] and they begin this book.

"Everything is in it," says our text, referring to the Torah. The ancient Rabbis saw their work—the Talmud and its interpretations of the *Tanach* (Bible)—as many interconnected webs of topics that, together, touch every area of life. As we learn together throughout this book, our discussions of nonprofit governance will be intricately interconnected with Torah.

Each chapter in this book begins with a *shiur* (plural *shiurim*)—a lesson on Jewish text. I've chosen selections from the Bible, Talmud, even Kabbalah to provide a new or original Torah lesson that takes just a few pages to place the chapter's specific governance

---

[4] I've adapted this translation based on the Soncino and the version at *shechem.org*. There is not unanimity on the numbering or sometimes the order of text in the Talmud. The Soncino's note 152 to Chapter 5 states that some scholars place this at the end of Chapter 6, the final chapter of *Pirkei Avot* which was added on after Mishnaic times, while *shechem.org* doesn't even show Chapter 6 as part of *Pirkei Avot* (and also shows these words as *mishnayot* 25–26; I went with the Soncino's numbering). In any case, these words were certainly intended as the end of *Pirkei Avot*. I finessed that issue by saying they end Mishnah *Pirkei Avot*. See the Soncino's note 2 to Chapter 6.

[5] The name *Pirkei Avot* means Chapters of the Fathers/Ancestors, or alternatively, just Important Principles. It is a collection of proverbs and life advice. It is sometimes called *Ethics of the Fathers* because its subject matter deals with ethics and upright living.

topic within the Jewish textual conversation. At the same time, the *shiurim* are intended to stand on their own as scholarship, and might be studied as commentaries on the Torah text.

"Everything is in it." Isn't it remarkable that millennia later, a book on nonprofit corporate leadership would turn out to take place within the Jewish people's ancient conversation, drawing meaning from our text and applying the text in ways both time-honored and new? What a privilege it is for me to add my piece to this ongoing conversation, on the way paved by so many scholars, readers, thinkers, leaders, and offerers of prayer.

1.2 ABOUT THIS BOOK

This is a companion volume to the many excellent resources out there on the governance of nonprofits. It includes my perspective as a rabbi, often taking Jewish examples but always with the intention of broad applicability. It is not a how-to, although it may suggest where and how to find resources. It does not provide model bylaws or structures, although it considers the benefits and drawbacks of many different organizational models.

I've devoted the limited space here mostly to explaining terminology, making sense of concepts from strategy to tactical management, with a particularly strong emphasis on ethics. I've duplicated little of what already appears in accessible, high-quality resources such as BoardSource.

BoardSource merits special mention up front. It is a nonprofit that exists to help other nonprofits be well governed. It provides a tremendous wealth of resources at *BoardSource.org*. I'm a member of BoardSource, and I recommend that you be a member, too.

I also especially recommend the excellent book by Mark Light, *The Strategic Board*.[6] Light is an extraordinarily astute observer of organizations and people. I agree with him often, but not always. His omnipresent charts make his ideas clear at a glance, and his explanatory text is friendly and sharp.

---

[6] Light (2001).

A Jewish Approach to Nonprofit Governance

I set out to write a book about synagogue governance, but quickly realized that 95% of this material is applicable to any Jewish organization, and 90% of it is applicable to any nonprofit. This book, therefore, presents a Jewish approach to nonprofit governance. Most of the examples taken are from synagogue governance, although other examples are also used.

This book is for board members, volunteers and staff alike—anyone interested in being of service through a nonprofit organization. Whether you're a synagogue, a Jewish advocacy or service organization, a secular charitable or educational organization, or indeed a church or other house of worship, this book is for you.

This book offers all that I wish that someone had told me before I began serving on nonprofit boards. I've tried to explain in plain language what's going on at the many levels of our organizations. There are also many new insights from emerging management best practices that have yet to be applied systematically to nonprofits. I believe nonprofits can and ought to be at the leading edge of management.

Structure of the Book

This book begins with the highest-level ideas and proceeds logically to lower-level issues. Roughly the first half of the book—chapters 2 through 5—deal with board oversight and volunteer leadership, while chapters 7 through 11 deal mostly with management issues. Chapter 6 deals with money, including accounting and revenue, and is a suitable fulcrum between the oversight and management halves of the book. But these lines are not hard-and-fast; the entire book is presented with the idea that it's good for boards to know about management best practices, even if they should let their managers manage, and it's good for staffers to know about oversight and ethics, even if they're taking, rather than making, the direction in those areas. From board president to entry-level staff, there's something in each chapter for everyone.

The book builds on itself, starting with the concept of an organizational decision, and moving down through strategy, fiduciary oversight, high-level policies, volunteer management, financial issues, people management, project management, productivity management, and process management. Each chapter can stand on its own, although each offers the richest meaning when read sequentially after those coming before it.

My Website: *npgovernance.org*
There's a website accompanying this book, at *npgovernance.org*. The website has a wealth of additional information and resources, stories from the trenches, and case studies, and it's also a place for conversation. Every post on the website accepts your comments, and I'll do my best to reply as people ask questions and post comments. You and I are colleagues, and we can consult and collaborate online.

Throughout the book, you will see *hard links* (also called *QR codes*)—those square dot patterns like the one on this page. These codes are actually website links, and smartphones are able to view the hard link and open your browser to the linked site. Try it if you have a smartphone handy. Smartphone or no, each individual essay in every chapter has its own section on the website, accessible through a menu, where all the resources for that essay are posted and more may be added as well.

I hope to see you on *npgovernance.org* as we comment, discuss, and learn together.

Chapter 2
STRATEGIC ISSUES

2.1 SHIUR

> *A spark of impenetrable darkness flashed within the concealed of the concealed, from the head of Infinity—a cluster of vapor forming in formlessness, thrust in a ring, not white, not black, not red, not green, no color at all. As a cord surveyed, it yielded radiant colors. Deep within the spark gushed a flow, splaying colors below . . .*
>
> Zohar I:15a[7]

Life is full of decisions. In a way, decisions are the building blocks of life.

I used to work in a company with an office in London, and whenever my British colleagues meant to say that they wouldn't have made the same decision, they said, "That was brave." Perhaps it was brave of me to start our discussion with a text that does not make sense. In this *shiur*, I will give one of an infinitude of possible interpretations. I want to make sure people don't think mine is the only or the authoritative interpretation: it's just the one that will do for our purposes right now.

Our text is from the Zohar, the great book of Kabbalah that comments on the Torah from a deep and convoluted mystical perspective. The Zohar is commenting on how creation happened. It envisions a "dark spark"[8] suddenly appearing, and from that spark a world formed.

---

[7] Translation by Rabbi Daniel Matt, in Matt (2004–2014), vol. 1, pp. 107–110. Also see Matt (2004–2014), vol. 3, p. 40, on Zohar 1:172a.

[8] The term "dark spark," *botzina d'kardinuta* in Aramaic, is unclear from the outset, a phrase rife with coded references to obscure sources and preexisting understandings. See Rabbi Matt's substantial footnote 4 on pp. 107ff (vol. 1). For now, although *botzina* does not usually mean *spark* and *d'kardinuta* does not usually mean *dark*, we will content ourselves with "dark spark" as a simple

Why dark? It's unexpected for the world to come from a dark spark, rather than a spark of light against a dark background. But darkness is not evil in Judaism. Light is a positive image throughout Jewish text, but dark, evening and shade are often positive images, too. Take it from me: living in sun-drenched Israel is one way to learn that light and shade can both be pleasant and necessary. That's an important key: Judaism is not focused on dueling dualities, like light against darkness. Judaism insists instead that everything is God.[9]

I see the dark spark appearing against a background of primordial light: the light of infinite possibility, an idea I got from a scene in Rabbi Lawrence Kushner's wonderful novel *Kabbalah: A Love Story*.[10] In this view, the first creation was an undifferentiated white light, symbolizing an infinitude of possibility. That's the raw material of reality. Everything since then has been a subtractive, rather than an additive, creation.

We often think of creative work as being additive: adding paint to a canvas, adding words to a page, adding musical notes to a score. But art can also be subtractive. When Michelangelo was asked how he created such beautiful sculptures, he is said to have replied that he could see the sculpture in the block of marble, and simply chipped away the material that wasn't part of the sculpture.[11]

So it is with the white light of possibility, the raw material of the world. Before creation, when everything was possible but nothing was actual, this white light shone with an undifferentiated brightness. But in order for anything to reach actuality, we must extinguish possibilities. All of a sudden it happened: an infinite number of *could-have-beens* collapsed into an *is*. God extinguished part of the possible to make room for the actual. In this view, the dark spark represents a multiplicity of possibilities condensing into an actuality. We understand this as a decision.

---

translation. It will become important that *d'kardinuta* also implies impenetrable hardness.

[9] See the highly recommended book of that name by Rabbi Jay Michaelson (Michaelson, 2009).

[10] Kushner (2006), pp. 190–191.

[11] I am not enough of a Michelangelo scholar to know whether and when the great sculptor actually said this, but it is attested in numerous contemporary sources. See, for an example pertinent to my life, Brohaugh (1993), p. 12.

All subsequent decisions are like that. Infinite possibilities lie before us, but in order to get anything, we must choose among our options. We cannot have all of the flavors of ice cream on one cone. In order to obtain a couple flavors at a time, we must choose to forgo all the rest. That is how our decisions work. The world began complete with all possibilities; our job is to whittle them down into realities. God has made the raw material, the possibilities of what could be. And we are God's sculptors, deciding what will be.[12]

In our text, white light is the presence of all colors at once. As we erase possibilities to make room for reality, in different places across the canvas of possibility, some of those colors go out. Now the light isn't an undifferentiated white anymore, but colors appear. Forms come to life. A foreground appears against the background.

Every decision today is a further dark spark to add to God's original creation. It may seem startling to say we can make our own dark sparks of decision, but this view of the Zohar text leads us there. Most of our decisions are much more mundane than that first dark spark of God's. But not all of them, for the Talmud teaches, "Whoever saves a life is credited as if they had saved an entire universe."[13] The Talmud appears to be saying that lifesaving is a

---

[12] The question whether God is also a sculptor—whether God makes decisions that change the reality of the created world—is too big for this *shiur*, but please visit *npgovernance.org* to discuss my take on it. In short, there is a lot of support in Jewish text for the view that God actively "sculpts," working with the originally created raw material of possibility to change the reality of the world—but that this activity is very different from that of the original creation. God may be active as a "sculptor," but God does not seem to create new possibilities that were not already possible at the first creation.

[13] M. Sanhedrin 4:5. Translation original. There is not unanimity on the Mishnah text, and the Mishnah student may have noticed that some texts have "Whoever saves a life *from within Israel*" (*miyisrael*), thus apparently restricting the matter of lifesaving to Jews. See, for example, the difference between Sefaria.org and the Wikisource Mishnah (best accessed through a search engine): the former has *miyisrael* in the text and the latter does not. I have omitted "from within Israel" from my translation, on the grounds that even Sefaria's English translation does not include it, and the sources I've consulted concur, importantly including Yad Vashem's website, which one would expect to be as focused on saving Jewish lives as anyone could be. I have stuck to the more usual, universal interpretation of lifesaving in deference to the unanimity of these sources. It doesn't change the argument I make in the *shiur*, in any case. All cited Internet sources accessed August 3, 2015.

decision that could preserve an entire world, so I don't think it's overboard to call that decision a dark spark on a par with, if not quite equivalent to, the original. Even though most of our decisions are not that momentous, all of them affect the course of the world. With large or small strokes, all of our decisions chisel God's block of possibilities into a sculpture of reality. It is in our power to make our work beautiful.

One pitfall that leads to indecisiveness is to fear the dark spark because it is dark. But we must choose what we want over what we do not want. If we don't decide, we create nothing at all. There is certainly a sense of loss to chiseling, but that's the price of art. So decisiveness is all about chipping off possibilities, like a sculptor chips off marble. Decisiveness is us following God in the beauty of co-creation.

2.2 MAKING DECISIONS TOGETHER

"Oh, I know what decisions are," readers will say. And they should, because we all know what decisions are. The question is what organizations are. The answer, for the purposes of this book, is that organizations are things that make decisions. They make those decisions on behalf of, and through the involvement of, people.

That's an interesting way of starting a discussion about organizations. You might define organizations as things that bring people together for a purpose. One of the great benefits of studying organizations from a Jewish perspective is that we don't have to content ourselves with only one interpretation at a time: multiple interpretations can be right. So let's spend some time thinking of organizations as making decisions.

Every organization makes decisions, from a restaurant dinner party with friends, to the most powerful nation on earth, to the oldest religious group still continuously practicing. What would we like to do together? What kind of pizza would our group like to order? What kind of building would our members like to build? Would we like to draw with crayons or play with trucks? Would we like to spend a certain amount of time or money creating beautiful music or offering a new educational program for the children? From earliest consciousness throughout our lives, we make decisions together.

The question "What's a decision?" now becomes more interesting. An organizational decision is more than just a personal choice of pizza. It's based on a process of taking into account multiple sources of information and preference, a process of coming to an answer, along with some form of commitment to the decision once made. Whether we're having a synagogue capital campaign committee meeting or a dinner party, a decision is the first thing that belongs to the organization corporately, not to any one individual.

If three people bring their own lunches and eat together, you have a group but not an organization. If one person brings lunch and shares it with others, you have a generous individual, but still not an organization. But as soon as multiple people participate in deciding together, the decision no longer belongs to any individual person. The decision belongs to the organization.[14] If there wasn't an organization before, there is now, as soon as a joint decision is made.

Decisions and Legitimacy

There's a certain magic to decisions. In some sense, a decision made by an organization has a higher status than the preference of an individual person. There's a decision-making process, agreed upon in advance and recognized by multiple people as fair. Such decisions command more attention and weight than they would if made by an individual acting alone. It's not about the decision being right: an individual could have the Right Answer and the organization could have the Wrong Answer, and the organization would still receive more deference because multiple people's opinions were taken into account through a fair, agreed-upon process.[15]

Legitimacy is the name we give to the weight organizational decisions carry. It is why many organizations get formed at all.

---

[14] My perspective is different from that of Light (2001), p. 115. The similarities and differences would make an interesting discussion on *npgovernance.org*.

[15] The delightfully complex Talmudic story of the Oven of Akhnai provides a quintessentially Jewish example of the "Wrong Answer" enjoying organizational legitimacy. Legitimacy does not always mean the decision is right! Majorities very often make decisions that are wrong. Visit *npgovernance.org* to read the story and my commentary. The tension between the legitimate decision and the right one could frame a great scholar-in-residence weekend.

Rather than remaining content to gripe about the policies of King George III, several dozen farmers incorporated the United States of America as a vehicle for the legitimacy of their mutual decisions and subsequent laws. Several generations later, a fragment of world Jewry did a similar thing, beginning with the World Zionist Congress in the late 19th century and culminating in the State of Israel.

Advocacy organizations like the ADL, JCRCs, AIPAC and J Street follow a similar trajectory: creating an organization gives a name to a decision-making process, and confers a legitimacy that individual letters to the editor cannot. Benevolent organizations like UJA, B'nai B'rith, the Jewish National Fund, Magen David Adom and the New Israel Fund form to pool their resources and direct funds as a group. Movement organizations and rabbinical associations like the Union for Reform Judaism, the Rabbinical Assembly, or Aleph: The Alliance for Jewish Renewal form to decide questions of Jewish identity and practice together. Synagogues, viewed in this light, come together to figure out what sort of community those involved would like to be, how to educate children, to hire rabbis and staff, and to make the decade-to-decade and day-to-day decisions that implement those organizations' larger decisions about shared identity and goals.

One corollary, to which we'll often return, has far-reaching implications for strategy, ethics and management: There is no such thing as fiat; there is only legitimacy. Nobody does anything just because they're told to. This is a general law. In Orthodox Judaism, legitimacy may have different components with different weightings than in Reform Judaism, but the general law is the same: free people follow rules, conventions or directions because they give those rules, conventions or directions legitimacy—not just because they are told to do so.[16]

We may support a legitimate organization because we agree with its identity, mission and values, because its internal processes are fair and we have previously agreed to them, because we are given a satisfactory chance for our voice to be heard, because our belief in giving our fellow members that same opportunity trumps

---

[16] I am excluding situations of duress for the purpose of this discussion, but even there the law applies. Compliance due to fear of punishment is not at all similar to compliance for its own sake. For people free of duress, legitimacy is what motivates compliance with rules. See *npgovernance.org* for a text study in which the Rabbis struggle with the legitimacy of Jewish commandedness.

our desire to have everything done our way, because we care about the organization and therefore to some extent take on its priorities and welfare as our own, because the organization is predictable in the process it uses to make decisions, so that we know what to do if we wish to influence it. These are several of the many components of legitimacy. They explain why we feel the organization's decisions matter to us.

Legitimacy is the coin of an organization's ability to make those decisions. It underlies the reason for our organization to exist. An organization's health can be measured in legitimacy. If legitimacy is low (may it not occur), by reason of poor decision-making processes, ethical violations, continued failure to reflect members' preferences, or other problems at the core of legitimacy, we naturally start wondering why we keep the organization going. High legitimacy, on the other hand, means not merely that people defer to the organization's corporate decisions, but also that those decisions are such, and are made in such a way, that people want to sign onto them and help implement them, and have a role in formulating them. In short, decisions are legitimate because people feel they own them.

Legitimacy comes from the heart. It can't be bought, and it can't be faked. Everyone knows when it's there, and everyone knows when it's not there. Later in this book we will discuss organizations' more tangible assets, from real estate to endowments to money in the bank, even including the commitment and love of members, leaders and staff. Legitimacy is intangible, and so basic that we're talking about it right here at the beginning of our discussion. Manage your organization's legitimacy as its most valuable asset.

Criteria for Revisiting Decisions

It is sometimes tempting to revisit a decision recently made—especially a contentious decision. Maybe someone missed the board meeting and now has something to add, or maybe a narrowly outvoted minority loudly demands additional time for argument. Reopening recent decisions is almost always a bad move. I can't say always because I don't believe in always and never, but having gone through this a half-dozen times on boards, I'm very skeptical.

Perhaps an issue was wrongly decided. But when we reopen a discussion that was just closed, we call into question whether any decision can ever be final. The organization's ability to be taken at its word is usually worth more than whatever could be gained by reopening the issue. The time to give everyone a chance to be heard is before, not after, the decision gets made.

This is not to say you should never reconsider decisions, just that reconsidering them too soon is usually a mistake. The following criteria may help determine when reopening a previous decision might be wise.

It is always appropriate to reopen a previous decision when:

- It comes up in a periodic self-evaluation. We will discuss self-evaluation below.
- Enough time has gone by that you can assess how the decision worked in practice. This length of time depends on the scope of the decision. If you've bought neon-colored staplers that the children don't like, it's probably okay to return the staplers already without further worry about legitimacy. If you've built an addition onto your building, wait several decades before knocking it down because the community no longer likes the architecture. Most of the decisions we make fit somewhere between those examples.

It is sometimes appropriate to reopen a previous decision when:

- There is a strong negative backlash that *surprises you*. If you were expecting flak, now is the time to show decisiveness and patiently explain what was decided and why. If you thought people would love the decision and they don't, find out why. Perhaps the decision can be adjusted without starting all over again.
- It is clear *to you* that a serious procedural mistake was made. By *you*, I mean the person or persons in charge of managing the decision. There are always going to be people claiming a procedural mistake in the aftermath of any contentious decision. If you're not convinced, do not reopen discussion. If *you* realize that *you* erred procedurally, consider reopening the issue.

  This strictly applies to procedural matters only. It is not about whether someone came up with a new argument that wasn't heard during the meeting. The question is not whether the discussion was complete (what discussion is ever complete?) but whether it was fair.

- New information becomes available. Give serious criticism to just how new, and just how important, that information is. Does it merely support a counterargument that's already been heard, or does it objectively change the entire discussion, rendering a previous decision invalid for incontrovertible moral or ethical reasons that had been either unknown or wrongfully overlooked?

If a person was found guilty of a crime, and they later find the real criminal at large, one would want to reopen the trial. But that's not because of the new information; it's because of the overarching moral imperative to catch the right person and not to penalize an innocent person. If instead the decision had been about choosing teams for the annual office volleyball game, and it turned out someone had been assigned to the team for last names N–Z when in fact their name was Calderon-Shapiro and not just Shapiro, it's probably not worth choosing teams again.

Or, if a group orders a pizza with green peppers and onions, and it turns out the friend who was in the restroom doesn't like green peppers, it's probably not worth sending the pizza back to the kitchen. Nobody wants to be part of a dinner party that sends back an order under such circumstances: it has low legitimacy. The friend who doesn't like green peppers can pick them off. On the other hand, if they ordered pepperoni and then find out that the friend who was in the restroom keeps kosher but eats vegetarian out, they would then reopen the decision, even if that means apologetically paying for the uneaten pepperoni pizza and ordering another one.

The information is not the issue. Organizational values are the issue. Perhaps those values include keeping kosher, or making space for those who keep kosher. If the group had illegitimately overlooked their values, one would want to correct the error.

In a way, each of these cases is about which course will best steward the organization's legitimacy. If some overarching value or imperative hinges on new information, so that the legitimacy of that value outweighs the legitimacy of letting decision stand, then reopening the decision can increase legitimacy by owning up to and correcting a mistake. If not, I doubt if any new information is worth the cost in legitimacy of reopening a recent decision.

Now sure, reopening one recent decision might not spell the end of your legitimacy. But it's a bad habit. We learn from Jewish text that one transgression leads to another.[17] These incidents add up, and you don't want to become accustomed to reopening decisions.

Stick with your decisions. If a decision was good enough on Tuesday, it's probably also going to be good enough on Wednesday. See your decisions through before taking them up again. That way, you'll know that the next time you make a decision, it will also enjoy the organization's legitimate commitment to see it through.

2.3 STRATEGY AND TACTICS

Not all decisions are equal. Some decisions are *higher-level* than others: they involve more resources, commit the organization more broadly, and have a greater impact on future decisions. Higher-level decisions should be given more time to work. Buying a stapler is a decision, and buying a building is a decision. But the building purchase is a higher-level decision than the stapler purchase. It commits more organizational resources, and it has a greater impact on the organization's future, including its future decisions.

Some decisions are very practical: what we're going to do together, what we're going to spend money on, what we're going to teach in a religious school, what prayerbook we're going to use for worship, what activities we'll support in our community, and what activities we won't. These are called *tactical* decisions because they have to do with the tactics of managing our organization in the moment. Procuring office supplies, creating text for a blast e-mail, scheduling two morning sessions for a religious school, creating a website, building or removing a choir loft, having the printer serviced, purchasing stickers—all are tactical decisions. Tactical decisions are about brass tacks. If your decision commits resources or causes something to happen, that is a tactical decision.

---

[17] "One good deed leads to another, and one transgression leads to another." M. *Pirkei Avot* 4:2.

These tactical decisions come at many different levels of impact and organizational commitment. If you decide to purchase cookies, that decision will have a small effect on your next event, and no effect after that event is over. If you decide to remove a choir loft, that will affect every future decision about your music. Removing the choir loft is a higher-level decision than purchasing cookies, although both are tactical decisions.

In organizational leadership, a key part of our job is to recognize not just the tactical decisions we make, but the values and goals we hope to serve by making them. This means looking up from those practical, tactical brass tacks and striving for a broader horizon of view. Who are we as an organization, and how does that guide us each day? What values do we hold and use in making all of our decisions? What kind of organization do we want to be five, ten, fifty years from now? In what circumstances, in what places, accomplishing what? What do we need to put "as frontlets between our eyes"[18] to guide all other decisions we make? These are some of the *strategic* questions we need to ask. Many writers have explained the difference between strategy and tactics, but we'll use a simple working definition that will serve you well: strategy means where we'd like to be; tactics means how we get there. Tactical decisions support, implement, and advance us toward strategic goals.

Strategic thinking demands the creativity to imagine very different possibilities, even if it's only for the confirming experience of deciding the group has been on the right track all along. Strategic thinking demands not just task completion but openness to the hearts and feelings of the people who are doing those tasks: are they happy? Fulfilled? Frustrated? Bored? Joyful? Strategic thinking requires us to articulate our values and critically self-assess how we're doing on fulfilling those values. It requires us to articulate where we fit in our broader community.

These strategic decisions are all very high-level because they inform and affect all tactical decisions. In fact, every tactical decision should consider the organization's strategy. So, if every strategic decision informs and affects every tactical decision, we can say that all strategic decisions are higher-level than all tactical decisions.

Strategic questions are generally not right-or-wrong questions: they are the yardstick by which an organization measures which

[18] Deuteronomy 6:8, JPS.

tactical choices are right or wrong for them. That's not to say the organization has no responsibilities. There are overarching obligations such as morality, law, and legitimacy, which apply to every organization; for Jewish organizations, our understanding of Judaism and our nonprofit mission are at the core of what is right for us. These overarching responsibilities are the core of our strategic identity, the core of who we are. Under their umbrella, our strategic decisions define what is right for our organization.

Strategic questions are always open-ended. In fact, among the benefits of a commitment to strategic thinking is that it gets us out of the rut of closed-ended questions. Strategic discussions are a time to think of third ways, creative solutions that transcend existing assumptions—or just to identify and reexamine those assumptions to ensure they still fit with the organization's desired vision. Strategic questions may be about broad goals, but they're never about how the organization will achieve those goals. Those "how" questions are tactical. By that token, strategic questions are never about feasibility, because they're never about specific plans. Feasibility is tactical. Of course feasibility concerns are important, but the time to consider them is when deciding how to achieve your organization's strategy, not when deciding what your strategy is.

I've arranged this book to proceed from the highest-level strategic issues down to tactical implementation. That is not an order of importance! But in my experience, getting stuck in the tactical weeds, forgetting to ask whether we're even moving in the right direction, is a more common mistake than concentrating too much on the strategic. This book's order of discussion will help us put first things first, understanding why we're here and how we fit into our mission before asking what we need to do next Tuesday.

Strategic Reviews and Strategic Planning

Every organization should pause from its work and take a strategic look at itself periodically. In this book, I use the generic term *strategic review* for the periodic activity of making time for strategic questions. It's a good practice to devote at least an hour each year for a strategic review during a board meeting—maybe more. This strategic review is not about changing the direction of the organization, but rather about checking in with the organization's movement and progress toward strategic goals and fulfillment of strategic identity. Tactical decisions might need to be steered or adjusted to conform to the organization's strategy, or members might need to resolve to take the organization's strategy more directly into account. Jewish organizations may find it meaningful to include the strategic review in their High Holiday preparation. There's no better season than the High Holidays to keep sight of core values, and no season when it's more tempting to get lost in tactics.

Less frequently, the organization needs to revisit its strategic assumptions from the ground up. This is the time to set the strategic vision for the next five, 25 or 50 years; it can be the work of a board subcommittee for several months to several years. Such a project produces written documents that articulate the organization's strategy and can guide lower-level decisions. They may include identity, purpose, mission, and vision statements, which we'll discuss below. Major decisions are made—for example, accepting the consequences of membership growth according to the organization's wishes expressed through legitimate deliberative processes. Strategic documents represent firm organizational commitments that are intended to last.

The annual strategic reviews I recommend are for measuring progress on the yardstick of existing strategy, not for designing a new yardstick. However, if an annual strategic review finds that the existing strategy is no longer a satisfactory yardstick, it's time to get a new one. Also, if board members don't know or have serious disagreements about why the organization exists, what it values, and where it would like to be in 20 years, the time for strategic planning may be now. Major strategic planning is often undertaken in advance of a capital campaign or other large project, but a capital campaign is ideally the result, not the cause, of strategic planning.

I think a small or relatively unstable organization, one growing or changing rapidly, or one that feels its situation is stagnant, would benefit from a full-scale strategic discussion every five to ten years. That's a short strategic time interval, and reflects the strong possibility that basic assumptions about identity, place in the community, or vision for the next phase of growth could change. For financially and organizationally stable synagogues or institutional nonprofits that own a building free and clear, I would not neglect strategic planning every 30 to 50 years, whenever either the organization or the broader regional and cultural scene looks different enough that the previous strategic-planning group's assumptions no longer apply. For most of us, decade or generational strategic planning is probably a reasonable guideline. The question is whether an existing strategic plan successfully addresses the current situation. If not, do strategic planning now. It will pay dividends in clarity of purpose, guidance in making future tactical decisions, and greater legitimacy.

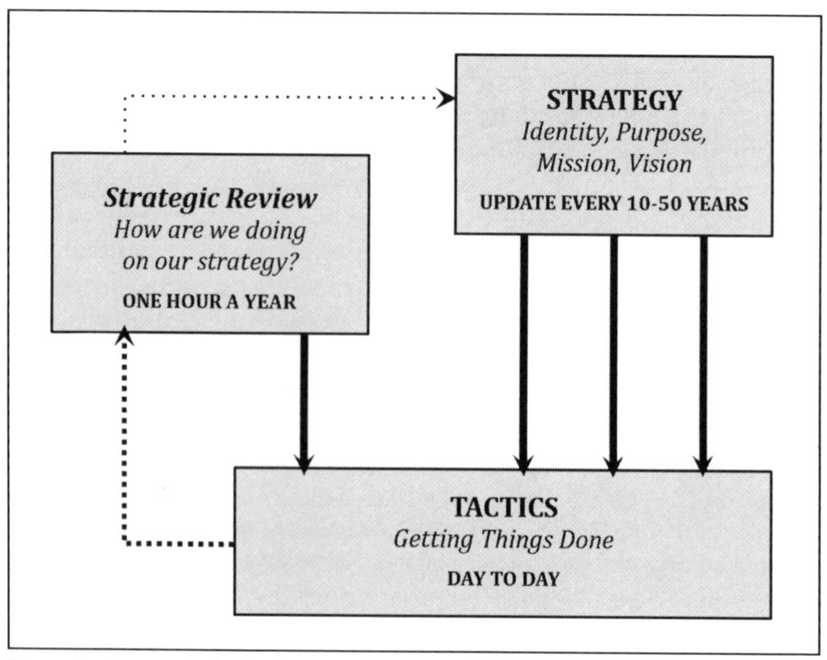

Figure 1. A strategic feedback process.

A strategic feedback process is represented above. Strategy comes first and guides tactical decisions. The big, bold arrows show that strategy influences tactics all the time, for every decision. Then periodically—I say once a year—a strategic review takes tactics into consideration, mostly to ask whether the tactics have advanced the organization toward its strategic goals. That reasserts and reinforces the strategy, sometimes suggesting how future tactics could better implement the strategy. Finally, a small arrow indicates that accumulated feedback from strategic reviews may play a small role in future strategic decisions.

The Internet is full of methods for strategic discussion, as well as consultants who can take you through them. It may be helpful to hire a consultant for your first strategic discussion or every once in a while, just to facilitate getting out of accustomed, possibly too tactical modes of thought. However, I don't think the choice of methodology matters very much, as long as it's an opportunity to ask whether all our work is leading us where we want to go. Choose a methodology that speaks to you, be it a bestseller how-to or just a disciplined board retreat.

One important tool is brainstorming. Brainstorming means making a space and time for people to generate ideas with no criticism—this is important, absolutely zero criticism or analysis—of those ideas. Some ideas will be better than others. But we get distracted from generating ideas when analyze them one by one. Brainstorming is a disciplined exercise in separating the impulse to innovate from the impulse to analyze. This separation offers at least two key benefits. First, the ideas generated will necessarily form a sort of funnel with a wide array of unready, infeasible or simply mediocre ideas and a smaller number of excellent ones. When we don't get distracted critiquing every half-baked idea one by one, we make time for generating more ideas, including great ones. Second, brainstorming is inherently creative and may lead to previously unseen issues being raised for future discussion. For both of those reasons, not to mention that the impulse to analyze usually tends toward the tactical, brainstorming contributes inestimably to strategic work. It also helps in many other settings, so we will often return to brainstorming throughout this book.

Using a KJ Diagram for Strategic Review

If you want a simple method that will spur strategic conversation, look no farther than the *KJ diagram*. This method is named for Kawakita Jiro, who is credited with developing it in the 1960s; it has become part of the lore of Total Quality Management (TQM) and has spread to all sorts of other areas, including now to Jewish organizations! KJ diagrams are a wonderful, inexpensive and versatile tool. Here's how a KJ diagram works:

1. Get a bunch of sticky notes and pens, and give everyone a small stack of sticky notes. Ask them to brainstorm things they like about the organization, things they'd like to change, and things that are particularly important to mention, with only one idea written on each note. Participants can mark "favorite," "to change," etc., on their sticky notes, or they can use different colors of notes or ink. Those three questions are really just three different approaches to generating

ideas; distinguishing among them is less important to the exercise than it appears. Participants can include tactical ideas—this is a brainstorming exercise, so everything goes. Give everyone ten minutes or so, and ask each participant to try to offer at least five different ideas, the more the better.

2. Place all the sticky notes on a large white board or table. The order doesn't matter, but each of the notes should be visible.
3. Now, participants work together to place like with like, repositioning notes so that those with similar topics are close together. Participants move around the room freely, and may grab a note and move it without asking anyone. They are free to talk, but the main activity is moving notes. If there's a disagreement, it will quickly become clear in conversation or because a note keeps getting moved back and forth. If that occurs, make a note of the disagreement, assuring participants it will be dealt with later, and move on. For this exercise, it's okay to copy a note that participants feel may belong in more than one place.
4. After 20 minutes or so, give or take, you should see the notes clumping up like cookie dough. These clumps are naturally emerging topic areas. For example, in a synagogue, one clump may seem to be largely about religious school, while another might be about food policy, or Shabbat morning services. Walk around together and investigate the clumps. Some may lend themselves to sub-clumps, and that's fine, but don't get distracted with sub-sub-sub-sub-sub-clumps for this strategic exercise.
5. Identify strategic questions that each clump raises. Some of the notes might already be about strategic questions. Others might be about dissatisfaction with something, which is an opportunity to ask how the community measures itself against its values, and what its applicable values are. Others might be about purely tactical questions, for which you have to think about their strategic context or, if the group agrees, put them aside for referral to the proper tactical channels. What do each clump's strategic issues say about who we are, what we value, how we relate to our surroundings? Refer to previous strategic-planning exercises if reports from them are available. They may help answer a question raised in the

KJ diagram, or maybe those previous strategic decisions need to be reviewed at this time.

There are, again, many excellent methods and much scholarship available on strategic planning. A survey of all the different techniques and approaches would fill more than another book. The KJ diagram is one of the simplest techniques that can spark a wonderful strategic dialogue. It is a good place to start.

As participants brainstorm their ideas, you might or might not wish to provide resources to jog their thinking, such as previous strategic documents, an organizational diagram of staff and committees, or a list of common strategic issues such as that appearing below in this chapter. The advantage of providing these resources is that participants may have an easier time focusing on the strategic, and will be less likely to forget something. The advantage of not providing them is that participants' thinking will be completely fresh. For a hybrid approach, let participants brainstorm for a period of time, then pass out a selection of resources and allow them a second period of brainstorming.

It can be very hard to stay strategic. Brainstorming naturally raises pet-peeve tactical issues that people urgently want to discuss. People may come to the meeting with an agenda to change policy in a certain controversial area. It's good when a strategic review brings those issues to the forefront. Sometimes we get so caught up in the daily grind that a strategic review is the only opportunity folks have to raise issues that need discussion. But if we allow the strategic review to get sidetracked off into debating a frustrating or contentious point, we will lose the opportunity to address our core strategic questions of who we are, who needs us and why.

Put the tactical concerns into a "*parking lot.*" Many facilitators draw an area on a board or use a flip-chart just for that "parking lot" of issues that need to be discussed, but do not need to be discussed right now. Acknowledge the parking-lot issues carefully, assuring participants that the tactical concerns have been heard. Repeat them back, making any necessary changes, to verify to the group that you've understood and recorded correctly. (These are techniques of Active Listening, about which many greater scholars than I have written.) Promise to give those parking-lot issues discussion time soon. Crucially, later, keep the promise to give those issues airtime. This tactical "parking lot" keeps the air clear. It bolsters legitimacy in three ways: by satisfying people that their concerns are heard, by accomplishing a strategic conversation as advertised without participants feeling the meeting was upstaged, and by keeping the promise to talk about those urgent tactical issues later and soon.

Strategic decisions serve as a guide for tactical decisions, so we record them in formal documents. That way, when questions come up in the course of implementation, the strategic documents will be useful as decision-making tools. Many organizations give prominent space to posting their key strategic statements—their values, their vision, the defining characteristics of their identity—so that everyone will see them as they go about their work.

2.4 SELF-CRITIQUE AND FEEDBACK

Figure 1 above shows a feedback loop: strategy influences tactics, and experience gained from tactics returns to raise questions for the next strategy session. This is the first of many opportunities for self-critique and feedback in our organizational life.

For good reason, Judaism emphasizes this process of checking in with ourselves and others. Regarding the Day of Atonement, it is written that for our errors between ourselves and God, the Day of Atonement suffices to make things right, but for errors between ourselves and other people, no religious ritual can suffice until the people involved have made peace.[19] In organizational leadership, self-critical feedback goes far beyond addressing things we've done wrong in relation to each other, although that can be part of the process. Self-critique is also about catching problems before they happen, about innovating new and creative ways to improve, and simply about keeping our values "before us always"[20] by continually checking in with them.

Let's face it: self-critical feedback is scary. It involves asking other people's opinions about our organization, and by extension about our own performance. It can be difficult and awkward to seek self-critical feedback. I don't want to sugarcoat the experience

---

[19] M. *Yoma* 8:9.

[20] Psalm 16:8 begins, "I have placed God before me always."

because the fear factor is very real, and it explains why so few rabbis, executive directors, and high-level lay leaders seek such feedback. But it is of paramount importance. We need to gently acknowledge that everyone shares the emotional, fearful reaction to it.

Now for some good news. First, although the performance of top leaders is fair game, strategic feedback tends not to be personal. Most personal-performance issues are tactical. Second, usually feedback is not as bad as we tend to fear. Still, it takes courage to open an organization under one's leadership to feedback.

Here are the benefits of strategic feedback. Strategy is all about where we are and where we're going, so without disciplined, periodic organizational feedback we are flying blind. Feedback provides strategic information, as an aggregate assessment of responses received and in specific answers to prompts or questions phrased to encourage strategic thinking. Strategy is nothing but guesswork without a disciplined process to encourage feedback.

Synagogues belonging to movements often receive significant strategic assistance, advice and experience from movement staff and colleagues. The same can be true of large, well-funded organizations. Small organizations and unaffiliated synagogues tend toward insularity simply because they benefit from far less official interaction with colleagues in other organizations. In insular organizations, this lack of cross-fertilization tends to ossify tendencies into habits, and habits into dogma. Strategically, this leads not only to aimlessness, but also makes it difficult to question assumptions about identity, core practices, values, etc., that once were helpful but may no longer be serving the organization well.

Self-critique and feedback allow us to be looser with our assumptions. That openness increases our resilience to challenges and facilitates our adapting to ever-changing circumstances. Having a clear sense of who we are is good strategy. But if our identity is not open to challenge and change, it is already outdated.

Recognizing and Removing Barriers to Honest Self-Critique

Suppose someone wants to discuss a particular lofty vision that your organization is unable to achieve. There's no reason to torpedo a thought experiment: perhaps a little time gaining clarity on where you'd like to be would be an achievement enough. Once you reach such a consensus, there will probably be small steps you can take to get even a couple inches forward toward the goal.

It's tempting to dismiss larger questions because you don't have time for them. But this is just another form of paralysis, because there will always be a more pressing tactical concern. My friend, the thought leader and educator Sarah Chandler, no longer allows herself to say, "I don't have time for that." She replaces that phrase with, "That's not a high priority for me right now." She is being more honest by connecting her use of time to her priorities. By extension, that opens the strategic question for her of whether those priorities are the right ones.

Strategy can always be postponed another day, week, or month, but it does not serve us to go about our very busy business never asking whether our hard work is moving us in the right direction. So we need the discipline of a periodic strategic review, protecting that time from pressing questions about who will make sure the envelopes are stuffed or the proposals are in. An hour a year for feedback, strategic brainstorming and honest self-critique might not be enough. It's definitely not too much. Why not start with that?

Stagnation is my name for widespread dissatisfaction with the organization, coupled with the general conviction that there is no way forward. Stagnation is no fun. Chronic dissatisfaction is dangerous to any organization's legitimacy. Why should there be such an organization, why should I be a member of it, if nobody is happy with it and there is no hope? Stagnation casts a pall over an otherwise warm and lively group of people. I've worked with many organizations facing stagnation, and even helped to lead a couple of them out of it. In my experience, stagnation is a symptom of a lack of strategic vision coupled with an incapacity to challenge negative or outdated assumptions that have calcified into stone. I've seen it mainly in small organizations, where lack of membership leads to the frustration of lacking sufficient funds, staff or volunteer power to accomplish programmatic ambitions, which then hardens the assumption that nothing can be done. But large organizations can also be stagnant, particularly if leadership makes little room for changing membership preferences. Strategic thinking prevents this kind of calcification by bringing us outside our assumptions. A periodic strategic review is therefore good preventative medicine for everyone, especially for small organizations.

Naysaying is a behavior that exacerbates stagnation. Naysaying insists that every idea has been tried before and didn't work, or isn't feasible, or isn't affordable. But nothing will ever change if no idea is ever given a chance to work. And that's not because the group is happy the way it is; it's because a few, some, or most members come to discussion feeling dispirited about the group's ability to change.

Naysaying is a fuzzy, imprecise way to block change. Not every new idea is a good one, but a responsible practice is to evaluate new ideas on their own in the context of the current situation. If something broadly similar was done a decade ago, it does not follow that it cannot work today.

Naysaying, then, is bad enough for tactical ideas. ("Oh, 15 years ago we tried bobbing for apples at the Purim carnival, and nobody liked it.") But strategic thinking is all about new ideas, larger ideas about advancing the organization's position and ability to do its work well. Strategic thinking by its nature requires imagination, fresh perspectives, the ability to see ourselves with outside eyes,[21] the ability to step back and ask if the assumptions underlying our task work are the right ones.

Strategic thinking, therefore, always opposes the paralysis of naysaying. Strategic thinking does not imply that everything will constantly be changing, but it does require an openness to change for which a naysaying attitude makes little room. "There was that law of life," wrote Norman Mailer, "so cruel and so just . . . that one must grow or else pay more for remaining the same."[22] A strategic review can reinvigorate morale by underscoring why everyone feels it's important to devote time to the organization.

There is nothing wrong with a small organization remaining small, if that is the preference of members. For example, small synagogues are often delightful, friendly places, inviting in ways large synagogues struggle to be, and may serve needs large congregations cannot. If your organization is small and you like it that way, celebrate that! A conscious choice to remain in a status quo because you are happy with it is the opposite of stagnation: it's a clear-eyed strategic vision of where you want to be. Stagnation is when you're stuck in a status quo nobody's happy with.

---

[21] "O wad some Pow'r the giftie gie us, / To see oursels as ithers see us!" — Robert Burns, "To a Louse, on Seeing One on a Lady's Bonnet at Church," 1786. Or, more understandably, "O would some Power the gift give us, / To see ourselves as others see us!" Board members would do well to memorize this couplet from Burns's altogether amusing poem. See *npgovernance.org* for a link to the full poem and some discussion.

[22] Mailer (1955), chapter 26.

Note also that the concerns of naysaying are without exception tactical: they're always about a specific case of failure or a perceived feasibility issue. Those critiques could be valid, but they do not belong in a strategy session. The president, committee chairperson or other discussion facilitator should be on the lookout to catch those tactical arrows in midair before they shoot down an important strategic discussion.

As we've discussed, strategic feedback is not primarily personal. Still, top leaders may not be used to it. Most of us enjoy the luxury of regular feedback. Employees get it from performance reviews; students get it from grades. Healthy relationships give us feedback. But top leaders who do not report to a supervisor face a structural deficiency in feedback. In synagogues, this means the rabbi (or senior rabbi), executive director or administrator, and congregation president may all find themselves lacking channels for critical feedback, and must proactively seek it out.

For top rabbinic, administrative and lay leaders, a large part of consciously seeking feedback is making sure the organization has channels for feedback and honest self-critique on a regular schedule, sticking to them, and using their leadership positions to create a culture where feedback is natural, honest, welcome, facilitated, and frank without the need to be judgmental. In return for the organization's nonjudgmental approach to feedback, top leaders must agree to take it seriously and answer it honestly. Leaders are not required to agree with criticism, but they are required to welcome it. Leaders' respect for criticism and for the courage of critics is a large part of the legitimacy of their leadership role.

On the other hand, personal defensiveness personalizes feedback even if the feedback was not intended personally. If someone says they'd prefer different worship music, the rabbi or music director could make the mistake of personalizing that feedback, taking it to imply that their job performance was not up to the critic's standard. Feedback sometimes but not always implies that kind of performance criticism; objectively, this example does not jump out as such a case. To the contrary, a congregant may have felt so comfortable with the rabbi's warmth and caring that they worked up the nerve to make a music request. Defensiveness does nothing but dig in heels without rational basis. Therefore, it is more than just an unpleasant turn of etiquette; it is inimical to the organization's progress toward its goals. Watch for defensiveness, especially in top leaders who lack regular feedback—and especially in yourself, the first place we can all start to benefit from feedback.

A good way to defuse our own defensiveness is to postpone our response. "Thank you so much for saying that to me, I understand"—after verifying that you do in fact understand—"and in this organization, we honor feedback and respond in a timely manner. I need a little time to think about what you've said. I'll keep you updated, and you're always welcome here" is a perfectly acceptable response in the moment.

For organizations facing anything that looks like stagnation, feedback is a way out and a way forward.[23] Never mind whether ideas haven't worked in the past or whether they raise personal emotions in leaders; feedback is what people now wish to express. Feedback can help tip the scale out of stagnation, especially if the organization separates strategy from naysaying tactical fears. Most of all, legitimacy requires the organization to hew to what members want over the long term. Sure, sometimes unpopular decisions are necessary. You could get away with general dissatisfaction for a few months to a few years without long-term negative consequences. But chronic dissatisfaction places the organization in danger. Why would people want to join or remain in an organization in which there's always an excuse not to bring their preferences to fruition? Feedback is an opportunity to remain in touch with what members want, recommit together to shared goals, and correct both the tactical and strategic courses as required.

Implementing Successful Feedback

One of the hallmarks of a well-managed organization is that the air is clear—by which I mean, people are generally happy with each

---

[23] "Clear a path through the wilderness for God" (Isaiah 40:3). Feedback provides the hope of a way forward by making time to discuss potentially difficult issues. Martin Luther King, Jr., takes the idea a step further, invoking "a Power that is able to make a way out of no way" (King, 1967)—an African American phrase brilliantly traced by Mieder (2010), pp. 181ff. All of our organizations aim to change the world in important and beautiful ways, and all of us need a way forward. You don't have to place yourself at the kind of personal risk King did to be taught by his image of God "making a way out of no way," or by Isaiah's call to "clear a path through the wilderness." All of us have obstacles in our path, certainly including the fear of feedback. Clear the path! Feedback is a way forward.

other in the workplace and in volunteer spaces, and where they are not happy with each other, those issues have been discussed and are at least known. We all have strengths and deficits, and what better place than a Jewish organization to work on both together? So the rabbi tends to yammer; we've all discussed it and he's working on it. So the administrator is better at day-to-day details than big-picture vision. Well, the Board has discussed it, and he can learn. So running meetings isn't the president's forte. There are many ways to work with that, from appointing a meeting chair to purchasing a good book on Jewish nonprofit governance with an essay on how to run a good meeting. Open feedback clears the air, replacing gripes with a cooperative atmosphere of improvement in which everyone trusts each other to speak honestly and to do the best they can.

I see three requirements for a successful feedback program: an atmosphere of openness, regularly scheduled meetings, and a commitment to answer every request seriously and honestly.

- *An Atmosphere of Openness:* People need to know they can approach their leaders at any time with feedback, that the organization values feedback, and that they will be welcomed and thanked for taking the trouble to offer their views. This must be done well every single time. One incident of poor feedback reception can destroy months or years of work building an atmosphere of openness to feedback. I did not say that leaders must agree with feedback. But at the risk of the organization's legitimacy and their own, they must solicit feedback, take it seriously, and give honor to those who offer it. Disagreement is often fruitful, but long-term dissatisfaction is a red flag suggesting that insufficient weight is being given to feedback, or that insufficient feedback is being collected.
- *Regularly Scheduled Meetings:* The suggestion box doesn't cut it. Organizations must actively solicit feedback. For all the passive activities that encourage feedback—informal conversations, encouraging committees to bring issues to the Board, the venerable suggestion box itself, website forms (which are fancy suggestion boxes), and more—there is nothing like a specific, actively planned activity to gather feedback and to reinforce for the rest of the year that the organization values and welcomes feedback. I suggest an

annual meeting specifically for feedback. While it is always advisable to collect ideas at an annual membership meeting, I would probably not do a specific feedback-gathering activity then, simply because (probably) not everyone there will have specific feedback they'd like to offer. At a feedback meeting, those interested could go into greater depth.

Because it is impossible to get participants to separate tactical from strategic feedback, I would attach a feedback-gathering activity to the strategic review. Do the KJ diagram as suggested above. Then, keep the ensuing discussion strategic, and at the same time review the sticky notes for useful feedback, be it tactical or strategic. It might be advisable to have one responsible individual review the notes for all-purpose feedback, while another reviews them for strategy and keeps the strategic discussion going.

- *Commitment to Answer:* It needs to be the ultimate responsibility of the organization, carried out by whoever is responsible, to answer feedback honestly and timely. Only when this is adopted as a core value supporting the organization's legitimacy can we expect it to occur. And only this will ultimately encourage members to offer feedback and participate in organizational introspection. Again, the right answer is sometimes but not always agreement. The only wrong answer is no answer.

  If leadership disagrees with feedback, they should accurately summarize the argument and dispassionately point out the differences of opinion, before rejoining the argument in favor of their point of view. It is a skill to cause people to feel listened to even while disagreeing with them; this skill can be acquired with practice. This book offers some thoughts and resources on it without claiming to speak with authority about it. It is a skill worth developing.

We are not listening to feedback until we are at least open to the possibility of changing our point of view. And if we aren't open at least in principle to changing our point of view, then there is little point in our engaging in feedback exercises because we should not be in leadership.

Feedback build habits of ethical leadership, strategic creativity, and tactical follow-through. I've offered just a few ideas out of many equally good possibilities for implementing honest self-critique in daily and annual practice. A climate of honest self-critique protects us from disasters ranging from the undesirable to the unspeakable. It is, above all, a worthy value that improves all who engage in it—individuals and organizations together.

Honest self-critique is not easy. Gently and honestly with ourselves and others, cognizant of the high stakes between its substantial benefits and the dangers of neglecting it, let us all commit to implementing honest self-critique in the way that we locally think best. After all, it is perhaps the most Jewish of values.

2.5 STRATEGIC ISSUES MOST SYNAGOGUES FACE

We've had theoretical discussions about strategy; now let's fill in more of the blanks. It would be impossible to compile a full list of strategic issues, nor is that our purpose here. These lists consider a synagogue example just to provide some focus, without claiming to have dealt with every possible strategic issue. With these lists I hope to illustrate by example the difference between strategy and tactics, and to help fertilize your own thinking.

I've provided a sample of strategic questions related to each key issue, along with number of potentially related tactical questions. The tactical questions are intended as a guide to recognizing the strategic issues that may underlie questions like them.

Remember, all strategic decisions inform and affect all tactical decisions in a well-governed organization. Although we're looking for specific connections here, it remains very possible for a tactical decision to be materially related to a wide array of strategic issues.

Don't let the importance of some of the tactical issues fool you. Remember, *strategic* choices define the goal, while *tactical* actions accomplish the goal. *Strategic* does not mean important and *tactical* does not mean unimportant. But the high importance or impact of a tactical decision does not make it any less tactical. We still need to identify the underlying strategic issues, the values we hope to serve through the tactical decisions we make. In this way, strategic clarity can guide you through the nitty-gritty. Note the diversity of high- and low-level tactical questions in the lists that follow.

These lists, again, are intended as food for thought, not as a complete compendium. I've undoubtedly forgotten many good issues, and there will be still more that will apply to your organization's strategy in particular. How would you expand these lists? How would you extend them for organizations other than synagogues? Those could be great exercises in strategic thinking.

Strategic Issue: Identity

Who are we as a synagogue? What are our core beliefs about Judaism, halakhah, kashrut? What sort of Jewish community do we want to be? How do we want a visitor to feel when walking in the door? To which demographics do we particularly appeal? What kinds of demographics characterize our current membership, and are we satisfied with that?

Tactical Questions: Can the synagogue host potlucks with home-cooked food, and if so, how? Should we invest in public-facing signage? What kind of music, if any, should we have at services? What are non-Jewish spouses permitted to do? Can Benjie Birnbaum's parents cater a very fancy lunch for his bar mitzvah? Should we join with St. Luke's down the street to co-host a soup kitchen? Should we have an alternative traditional minyan in the building's small chapel during the larger, less traditional service in the sanctuary?

Strategic Issue: Membership

Who belongs to our synagogue? What relationship do we have to our members (for example, are they users funding events through fees, do they have a strong sense of overarching ownership)? Are there groups of people that we need to attract? What kinds of needs do our members have, for life-cycle events, for social connection, for social-action opportunities, for worship, for pastoral care?

Tactical Questions: What should we charge for dues? How should we structure dues? Should we have individual or household member units? Should we build a new classroom wing or a new soup kitchen? Who has access to a rabbi for private celebrations? What time should we schedule services? Do we need a membership cap? Should we be advertising? Do we need multiple types of worship services? Should we offer a full-scale religious school, and if so, whom should it serve? Should we keep the building open for adult education or socializing opportunities during the week? Are we offering the right kinds of programs for our current and desired members?

Strategic Issue: Growth
Is our congregation the right size? Would we like to be larger in order to have greater economies of scale or to offer new programs, and is that growth realistic given our surrounding community? Are there people we could realistically attract to membership? Do we need to do better attracting new members, retaining current members, both, neither—based on our own intuition and based on data? Are we happy with the size we are? Are we too large to foster the kind of community we desire? Have we grown too large too fast, so that we need to slow down and let our programs and activities catch up? What is our core character as a community, that we would never want to change?

Tactical Questions: How much of our budget should support growth? Should we do more of what brought our new members in? What membership size would be able to support our programmatic ambitions financially? Can we make do with the budget we have? Are our programs matched to our community's needs? How should we advertise? What do we need to do to be ready for growth—in our physical space, in the school, in the office? Just how much growth are we ready for right now? How can we gather the data we need to make higher-level decisions?

Strategic Issue: Physical Plant
What are the purposes of our physical space? How does our physical space reflect our values? How does it fail to reflect our values? What styles of architecture, interior design, aesthetic fit with the surrounding landscape and community, social gathering space, reception, utility consumption, Internet readiness reflect our values? For what functions do we use the space? Where are we currently crowding or underusing our space? How does the space support or limit our programmatic ambitions?

Tactical Questions: Should we launch a capital campaign to expand our building? Should we build an access ramp to the bimah, and how does that compete with other priorities? Should we subdivide the Multi-Purpose Room into classrooms? Should we remove walls to join underused classrooms into a Multi-Purpose Room? Should we open a soup kitchen on the ground floor facing the street? Should we keep the choir loft, expand it or remove it? Should we name areas or rooms after high donors? What are the specific needs for space of our existing and desired programs, and how can they be balanced in a shared space?

Strategic Issue: Education of Children
What values do we want to pass on to our children? If we had to prioritize, how would we rank the importance of preparing a child for Bat/Bar Mitzvah, inculcating a love of Judaism, fostering Jewish friendships, developing knowledge of Jewish text (Tanach, Talmud, midrash, responsa, etc.) and Jewish history (Ashkenazic, Sephardic, Mizrahi, African, Asian, world), developing proficiency in Hebrew, other educational goals? How would you answer a child who asks, "Why do I have to go to Hebrew school?" What are our community's preferences and trends with relation to day school?

Tactical Questions: Should students be expected to continue with Hebrew school past Bat/Bar Mitzvah, and if so, how strongly should they be encouraged? What should we do with students who appear in fifth or sixth grade and want a Bat/Bar Mitzvah on time? What should be in the religious-school curriculum? When should religious school meet? Do we need to offer in-depth religious school if many of our families are sending their children to Jewish day school? Should we teach modern Hebrew?

Strategic Issue: Diversity
What is the current demographic makeup of our community? Do we tend to identify Jewish culture (food, history, politics, observance) with the culture of a particular Jewish ethnicity, such as Ashkenazi or Sephardi Jews? If so, is that part of our synagogue's core identity (more common in Orthodoxy) or should we broaden our Jewish horizons? Does our community have knowledge about Jewish ethnicities other than the majority ethnicity in our synagogue? What about women, LGBTQ families, Jews of color, Jews by choice, intermarried families, disabled people, and single people—in what ways do they or can they enrich our community? Do any of these groups face barriers to full participation in our community? Are we able to broaden our sense of Jewish identity to include more people?

Tactical Questions: What Jewish history curriculum should we teach our children? What should we teach children about the family? Should we make an effort to feature different kinds of families and people of different races in our official photographs and brochures? Do we require training for staff and volunteers, or other internal action, to check our assumptions about whom we are welcoming to? Should we build an access ramp? Should the rabbi perform interfaith marriage ceremonies? Same-sex marriage ceremonies? Should we encourage non-Jewish spouses to convert to Judaism? Are there limitations on the participation of non-Jews in our ritual and organizational life?

Strategic Issue: Place in the Surrounding Community

What does our surrounding community need? Which of those needs do we serve; which do we wish to serve? With whom do we compete, and for what do we compete with them? With whom might we collaborate, and for what purposes? How has our surrounding community changed over time, how do we expect it to change over the next years and decades, and how does that affect our strategic direction? How does our location—our local neighborhood, access to transportation including roads, transit and parking, impact our strategy and expand or limit the range of our tactical options? How do we relate to our neighbors—abutters, members of our local community, people of our town, city or region? How do we participate in the civic life of our municipality, county, state, nation? To what extent is our neighborhood part of our core identity—could we be the same congregation elsewhere? Do we wish for our neighborhood to play a greater or lesser role in our identity?

Tactical Questions: Should we expand in this location or move to a different neighborhood? How can we address a nuisance complaint from an abutter? Should the Social Action Committee co-sponsor a rally to raise the local minimum wage? Should we participate in a community-wide Simchat Torah celebration, or celebrate at home in our building? What should our policy be on closing due to inclement weather? At what times should worship services be scheduled? Should we co-sponsor a ballot measure? Should we build a homeless shelter? If we advertise, which newspaper or radio station would be the best choice?

Strategic Issue: Image and Brand[24]

What do we want people to think of us? What do they actually think of us? What sort of feeling do we want people to have when they first find out about our congregation? Is our image closely tied to particular spokespeople (a rabbi, a congregational leader) and if so, are we satisfied with that? What do we want people to know we are most enthusiastic about, that we love most, that we feel most obligated to? What five words best sum up our current answers to all of the foregoing strategic questions in this section?

Tactical Questions: How much should we spend on a print or radio ad? How should an ad look? What should be on our signage? Which specific words should we be sure to use in talking about our community? What are some talking points that would help our membership committee and staff explain our community to new faces? What, if any, changes do we need to make in the short term to our organizational structure or physical plant to make them consistent with the way we wish to be perceived? Does our website reflect the image and brand we want to communicate?

There are also issues of strategic importance to the broader Jewish community. Many synagogues decide that a core part of their mission as a synagogue is to serve the interests of the broader Jewish community in a selection of the following and other ways.

Strategic Issue: Welcoming People to Synagogue

How high a priority is it to welcome new faces? Are we focused on signing up members or are we also a place for long-term non-members to come and participate? How should the Jewish visitor's path and timeline toward membership, if they should choose it, feel and be managed? Is there a particular niche within the broader regional Jewish community where we need to focus on welcoming? What is our vision for how a visitor is greeted and feels when entering the synagogue? Should we participate in outreach programs, with the regional Jewish community or independently? Are there financial or other barriers to membership that are faced by people who would otherwise choose membership? Are there

[24] Don't shy away from terms like *image* and *brand* just because you're a nonprofit. These ideas are no less important for nonprofits. See Chapter 11 for more.

channels other than worship services and religious school—social events, social action, others?—which might lend themselves to welcoming Jews from the broader community? Are there political or other issues which might either encourage or limit unaffiliated Jews in our community checking us out?

Tactical Questions: Should key leaders (rabbi, president, etc.) make it a point to talk to unfamiliar faces at all events? Are our priorities for promoting our events the right ones? Does our website facilitate people finding us, and finding the programs they're interested in? Is there anything we can or should do to foster friendships within the community? Should we change the financial structure of membership? Should we do joint activities with Jewish or interfaith community organizations? With whom should we march in the Yom Ha'Atzma'ut parade, or should we march by ourselves? The LGBTQ Pride parade?

Strategic Issue: Supporting Jewish Identity

What priority do we place on forming adults' and children's identity on Jewish practice, Shabbat, kashrut, halakhah, Israel, other issues? How do we view Jewish identity and how should we support that view? Are there some ways of being Jewish that we see as more ideal than others? Do we need to redouble efforts for pluralism on the bima, or do we need to stand for a clear and consistent principle (on any number of issues)? Which values do we want to inculcate in our children to take with them into Jewish adulthood? Are there non-members for whom we as a synagogue are expected to speak in the surrounding local community?

Tactical Questions: How active should our rabbi(s) be within the broader community? Should we offer programs directed toward Jewish non-members in the broader community? What about those Yom Ha'Atzma'ut and Pride parades? What curricular decisions for our religious school will support our understanding of Jewish identity? What Jewish values should our rabbi exemplify in her or his personal behavior? What policies or programs will help our congregation exemplify and model pluralism to the surrounding community?

Strategic Issue: Supporting Jewish Continuity

How does our children's education program support the broader goal of Jewish continuity? How does it not support that goal? How does the value of Jewish continuity affect our strategic choices in education? How about our adult education program? In which areas other than education might we contribute to Jewish continuity? Does our surrounding community have particular needs in the area of Jewish continuity that we might be positioned to address? How does Israel figure into Jewish continuity for us? What is Jewish continuity anyway? What role does contemporary Jewish innovation—in music, literature, art, fashion, entrepreneurship, science—play in Jewish continuity?

Tactical Questions: Should we measure the results of our religious school in terms of Jewish continuity? How can our religious school better support Jewish continuity? Are there ways we can support our members or local Jewish non-members in religious observance in the home? Should the rabbi(s) perform interfaith weddings? Can we make it easier for our members to find Shabbat candles, Hanukkah candles, matzah, challah? Should we offer cooking classes, and if so, should it be matzo-ball soup or shakshuka?

2.6 PUTTING OUR DECISIONS IN WRITING: PURPOSE, MISSION, VISION, POLICY

If the ideas in this chapter have been new to you, it can be very difficult at first to keep strategy and tactics separate. As we begin to discuss some tools to articulate your organization's strategy and tactics, I hope the chart below will help with the distinction. Remember, every tactical decision should be in keeping with all strategic decisions.

Remember also that some tactical decisions may be very high-level, like constructing a new building; sometimes such high-level tactical decisions are mistakenly called strategic. They are not. Building a new building is a tactic. It's a large-scale, big-money, high-level tactic, but it's very much a tactic. *Why* you're building the building, how you hope it will position your organization, the values guiding the use of space, the vision you have of the building fully utilized: those are the kinds of strategic decisions that ought to guide you as you execute the tactic of building it.

Tactical Decisions Are . . .	*Strategic Decisions Are . . .*
Mostly short- to medium-term	Long-term
Detailed and factual	General and global
Specific ideas	Values and goals to guide ideas
Ready to implement	Universally applicable
In keeping with your goal	Deciding what your goal is

Statements of Purpose

In the United States, nonprofit organizations are required to have a statement of purpose. Your statement of purpose was filed with your state when you incorporated; it can be found on file with the official charged to keep your state's corporation records. If you have 501(c)(3) recognition, a statement of purpose was also filed with the Internal Revenue Service in your application for tax-exempt status (Form 1023). These records should also be available online or from your organization. (I apologize to my non-U.S. readers: I am less familiar with other jurisdictions' regulatory systems.) Your *purpose* is why your state and the IRS allow you to be a nonprofit corporation. Your legal responsibility is to fulfill that purpose.

However, because purpose statements are legally binding, good ones leave as many options open to the organization as possible, and therefore do not typically say much. Look up your statement of purpose if you haven't seen it recently. More than likely, it says little more specific than that you are a nonprofit, with a certain type of work (a synagogue, an advocacy organization, etc.), and will do such other legally permissible activities as the organization may decide. But even that isn't bupkes: it's a starting point for everything else.

Mission and Vision

The words *mission* and *vision* get bandied about, but they have very specific meanings—cognizance of which may help prevent a mission-statement meeting from floating off into space. In organizational strategy, *mission* means what you are here to do, and *vision* means what life will be like when you do it well.

Theoretically, purpose and mission answer the same question: "What are we here to do?" But purpose statements are terse to avoid limiting the organization's legal options, so the mission statement finishes the job. A good mission statement encapsulates all of the various areas of the organization's strategy, and can be read as a summary of strategic decisions to date. It can be very challenging to accomplish that in a couple of sentences.

A little wordsmithing is not so bad. But people dread mission statements because discussing them too often turns into drawn-out discussions comparing synonyms. Here are a few suggestions. First, the mission statement or vision statement is never as important as the mission or vision itself. Agree in advance not to argue shades of dictionary meaning. Write in simple, natural language. Use active verbs and nouns, a few adjectives, and a minimum of adverbs and the verb *to be*. Avoid superlatives and self-compliments; they do not add meaning. Instead of saying, "Our mission is to be the center of Jewish learning in North Anytown, excellently and caringly, and to be a welcoming place where anyone can come," you might write, "We teach and learn Judaism in North Anytown. We care about each other and welcome all."

Draft a statement if you feel it will help. Don't let it become busywork that detracts from your strategic awareness rather than adding to it. If you find that a bullet-point write-up of the KJ diagram from your last strategic review suffices to remind you what you're trying to do (mission) and achieve (vision), then that may be enough right now. Certainly don't neglect the KJ diagram or equivalent brainstorming exercise in favor of "winging it" straight into wordsmithing: that is like painting window shutters before a house has been designed. On the other hand, sometimes it is helpful to have a concise, intentionally worded statement that conveys your strategy through clear, elegant language. In fact, that was not a bad mission statement for mission statements, just now.

In a way, your vision and mission are complementary; in another way, they may be duplicative. Mission asks, what are we here to do? And vision asks, where do we want to be? While these questions are not identical, they're close enough that the work of answering both may not be worth it. Many organizations seem to have only one or the other. This is not wrong.

Many great sermons could come from the idea of vision. I'll mostly spare you for the moment because this is a down-to-earth book about governance, but *vision* is a very Jewish word. Biblical figures constantly have visions, even if we restrict our meaning specifically to organizational-strategy visions. It might be fruitful to consider how the visions of Abraham,[25] Jacob,[26] Joseph,[27] Moses,[28] Joshua,[29] Ruth,[30] David,[31] Zechariah,[32] Esther[33] or others might teach us in our efforts today forming our own visions.

There are many online resources for sample mission and vision statements, including a wealth of resources just for synagogues. Rather than duplicating them, I'll offer just a couple ideas.

First, some of the vision statements out there are enormously long. I do not recommend that. Internal strategic documents longer than a few sentences should be in bullet form. Wordsmithing a multipaginous opus by committee is not worth the time spent. Also, paragraphs tend to obscure points that would be clearer as bullets. You may legitimately need a lengthy document, but the longer a bulleted statement gets, the more it duplicates the bulleted summary of your strategic review. So either keep these statements short, or stick to the summary of your strategic review.

Second, stay out of the tactical weeds. This is not the place to talk about pet peeves or choices of policy.

Third, avoid floating off into space. Make sure each word adds meaning and do not give yourselves latitude for platitude. Far too many mission statements end up amounting to the obvious. It doesn't have to be that way. If you feel you may be on a spacewalk, a good way to tether yourself back to the mother ship is to ask if the opposite of your words would be plausible.

For example, "to live the ideals of Conservative Judaism in a welcoming, egalitarian way that honors the State of Israel" gives me useful information about a synagogue and probably summarizes their strategy pretty well. I can plausibly imagine a congregation with the opposite of each of those attributes, so I can narrow down my understanding of who these folks are. But for a synagogue "to serve the Jewish community by providing worship services and

---

[25] Genesis 15:12–16.

[26] Genesis 28:12–22, Genesis 32:25–31.

[27] Genesis 37:6–7, Genesis 37:9.

[28] Exodus 3:2–4:17, Exodus 33:18–34:8, Deuteronomy 34:1–4.

[29] Joshua 1:1–9.

[30] Ruth 1:16–17.

[31] II Samuel 7:1–16.

[32] Zechariah 4:1–5:11.

[33] Esther 4:16, Esther 7:3.

educating children" was not worth a meeting's time to articulate. What else were they going to do, open a Chinese restaurant?

On the other hand, "to provide regular Sunday morning instruction in the Hebrew worship service, life-cycle events for members, as long as they are registered in advance with the office, and rent space until a permanent location can be found" is a task list, not a mission statement, however high-level or important those tasks may be. The task list needs to be guided by values. What are they? A mission or vision statement speaks not to what you do each day, but to the values and strategic goals that guide you.

Policy Documents

In this book, a *policy* is a written tactical decision by an organization. Let's explore this definition.

I say policies are written. You might say an organization has verbal policies, but I don't think a policy can truly be set until it is written down. The organization is free to change its policy through a legitimate process, but if the policy has not changed from Wednesday to Thursday, it needs to be the same when Bob consults it on Thursday as it was when Claire consulted it on Wednesday. This requires writing the policy down.

A policy is an organizational decision. I know people who say they have personal policies, but as far as we're concerned right now, that's just a figure of speech. There is a difference between a personal decision and an organizational one. Organizational decisions are legitimate: they arise by legitimate processes. Words like *strategy* and *policy* recognize them as such.

Policies are tactical. Policies are always tactical. Policies are about what the organization, its staff, leaders and members do. Specific activities are always tactical, so policies are always tactical. Strategy explains, or should explain, why each policy was adopted.

Policies can be large or small, high-level or low. Technically, purchasing staplers is a policy. It was the policy of the organization to commit funds to the purchase of those specific artifacts at that specific time. That very low-level policy implemented other, higher-level policies: that the office manager is in charge of purchasing office supplies, that minor purchases can be charged to a general expense item for office supplies, that the office should be well stocked, that there should be an office, etc.

The word *policy* is usually reserved for higher-level policies that deal with general cases. Whenever a situation meets criteria *X, Y* and *Z*, our policy is to take actions *A*, *B* and *C*. We usually don't honor specific, situational decisions by calling them policies. We usually don't say that it's the policy of this organization to purchase a kosher pizza for staff who worked late into the night stuffing envelopes. But it is, and reminding ourselves of that helps us be aware of whose money we're spending, for what purposes, and in keeping with which values that define our strategic direction.

The generality of criteria-driven policies doesn't make them any less tactical. Requiring seat belts on field trips is a tactical decision. It does not apply to any one field trip, but to all of them; conversely, it is also possible that a field trip will never materialize even though the policy has been adopted. It's still a tactical decision. There are strategic reasons the policy is important, such as safety, setting a positive example for children, and liability prevention.

Every policy has such a relationship to the strategic goals it serves. It may be enlightening to open your policy handbook and try to think of the strategic values or goals behind three policies chosen at random. (What's that, no policy handbook? See Chapter 4.)

Policies ensure fairness and consistency. They help manage expectations. They help ensure the tail doesn't wag the dog. If there is an emotional situation, a favorite donor, or some other temptation to tip a decision for or against someone, a good written policy can help defuse a situation that might otherwise become personal. Policies promote community by ensuring everyone follows the same rules. Policies promote legitimacy in those ways. Sure, we may occasionally find ourselves having to "wing it" with a decision about an unforeseen situation. But it is always more legitimate to follow a policy, and so it is always advisable to have policies in place.

Chapter 3
THE BOARD

3.1 SHIUR

Rabbi Simon said: At the time that God came to create the first human the ministering angels formed themselves into two groups. One said, "Create!" and the other said, "Don't create!" as it is written: Kindness and Truth met; Justice and Peace kissed.[34] *Kindness said, "Create him, because he does much kindness." Truth said, "Don't create him, because he is full of lies." Justice said, "Create him, for he acts justly." Peace said, "Don't create him, since he's full of argument." What did God do? God took Truth and threw it to the earth, as it is written:* And he threw truth to the earth.[35] *The angels said to God: Master of the Universe, why are you insulting your royal stamp [Truth]? Raise Truth up from the earth! As it is written:* Truth will sprout from the earth.[36]

Midrash Bereshit Rabbah 8:5[37]

This story is a wonderful example of *midrash*, a genre of rabbinic literature in which the Rabbis take imaginative excursions from Biblical text. Here the Rabbis have filled in a story between the eleventh and twelfth verses of Psalm 85. The "ministering angels" are personified as Kindness, Truth, Justice, and Peace, each with its own agenda that explains its advocacy for or against creating Adam. Only the Rabbis' familiarity with committee deliberations could explain their choosing to personify these angels —all representing the good—in a debate not very different from our own deliberations. At last, God takes the mysterious, extraordinary step of throwing Truth down to the earth, to sprout from the ground.

---

[34] Psalm 85:11.
[35] Daniel 8:12.
[36] Psalm 85:12.
[37] Translation from Margalit (July 2012).

Students new to Talmud should not be surprised by the Rabbis' wild, almost koanic approach, which is not typical of the much more forthright, declarative style of the Bible itself. Take the story as it is, without worrying too much about its fealty to the original intent of Psalm 85 and the Book of Daniel. The Rabbis are having fun in order to learn something from the text, and so might we.

My teacher, Rabbi Natan Margalit, offers a remarkable teaching on this passage and the verse "truth sprouts from the earth."[38] Natan imagines truth as a plant sprouting from the ground, with branches reaching toward Heaven. Some things are true for all of us, just as all the plant's branches reach toward the same sky. Other times, something may be true for us on one branch, and someone else may have their own truth on another branch; although both of our branches yearn toward the same Heaven, they are not the same. Heaven forbid, indeed, there should be a single, uncompromising Truth reigning in Heaven, instead of the truth that God in divine wisdom decided to cast as a fruitful seed to earth. Without the multiple branches of our mortal, imperfect and yearning truths, there would be no room for diversity, harmony, even friendship. Humanity in its richness and imperfection could not exist. God had to cast truth to the earth in order to create humanity.

In our deliberations, we remain free to claim we represent the common direction of all branches, not just the characteristics of our own branch. But before we insist ours is the only way, let us seek earnestly to understand our colleagues' branches of truth.

This story sheds light on the Rabbis' view of human nature. They understood—they say God understood—that we are imperfect but great, capable of kindness and war, yearning toward justice but full of lies. Organizations are made of, by and for us, with upward steps just the right size for our feet to take them, with guardrails to hold our greatness and our error, our love and our war. In governance, these safeguards are collectively called *ethics*.

I wish to imbue our discussion of leadership with a clear sense of ethics. It is not easy to run a Jewish organization, and it is not easy to run an ethical organization. If these endeavors feel too easy, we are probably overlooking something. Both require self-critique and feedback from

[38] Margalit (July 2012).

others. Both share the interplay of kindness and stringency required to ensure that we behave justly in the challenging situations in which organizational leadership places us.

We are kind to ourselves and others by recognizing that everybody errs. For that reason, we are stringent with ourselves and others by recognizing that we need safeguards, and we recognize those safeguards in the form of rules. It is kind to our members to be stringent with our leaders, recognizing that a lack of ethical safeguards invites an ethical breach. We accept the stringency to require adherence to those rules in all cases, not because we personally cannot be trusted without them, but because ethical problems generally arise without them. Therefore, ethics requires of those in leadership the kindness to yield to ethical rules.

Let every branch of our organization yearn and correct its course toward ethics. Even as we in our autonomy branch out in different ways, let us yield to the law which requires us to bend our standards and practices upward.

3.2 THE FIDUCIARY BOARD

I've spoken of organizations making decisions. You might object: aren't decisions made by people? If we wish to be effective, we need to understand which people make decisions and why.

Nevertheless, I've argued that organizational decisions belong not to any one individual but to an organization corporately. I've argued that they enjoy greater legitimacy than private decisions.

This chapter discusses how organizational decisions come about. We will learn where an organization's legitimacy comes from, as well as how that legitimacy can be conferred on certain people at particular times in order for them to act on behalf of the organization. We will consistently emphasize the ethical obligations by which people become bound when they become empowered to decide for an organization.

Who is responsible for your organization—to make policy, to bind the organization to agreements with outside entities, to speak for the organization? Who is in trouble if something happens (may it not) and an injured party brings a lawsuit?

In this book, we will be talking mainly about *independent* organizations—by which I mean that the organization is fully empowered to make decisions for itself. The alternative is for an organization to be subordinate to a larger (often national) umbrella group that allows local organizations some autonomy but is ultimately responsible for them. A local chapter within a national advocacy organization, a synagogue organized as a campus of a single national movement-based organization (not uncommon outside the United States), and the structurally similar case of a single campus of a large, multi-campus synagogue, all are examples of arrangements that are not *independent* for our purposes. Within certain defined limitations, local chapters or campuses might enjoy most of the autonomy an independent organization would have. This book's advice assumes an organization is independent, although most of it ends up applying to all sorts of organizations.

Member-governed synagogues in North America often hold a movement affiliation. That does not make them any less independent for our purposes in this book. We are talking about independence in the decision-making sense.

Finally, I will be referring to nonprofit legal structures in the United States. I hope that especially my non-U.S. readers will augment this book with local expertise on corporate structure. I will gratefully post such information on *npgovernance.org*.

I am not a lawyer, and nothing herein should be read, construed, or assumed to be legal or tax advice. You should hire a lawyer, preferably a highly paid one. I heard that lawyers would come and chase me down if I didn't say that.

What Is a Fiduciary Board?

Nonprofit organizations in the United States are governed by a *board of directors*, or just a "board" for short. Board members take on a legal obligation to ensure that the organization operates legally and toward its declared purpose, and to ensure the organization's well-being and sustainability. This is called a *fiduciary obligation*, and it is the bedrock of governance ethics. People under such obligations are called *fiduciaries*. A fiduciary obligation means that the person is required to act in the interest and toward the purpose of the organization as a whole, not merely in their own interest or according to their own preferences. The word *fiduciary* comes from the Latin *fidere*, to have faith in, or to trust. A fiduciary is someone in whom you can have faith, who acts in good faith and who is faithful to the interests of the organization. Board members share those basic ethical obligations.

That does not mean everyone on a board always agrees. Board disagreements are essential to progress, as the board hashes out different sincerely held views of what is in the organization's best interest. That's what board members are there to do! In general, board members should assume that colleagues' actions are motivated by their personal views of the organization's best interest. After all, that is their shared legal obligation.

A word often encountered in these contexts is *trustee*, but it is used to mean different things. If trustees appear in addition to a board, a trustee may be a particular officer, often someone with a fiduciary obligation to the organization's endowment. Trustees could be financial guarantors of the organization. Some organizations define a trustee to simply mean a member of the fiduciary board, which they may call the *Board of Trustees*. Others call it a *Board of Directors* and use the term *director* for a member of that board. In this book, we will simply use the term *board member*.

The board makes decisions for the organization. The power granted to board members to vote on these decisions comes subject to their legal obligation to act as fiduciaries, in the best interest of the organization and its purpose. For that reason, **board members are individually liable** if something goes wrong. If someone slips on a banana peel while you're a board member (may it not happen) they could take your car to pay for it (may it not happen).

Wait a minute, what?

I want to make sure everybody understands this. As a board member, you are individually liable for the organization's mistakes. Let that sink in before I offer some good news about it. I constantly emphasize to board members that you have an individual duty to satisfy yourself that the organization's actions are right. Your personal liability is on the line. Most board disagreements do not rise to this level, but if you feel concerned about a potentially illegal activity in the organization, it won't be a defense in court that you allowed someone to talk you out of your duty to satisfy yourself.

I doubt anyone would sign up for that kind of liability if there were not Director & Officer (D&O) insurance. This insurance protects board members ("directors") and officers (the president, secretary, etc., who may not be technically required to be board members) from their personal liability arising from actions of the organization. Premiums are paid by the organization and board members are named beneficiaries. Never, ever, ever join a board without D&O insurance. The organization should give you proof of your coverage after your election and before you take office. Examine the insurance policy and ask any questions you have.

But beware: if you break laws or break your fiduciary obligation, or if you took action or failed to take action that you knew could lead to liability, or if you were grossly negligent (not paying attention) and should have known about such a situation, your D&O policy may deny your claim. D&O insurance allows people who act ethically and carefully to serve on boards without having to fear liability from events they could not have prevented, but that protection is entirely contingent on their fulfilling their fiduciary obligations.

Being a fiduciary, then, is a serious matter. If you serve on a fiduciary board:

- You are empowered to vote on decisions for the organization.
- You are required to act as a fiduciary for the organization, in everything you do in that position.
- You are personally liable if anything goes wrong. Your D&O insurance will protect you if you have fulfilled your fiduciary obligations, but could deny you coverage if you acted illegally, unethically, or negligently.

Exceptions and Complications to the Fiduciary Board

The word *board* is often used for any top-level non-staff decision-making body for an organization, even if it does not have fiduciary responsibilities. We've mentioned multi-campus and hierarchical movement-run synagogues as well as chapter-based organizations, which may very well have "boards" for each location, even if the fiduciary board is located centrally. Government agencies often have citizen "boards" whose members take on certain fiduciary obligations but do not exercise power over the agency, which remains a unit of the government. And especially outside the U.S., fiduciary obligations may be structured differently.

A fine example of a non-fiduciary "board" may be a synagogue religious school board or committee. The school committee is (probably) structured as a committee of the fiduciary synagogue board. School committee members therefore do not have individual personal liability for the school: like all other functions of the synagogue, this liability falls to members of the fiduciary board. But school committees take on many typical board roles, such as setting budgets, overseeing a complex organization, and hiring and firing the principal. Although they may not be at personal liability, members of such committees do, or should, take on ethical obligations to decide in the best interest of the religious school. If this arrangement works well, the fiduciary board will seldom need to intervene. While it's important to remember who bears ultimate responsibility and is therefore finally in charge, service on this type of body can be a valuable fiduciary experience.

There are also *advisory boards* and *honorary boards*, of which organizations make all sorts of different uses. The word "board" in these cases is just an honorific; they are outside our discussion here.

Finally, an exception to these principles occurs for "religious corporations" in the State of New York. The Religious Corporations Law (RCL) legislates that for religions without a hierarchical structure, the powers of hiring, firing and setting the compensation of clergy are not exercised by the board but by the general membership. The RCL results from eighteenth- and nineteenth-century church politics, and in its original form predates the Bill of Rights. Its unconstitutionality[39] and the reasons it is still in force are far beyond my ability to make sense of. It has the practical effect of making it very difficult to fire a rabbi for cause in New York.

I wonder what would happen if a rabbi in New York were to commit misconduct necessitating his removal in the Board's opinion, then defy the Board's dismissal based on the RCL, and then commit further misconduct bringing liability against the synagogue. Would D&O insurance refuse to pay on the grounds that the liability did not stem from a Board action, or that the congregation was negligent in not firing the rabbi, or that the issue fell outside the D&O policy because it was not a board power according to state law? Does the RCL place individual synagogue members at liability, or does it remove the concept of personal liability altogether? If you are in New York, please consult an attorney to understand these thorny issues. In any case, with respect to the RCL, congregations in New York fall under the category of non-fiduciary boards as described above, because the RCL removes the board's power to act.

[39] Cohn (2005), pp. 32–35.

The difference between fiduciary and non-fiduciary boards is major. Nevertheless, I would argue that the same ethical obligations are incumbent on everyone claiming the title of a board member, even if for non-fiduciaries those obligations cannot as easily be enforced at law. I recommend, therefore, that non-fiduciary boards emulate the fiduciary model to the extent possible, accepting individual fiduciary obligations and taking them seriously, as a matter of ethics if not of law. For the remainder of this book, the word *board* always means a fiduciary board unless stated otherwise.

Tax Exemption and Tax Deductibility

There is a lot of confusion over tax-exempt status. In the United States, we have overlapping state and federal jurisdiction. Your state grants you incorporation and recognition as a nonprofit corporation. A nonprofit has no stock—nobody "owns" the corporation or its assets—and unlike for-profit corporations, nonprofits cannot lawfully distribute funds to members. (They can certainly pay people a reasonable salary for work, but they cannot sell a building and send everyone on the membership list a check.) A nonprofit exists to serve a recognized purpose. Nonprofits are exempt from business taxes and most government fees. Your state also enforces board members' fiduciary obligations.

Additionally, the United States offers an important tax benefit to organizations recognized under Section 501(c)(3) of the Internal Revenue Code—called 501(c)(3) organizations. Section 501(c)(3) says that anyone who donates to a corporation organized for religious, educational or charitable purposes may take the donation as a deduction on their personal federal income taxes. That's why organizations apply to the Internal Revenue Service for this recognition. There are arguments that religious organizations are not technically required to be recognized, but let's ignore that; 501(c)(3) recognition carries large benefits including much greater ease of accepting donations and being able to use online donation systems that require 501(c)(3) status.

Let's review. Nonprofit status, including tax exemption—the organization's ability to avoid paying business taxes—is granted by your state. The ability for donors to deduct donations to you from their federal income taxes is granted by the federal government, specifically the IRS. Your organization is governed both by your state's corporation law and by federal tax law. Also, as a condition of granting 501(c)(3) recognition, the IRS requires certain language in your statement of purpose to ensure that your activities remain religious, charitable, or educational.

There is a widespread misconception that organizations endanger their 501(c)(3) status by engaging in any political speech at all. Not so. The prohibition is against supporting or opposing a candidate for elective office, and against devoting too much of your activities or revenue to lobbying activities. Many board members are overly cautious on political speech out of misinformation. Please consult an attorney knowledgeable about 501(c)(3) political speech to learn where your organization should draw the line.

To Whom Are Board Members Responsible?

To whom, exactly, are board members responsible? Most people would probably say they are responsible to the members of the organization. Members benefit from board members' obligation to act in the organization's best interest, and as we discussed above, long-term failure to follow members' preferences leads to low legitimacy. For trivia buffs: In the United States, board members owe their legal obligation to the people of the state in which they were formed. Nonprofit organizations are chartered by states, and the state maintains a public interest in your organization upholding the purpose for which the state granted incorporation. If you try to dissolve your organization, your state Attorney General will represent the public interest in court.

I was on a nonprofit board (not a synagogue board) in which some people wanted to sell our building and distribute the proceeds to members. Before joining the board, I visited a meeting, and happened to point out that distributing funds to members would be a criminal offense. An attorney had been presenting the plan, and he had his back to me. He turned around very slowly, gave me a quizzical look, turned back around and said, "That guy . . . is *right*."

Nevertheless, the effort to sell the building continued. Even if the money could not be distributed to members, it could be used to drastically reduce dues. Along with a narrow board majority, I did not judge this plan to be in the organization's best interest, although it may very well have been in the best interest of members. Those two interests may align most of the time, but in this case they did not align. On that board we had some interesting discussions about nonprofit law, and the building did not end up getting sold.

The point of this story for us is threefold. First, board members' fiduciary duty is a public duty, and your state government will enforce the public interest if necessary. Second, do not be afraid to raise an ethical concern. Board members are to assume the best of each other's motivations, but the fact is that sometimes people want to do things that are unethical or illegal, either out of misinformation about their obligations or out of genuinely nefarious motives. None of our organizations is above the possibility of this. Third, the board is the place for serious concerns to be raised, and you as a board member are obligated to raise them if you have them. It can be an unpleasant duty, but it is an absolute duty. Even if they would rather not spend time discussing something, even if they fear losing friendships or facing hostility, each board member has an individual fiduciary duty to satisfy themselves as to the legality and ethics of every decision. Do not fear to raise such a question, and do not shut down another board member if they raise one.

3.3 ETHICS

In nonprofit organizations, leadership is about responsibility. It is not about power, vision, charisma, honor, financial largesse, recognition for past accomplishments, or any of that. It is about being the one responsible for whatever else goes on. Could there possibly be a more Jewish idea? The Rabbis say that Moses was chosen to lead because of his performance as a shepherd: when a sheep wandered away from the flock (a common event that would have been considered an acceptable business loss) Moses searched for the sheep and carried it back to the herd.[40] Board membership in a Jewish organization is Jewish leadership. Board members are leaders by virtue of their accepting this responsibility.

A Word about Secrets

A secret is a potential red flag. When we encounter a secret, our ethical duty is always to examine it critically, asking what information is being kept from whom, and why. Marilyn Peterson

[40] Midrash *Shemot Rabbah* 2:2.

observes that "secrets tend to produce three-person triangles of deceit,"[41] that is, two or more in on the secret, and at least one who is excluded from it. Secrets involve deceit because they have to be maintained. Excluded parties must be prevented from finding out.

Some secrets are necessary and desirable. Personnel records are a great example. Salaries, performance reviews, disciplinary records, etc., are usually confidential for good reasons. However, many organizations make their top employees' compensation public in order to serve a transparency interest. And you bet, if anyone were found to have committed misconduct that could put others in danger (may it not happen) there's a public right and need to know. There's a limit, therefore, even to information usually kept secret. In a well-governed organization, confidentiality is the exception and not the rule—an exception made only in specific cases and only for formally defined, well considered, very good reasons.

No secrets should be kept from the organization's president. That person was democratically elected to lead, and secrets kept from them undermine the legitimacy of any leadership. As a corollary, the president must be privy to every proceeding. The president doesn't necessarily need to have their inbox flooded, but they do need to be permitted to obtain any information they ask for. Perhaps this is obvious; I mention it because I've seen it breached. The president should always be an *ex officio* member of the organization's personnel committee or equivalent, for this reason.

Conflicts of Interest

Board members must act in their honest assessment of the organization's best interest. That is the only interest that board members are allowed to consider. A *conflict of interest* arises for anyone with a fiduciary responsibility when they could plausibly be influenced by an outside interest. These situations are extremely common and often happen without board members realizing it. Here are some of the most common conflicts of interest:

- *Self-interest:* A board member votes to hire themselves or their company. The board member has a personal financial interest in an affirmative vote, so they cannot do their duty to act in the sole interest of the organization in such a case.

[41] Peterson (1992), p. 81. See Peterson, pp. 80ff, for a detailed examination of the ethical issues posed by secrets.

Hiring a spouse or other close relative is also considered self-interest. A spouse's hiring directly affects the board member's personal finances; therefore, this and any other arrangement with a close relative is self-interest.

- *Other organizational interest:* A board member who serves on the board of another nonprofit, and votes to merge the two organizations, or to hire the other nonprofit, or to do anything that benefits the other organization, is conflicted between their equal fiduciary duties to both organizations. In situations involving both organizations, they cannot act in the exclusive fiduciary interest of either.
- *Favoritism or Animus:* A board member who is trying to get a date with the office manager is in a conflict of interest. The board member's personal interest is inextricably entangled in their business dealings with the office manager. This situation can turn just as quickly to animus, as you can imagine, which is the same conflict only with the opposite inappropriate influences. (This situation may also violate other laws, such as those prohibiting sexual harassment.)

These cases do not require there to be actual corruption. All a conflict of interest means is that a person has incentives to act in an interest other than that for which they have a fiduciary obligation.

The generally accepted remedy in advance for a conflict of interest is *disclosure* and *recusal*. Disclosure means that the person in a conflict of interest discloses all details of the situation to fellow board members, and, unless there is some good reason not to, to general membership and to the general public. Disclosure always protects the discloser. The board's continuing legitimacy depends on everyone's forthright honesty around conflicts of interest. They happen. We get into trouble mainly when we fail to disclose them.

After disclosure, the conflicted party recuses themselves from any decision about the matter in question. In most cases, recusal is sufficient to mitigate a conflict. Here are some recusal options:

- *Full Recusal:* The conflicted board member does not vote on the matter, is not permitted to be in the room when it is discussed, and is not privy to discussions that take place about it. It may be necessary for the board to meet in *executive session* (closed session, without minutes, to be used sparingly) to make this possible, which could constrain the feasibility or advisability of this option.

- *Recusal from Discussion and Voting:* The conflicted board member does not vote or discuss the matter, but is privy to the minutes of past discussions about it. This is a common way of handling conflicts.
- *Recusal from Voting:* The conflicted board member is permitted to discuss the issue as a board member, but must abstain from voting. I don't think this is a sufficient level of recusal for personal-benefit conflicts, but it may be sufficient for outside-organization conflicts.

In addition to recusal, *dealing at arm's length* may be a way to mitigate a conflicted situation. In arm's-length dealing, special steps are taken to make sure there is no familiarity in a conflicted negotiation, and that any compensation arrangement is at a fair-market value. Arm's-length dealing is not sufficient to mitigate most conflicts. It will not (usually) help to deal at arm's length with a board member's painting company when the building needs to be painted. But arm's-length dealing can help as an additional step.

Some conflicts of interest cannot be mitigated even through recusal. A good example is hiring the spouse of a board member. That presents an ongoing situation in which the conflicted board member has oversight authority over someone who manages their spouse. Almost everything such a board member does would necessarily be conflicted. And even if they take no explicit action, their presence on the board would unavoidably cast a pall over the administrative leadership's ability to manage the spouse. There would always be the specter of favoritism if not the fact. It can't happen. For such conflicts, and for conflicts in which for some reason the appropriate level of recusal is not feasible, the only acceptable answer is for the conflicted board member to resign.

Conflicts of interest are not just for board members. Committee members have authority delegated by the board, and are ethically required to act in the organization's interest within the scope of their delegated authority. A synagogue's Ritual Committee choosing to purchase silver candlesticks from the chairperson's husband, who just so happens to be an antiques broker, would give rise to a conflict of interest quite along the lines we've discussed.

Similarly, managers, purchasing staff, and many other roles receive delegated authority to act for the organization, and are thereby required to decide in the organization's best interest. The office manager purchasing pencils from his wife's pencil company could be a problem (though it could be resolved by asking for permission from a nonconflicted person with higher managerial authority). A rabbi hiring her daughter as camp director would certainly be conflicted, though again if the school committee makes the hire and somebody else manages the daughter, it is not problematic. If the rabbi usually manages the camp director but special arrangements are made to manage the rabbi's daughter, that would be an example of arm's-length dealing in the workplace.

It is an ironclad rule that an organization may absolutely not under any circumstances hire a board member or their immediate family for an ongoing employment position. It is a conflict of interest to manage or exercise oversight over one's family member. This is not because anyone involved is doing anything wrong, but because the situation is wrong. No good comes of giving a board member's relative a job. It goes without saying that the same is true of board members' business partners, or board members themselves. Direct compensation to a board member could constitute what regulators call *private inurement* and call your nonprofit status into question.[42]

It is a conflict of interest for a synagogue to hire a synagogue member. This is because the member's right to vote and organize on the general management of the community is not consistent with reporting to a manager. It can be awkward to talk about synagogue policy with a member who is employed there; the awkwardness is a red flag that this is a conflict of interest. For nonprofessional positions, I tend to think this conflict could be mitigated by

---

[42] Synagogues often make one exception to this "ironclad rule" that I feel compelled to mention. I can think of no solid ethical reason teachers in a synagogue religious school should be an exception, but they often are. It is good for congregational members and leaders to teach children, and these aren't anywhere close to full-time jobs; they're generally for low pay, a small number of hours, not competitive for hiring, and they sometimes demand the particular expertise of a narrow range of people. If a board member's wife is the only person in a small community who speaks fluent Hebrew, what can you do? I can't tell every synagogue to restrict board members' families from teaching in the school. Having said that, I offer a few mitigation suggestions on *npgovernance.org*.

disclosure, public advertisement of the position, and recusal by the member and their family from hiring and from all issues pertaining to that role. For managerial or professional positions I don't think it's possible for the same person to be both dues-paying member and paid staff. The professional should resign their membership if they wish to take the job, and the congregation may need help to make the transition in their relationship with the person.

Conflicts of interest may fail to be disclosed and mitigated in advance. This can happen because nobody thought of them until after they occurred, or because a problem happened while a conflict of interest was current. It's never too late to make things as right as they can be. The first step is disclosure. If a fiduciary board failed to notice a conflict until a problem occurred, they should own up and say to the members, "Oops, we failed to notice this until it occurred." Never cover anything up. Disclosure can be a teaching moment. If everyone has done their best and simply did not have training or for some other reason failed to predict the problem, then there's nothing to be embarrassed about. It's an opportunity to learn together. Just disclose.

Once you've disclosed, mitigation during or after a problem is generally more severe than mitigation before the problem. This is because mitigation now must redress, not merely prevent, an ethics problem. Higher levels of recusal will generally be required. Resignation may be necessary, even restitution of funds. It all depends on exactly what occurred. There is nothing wrong with making an innocent mistake, and there is everything right with noticing and correcting a mistake. The goal is to restore confidence in the organization's legitimacy.

Whenever a breach of ethics catches an organization unawares, it comes at a cost to legitimacy. It's never too late to patch things up, but it's wiser to brainstorm conflicts of interest that could arise, adding mitigation plans to your policy manual as you think of them.

Appearance of a Conflict of Interest

Finally, there are situations in which no conflict of interest exists, but there is a perception that it could exist. This is called the *appearance of a conflict of interest*. For example, a synagogue board member and the preferred kosher caterer are close longtime friends and second cousins. Let's say the preferred-caterer relationship long predates the board member's fiduciary service, and is renewed every four years by a board vote. There is no particular reason to believe the board member's judgment is compromised, nor that the caterer received preferential treatment due to his relationship with the board member, nor that the board member enjoys any sort of personal benefit from the business (the familial relationship is too remote to warrant that assumption). Still, the situation could raise uncomfortable questions.

The appearance of a conflict of interest is much more subjective than a conflict of interest itself. A wide range of situations could lead to the appearance of a conflict. The best course for all concerned is to get them out on the table. The appearance of a conflict of interest may not be that big a deal. Why not disclose it and get it mitigated, rather than waiting for someone to bring up a concern later?

Treat the appearance of a conflict just like a known conflict: disclose it and mitigate it. Mitigation for the appearance of a conflict could be a level or two less severe than it would be for a substantiable conflict. In our example, disclosure and a couple arm's-length precautions may take care of the matter in everyone's eyes. I think recusal from voting in such a case would be a laudable extra step from a board member who wanted to bend over backward for transparency. These decisions are your organization's to make, in the open after the matter has been disclosed.

Some authorities say that the appearance of a conflict is a conflict, and urge that no distinction be made at all. I don't agree. There is a night-and-day difference between hiring a board member's wife and hiring a board member's second cousin. The idea of appearance of a conflict gives us a language with which to prevent awkwardness when a fiduciary might seem unduly subject to outside influences, even when they actually are not.

If someone suggests that you may be in a conflict or the appearance of one, take it as an opportunity to get things out on the table. Doing so protects you personally more than anyone else. Say, "Hey, that's a good point, I'm glad you brought it up, let's figure out how we can get everyone comfortable about this." You are not being accused of corruption or wrongdoing. A friend is giving you an opportunity to protect yourself. Take it.

If you are concerned about a potential conflict, bring it up. Your job as a fiduciary is to say those words if you feel those feelings. I would much sooner trust the legitimacy of an organization that discloses 25 conflicts of interest by board members each year than one in which no conflicts of interest have been reported in 25 years. Conflicts of interest happen constantly. The proper handling of them will increase your organization's legitimacy.

The Talmudic sages over 1,500 years ago already knew about conflicts of interest,[43] and offered sophisticated thoughts about them, on which a great deal of *halakhah* (Jewish law) is based. That would be a good subject for a scholar-in-residence weekend. Jews have managed these issues for millennia, so you're on the right track if you're managing them, too.

Crime

We are not immune from rabbis, staff or volunteer leaders doing the unthinkable, nor are we immune from embezzlement and theft. On the bright side, everything gets better from here. But for the next few pages, we have unpleasant business.

I have served on eight boards, including two synagogues, two non-synagogue Jewish nonprofits, three non-Jewish nonprofits, and one government agency. Four of those were fiduciary boards of the type we're focusing on in this book. I've also been involved in senior staff leadership and non-board volunteer leadership at a third synagogue and many nonprofits. I have seen money stolen four times, unethical money handling many times, physical assault once, physical intimidation without assault once, witness tampering once, a sexual felony once, and fiduciary breaches many times. Most people will never do any of these things, but there are some who will if given the opportunity. And as recent news has unhappily proven, synagogues are not immune from the bad side of human nature. The only way to keep our communities safe is to talk transparently about this unpleasant subject, and prevent it through policy, vigilance, and clear understanding of the danger. On the other hand, denying the possibility of crime creates the ideal conditions for crime to happen.

Rabbis in particular have a lot of power in synagogues. If they don't answer to anyone, that's a red flag. I believe every rabbi should have a regular check-in with a peer accountability group, Jewish or interfaith, movement-based or not. The rabbi and board can also check in with each other. Rabbinical associations are supposed to

---

[43] See Fogel and Friedman (2008). Available online at the website http://link.springer.com/article/10.1007%2Fs10551-006-9327-7, accessed August 4, 2015.

police their members' ethics, but some have better track records than others. Regardless of any other structure, if you're a board member, the fiduciary duty toward your organization is yours.

Anyone can commit a crime. Top-level employees (executive directors, rabbis) may be at greater risk because they do not report to a manager. Rabbis are given a lot of personal deference, so they need to be extra careful to be accountable for that responsibility. But financial, sexual and other crimes can come from anywhere.

The embezzlement cases I've seen have been crimes of greed, not crimes of need. Whether powerful staff or just very good talkers, these thieves found personal gratification from taking money. Theft of funds could certainly be a crime of need, but we err when we assume that only the needy will steal.

I call it a *crime of trust* when an individual abuses the trust granted them in order to gain something, typically money or sexual gratification. Sexual harassment alone may not be a criminal offense, but it is a serious violation of workplace trust that opens the organization to civil liability, and it is just as unacceptable.

Crimes of trust erode confidence in your organization, so much so that the impulse may be to cover them up. You may feel the organization's mission will fare better if a $10,000 embezzlement is not revealed right at the height of a $10,000,000 capital campaign. My emphatic advice is that the cover-up is always worse than the crime. Every time I've been through this situation as a board member, I've wished I'd said something sooner. Being vigilant and trusting your instincts is the only right answer. Assuming "it can't happen here" and letting people talk you out of your duty to satisfy yourself is the only wrong answer. Silence will buy you an unknown period of time before the incident happens again, and if you covered it up, you could share in the liability next time. And I wish it were needless to say but it is not: shame on anyone who covers up the sexual or financial crime of a trusted community leader.

Every board member must be immediately and fully informed of any concern about illegal activity. They are individually at risk, so it is their right to know. The Board will decide how to handle it and may decide to handle it privately. But the situation may not be kept from board members. It is not acceptable to restrict this kind of information to the president, the rabbi, a personnel committee, an executive committee, or any other subgroup. Everything that could put board members in personal legal jeopardy must be disclosed to the full board—completely, immediately, without exception.

Let's get to some recommendations and close this unpleasant section. First, if you do not have a sexual-harassment policy, please ask another organization for one right now and copy it right away, to give yourselves a starting point. The same goes for policies on the handling of money. If you know that a crime has been committed, notify the police without delay. And if you know that something has exposed or could expose the organization to liability, report it to the full Board and do whatever you can to prevent it.

If you find yourself in a terrible situation, be like the board of Congregation Kesher Israel (Orthodox) in Washington, D.C. In one of the worst cases of Jewish clergy abuse to surface recently, they caught their longtime rabbi, Barry Freundel, filming women within the congregational mikvah. As soon as she found out, the board president called the police to turn Freundel in. No doubt it was a highly emotional time, but the board and its president did their duty under pressure, and in so doing protected who knows how many further women from abuse. Freundel, for his part, was provided his full due-process rights by the American judicial system.

The situation was terrible. But imagine how much more terrible it would have been if the congregation had dithered with some amateur internal investigation when they already knew Freundel's crimes were continuing. Imagine how many more women would have suffered if the board had allowed bromides like "it can't happen here" or "this is confidential" or "we can't let this damage our reputation" to lull them into complacency and cover-up.

There was nothing good about this situation, but *kol hakavod* to the Kesher Israel board for teaching us what to do if it should ever happen to us (may it not). They are heroes of integrity.

Must a Crime Be Reported?

In a word, yes. Often only a few people know about a crime at first, and it can be deceptively easy to try to buy time. Nobody wants to deal with a situation like this. There can be a strong temptation to justify watchful waiting, which is nothing but an excuse for inaction.

If you are informed of a crime by someone who wishes no action to be taken—whether because they are guilty of it, because they believe the organization will fare better not reporting it, because they are of the opinion that crime should be handled by an internal or religious investigation rather than by police, or because the known information is suspicious but inconclusive and they do not want you digging—they may say to you that the information is confidential. This has happened to me on two different boards. If it happens to you, get legal advice immediately. The confidentiality excuse may not only be false but also constitute witness tampering, itself a serious crime. Do not get drawn into such activity.

In three of the embezzlement cases I've witnessed, there was a concern that reporting the crime would undermine donor confidence and harm the organization further. For other crimes, there are always concerns that if publicized, the incident will reflect poorly on the organization's reputation. I strongly believe we're better off disclosing. Cover-ups take a lot of effort and always reflect worse on the organization once the cover is blown.

Sometimes religious mercy is invoked to justify cover-up or diversion from civil to religious authorities. Yes, perpetrators need love and support to repent and become better people. But paralyzed complicity and misplaced benevolence only hold them back from repentance, while endangering others by enabling their misdeeds.

The urge to keep secrets can result from the devil-we-know fallacy, in which we naturally prefer a bad known state (the status quo) to an unknown state (reporting). It can also come from the uncontrolled-risk fallacy, in which we fear risks outside our control (like flying in an airplane, or reporting a crime) more than risks within our control, even if the latter are objectively more dangerous (like driving a car, or covering up the crime).

More importantly, the fear of a properly handled incident reflecting badly on the organization is predicated on the dangerous fallacy that crimes don't happen in nice Jewish organizations like ours. We must dispel that nonsense with integrity and education. Catching and prosecuting a criminal, while unpleasant, can be a teaching moment.

Always ask a lawyer for specific advice. There are many factors to consider, and there's also a notion of scale: I'd immediately report a $10,000 theft to the police, but maybe I'd let a $10 theft slide after an honest apology and conversation—and disclosure to the board.

Before we get to weighing the factors, there are two important exceptions:

- Crimes victimizing children or those with disabilities invoke what are called *mandated reporter* statutes. Everyone involved in a responsible position in an organization should know whether they are *mandated reporters* according to local law. An attorney can tell you. If you are a mandated reporter, you can be criminally prosecuted for knowing that a child or disabled person was victimized and not reporting it promptly to the authorities.

- Clergy and certain other professionals, including lawyers and mediators, are covered by *shield laws* which may differ by jurisdiction in their specifics. Shield laws could exempt a professional from reporting, and could protect them from having to testify in court about something they heard. To be applicable in a given case, shield laws require that certain criteria be met about the professional, their relationship to persons in the case, and the conversation. Clergy and other applicable professionals should be aware of the extent to which they are covered by shield laws in your jurisdiction.
- The interplay between shield laws and mandated-reporter laws, not to mention any organizational rules imposed on clergy by their professional associations, can be complex and is a very important question to ask your attorney.

Having discussed those exceptions, I can say a few things about whether to report to the police, where it isn't immediately clear.

1. One board member may decide not to report, but they cannot dictate to a board colleague that the organization's interest is in not reporting. That is for each board member to decide individually. Lying to a colleague or twisting their arm in an effort to prevent them from reporting could constitute a new crime of witness tampering.
2. It is never acceptable to keep damaging information from any board member. It is their right to know because they are personally liable for it. Immediate disclosure at least to the full board is a non-negotiable, absolute requirement.
3. The board should consider who is harmed or at risk from the crime. In a case of modest financial embezzlement (may it not happen), let's say the money was returned after the thief was confronted, I could see an argument that it was a crime against the organization, and the organization therefore gets to decide what to do about it. On the other hand, a crime involving sexual abuse (may it not happen!) has individual

> victims; furthermore, sex offenders tend to reoffend until stopped. The only reason not to report sexual abuse is if the survivor decides not to report it, without any kind of pressure, with adequate advice, and is an adult. Otherwise, any decent organization should be willing to take whatever political hit may come if it means stopping or preventing such a thing and putting the offender away.

While there is a non-negotiable duty to disclose all concerning information to the full board, board-only disclosures run the risk of devolving into rumor mills. I would disclose to general membership as soon as possible, just to get ahead of the rumors. A membership disclosure is a public disclosure for all practical purposes. Although it is sure to be unpleasant, I think we're best served by disclosing.

Consistently shared values of reporting and transparency make your organization an unattractive venue for misconduct. When there is clear evidence of crime—an eyewitness, an incontrovertible breadcrumb trail, a clear lack of any other explanation for the disappearance of $1,100 from the cash box—the only appropriate audience for that kind of evidence is your local police department. If there is clear evidence of non-criminal misconduct, or unclear evidence of crime, inform all board members right away.

Reporting in Ambiguous Situations

When you don't have clear evidence but merely suspicion of wrongdoing, there is more latitude and also new dangers. Making an accusation can cause someone to sue you for slander, even if the accusation was made in good faith and perhaps even if it was true. (Truth may be an absolute defense against slander charges, but it costs money to make that defense.) There may be social or other intimidation, even though that is illegal. If other board members don't share your assessment, there may not be a lot you can safely do on your own. Always consult a lawyer in those sticky situations.

It is unethical to maintain fiduciary ties to an incorrigibly unethical organization: your fiduciary responsibility implies that you publicly vouch for the organization. Your responsibility as a fiduciary is to exhaust all reasonable options to correct the organization's course, and failing that, to resign. In less serious situations, for example a conflict of interest on which you have an irreconcilable difference of opinion with the board majority but which you do not feel necessitates your resignation, you may nevertheless wish to document what occurred.

As a last resort, there is a way to discharge your moral obligation even if you don't feel you can act to alleviate your concern. Compile a carefully documented chronology of events, including evidence you found, communications you had, and responses you made, in consultation with your attorney. E-mail provides an easy paper trail of records, which is why I always use e-mail for important communications. If you resigned, include your resignation letter, or the date of your coming off the board. If you didn't feel the situation warranted your resignation, you might explain in writing why you felt you could continue as a fiduciary.

Then, should there ever be a question about your role, this compilation will prove that you did all the diligence you could. Such a compilation is called a *memorandum to the file*. Mail it to yourself to create an evidentiary timestamp, and keep it for your records. I just went through this, not a month before this writing, in regard to the sexual felony I mentioned. A memo to the file is unpleasant and frustrating, but it will establish that you did all you reasonably could to discharge your ethical obligations in good faith.

3.4 BOARD COMPOSITION & STRUCTURE

A board is composed of members of the organization, democratically elected to serve for limited terms. None of these are technically requirements, but this book will treat them as if they were. A board is *deliberative*, meaning that it is the place for discussions and exchanges of views. A good board consists of about 7 to about 18 members, depending on the size of the organization: enough to bring a richness of expertise and views, but not so many that discussion becomes stilted by procedure. A good rule of thumb is that your board should fit around your conference table.

Officers are typically, but do not technically have to be, board members. These usually include the President, Secretary (or Clerk), Treasurer, one or more Vice Presidents, and often others. We will talk briefly about these offices in Chapter 4, but there are many resources on their typical duties online, through communal organizations, and through government agencies.

It is essential that board members and officers serve limited terms in their respective roles. When the president is going on their twentieth year, and the same board members have served for most of that time, the organization tends toward stagnation. Board members may convince themselves and others that nobody else wants to serve, when in reality other leaders might emerge if terms were limited. Legitimacy demands that leaders, however dedicated or irreplaceable, eventually relinquish control. This is why a well-governed organization rotates its volunteers through the chance to lead by limiting terms. This may be difficult in small organizations, but it is even more important there: the dangers of stagnation and undue attachment to individuals[44] are greater.

Many boards specify two-year terms for members and officers, with officers holding only one term, and board members serving no more than two (for a total of four years) or three (for a total of six). They may once again become eligible to serve after being off the board for one or more terms. I think these are about the right amounts of time, perhaps with the exception of officers who could serve as board members first and then be elected to office. Two- or three-year terms of board service are great for staggering members: half the board could turn over in odd-numbered years, and the other half in even-numbered years. That way, the board's membership always offers both continuity and fresh pairs of eyes.

Many organizations have a succession plan for the President and Vice President(s). Members might be elected Vice President with the expectation they will subsequently serve as President, and then remain on the board as Immediate Past President. This means a longer term of service for individuals going through that cycle, while also providing an opportunity for on-the-job training and continuity. Sometimes this model includes First, Second, Third, even Fourth Vice Presidents, the number depending on the organization's size. I really would think twice about having more than three Vice Presidents, if that, simply because a deliberative board should neither be too large nor composed mostly of officers. There needs

[44] Undue attachment to individual leaders may be an example of *heroism*—not a positive thing in this context—discussed in the later chapters of this book.

to be plenty of space on the board for members whose only job is to think about the issues before the board.

It is very important to keep the presidency rotating, for all the reasons that board members must rotate and more: the presidency holds a lot of power. I think a two-year term makes sense, maybe three in the largest organizations. That gives a leader enough time to get acclimated, get their agenda done, prepare the next group of leaders, and pass the torch. If you use a succession plan through one or more Vice President roles, I suggest sticking to a two-year term.

I don't recommend one-year terms for officers or board members. I don't think that's enough time for leaders to get their sea legs before they have to move on.

Composition of the Board

I've belonged to five synagogues and many other organizations, and each organization had a different board structure. Here are some of the choices. I present mostly pros and cons because there are few right or wrong answers here.

One contrast is between boards composed largely of *ex officio* committee chairs, and boards whose members' only job is to be on the board. *Ex officio* ("from the office") means that a person sits on a committee as part of a different volunteer or staff position. For example, the president may be an *ex officio* member of every committee, meaning that she is involved on those committees because of her presidency, not because she personally joined each committee. Very often, staff sit on committees *ex officio*: for example, your executive director might be an *ex officio* member of your finance committee, because their job gives them knowledge that the committee needs. When their job as executive director ends, so does their membership on the finance committee.

It's a common misconception to think *ex officio* means nonvoting. Perhaps people mistake the "*ex*" for meaning "out of office." When staff such as the Executive Director sit on committees *ex officio*, they generally do not vote, but that's because they are staff, not because they are *ex officio*. If your bylaws place committee chairs on the board, then those chairs sit *ex officio* on the board: they sit on the board as a consequence of being a committee chair; their term on the board would end when their term as committee chair ends. These would typically be voting board members, however.

If you mean to specify that an *ex officio* member of a board or committee will not be voting, do that in the bylaws by defining the position as "*ex officio* nonvoting." Otherwise, the assumption should be that members of the organization sitting *ex officio* vote, while non-members do not. Better to specify these things in advance.

Boards featuring committee chairs *ex officio* offer good communication with committees, easily keeping updated about accomplishments and challenges. Escalating an issue to the board becomes natural: the committee chair simply brings it up. The board may receive committee reports easily this way. Also, this kind of structure can help committee members feel involved, which in turn helps with recruitment of new leaders.

The main disadvantages of committee-chair boards are that they can result in staid leadership, and that they can cause the board to become too tactical. Regardless of their other duties, chairing committees or otherwise, board members remain responsible to the organization as a whole and cannot afford to overlook strategic leadership, fresh thinking, developing expertise outside their committee area, and most importantly their overall fiduciary duty. Also, the fiduciary role plus the committee-chair role can sometimes be too much for one person. They may become overwhelmed and not function in either role effectively.

The practice of appointing board members explicitly or implicitly as "representatives" of constituency groups presents similar pros and cons. A synagogue may wish their board to have a representative from the religious school, at least three members under 50, whatever the case may be. In advocacy organizations this can make even more sense. I once advocated in one of my synagogues for board liaisons from each committee, who were not the committee chair. These arrangements offer similar advantages and disadvantages as the committee-chair board, without the disadvantage of potentially overburdening the same person with a chair and a fiduciary role. Be wary, however, of enumerating too many constituency groups, lest you end up dealing with the politics of forgetting one, or of a new one demanding representation.

Every board should have at-large members. You might choose to have an at-large board, which is absolutely fine. If you choose to have a committee-chair board or some other largely *ex officio* arrangement, there need to be at least a few board members who have no job but to be board members. At-large members remind the board to look after the organization's overall best interest and strategic concerns, not just those of a particular constituency.

Avoid the word *representative*, because it conveys a misimpression. Unfortunately, the existence of a whole field of important research on nonprofit governance representation theory doesn't help us avoid confusion right now. Here's the distinction. It is important to make sure everybody *feels* represented, and in each decision the organization must consider the interests of its whole membership and even nonmember stakeholders (e.g. kids, seniors, future generations of Jews who haven't been born yet). However, no board member "represents" a constituency in the sense of fighting for their interests against other competing interests. This is not a legislature. The duty of every board member is always and only to the organization as a whole. It is a conflict of interest for board members to feel or express any other representative duty. Even if your bylaws provide for a board member to be appointed by some subset of the general membership, once in office that board member serves only the whole organization itself.

Board diversity leads to more and better ideas. When recruiting and developing a diverse slate, nominating committees should be aware of factors like gender, ethnicity—not all Jews are Ashkenazi—age, LGBTQ identity, financial status, household arrangement and size, Jewish practice as appropriate to the organization, area of interest within the organization, and other factors. If it ever was possible for a group of straight white men of comfortable means to do a good enough job as a deliberative board, it is no longer. Your organization needs the interplay of multiple perspectives that a diverse membership will bring to a deliberative board.

It used to be traditional to have a required donation for board members. I recommend against this. Before going into the reasons, let me clarify that board members should absolutely donate to the extent of their ability. They should be current in their financial obligations, because they care about the organization and because they set an example for others. They should donate as they are able above those obligations for the same reasons. And when the organization needs to raise money, board members are the ones whose job it is to raise it (it's not anyone else's job, honey) and so they ought to be the first to give.

Nevertheless, I think the time for required board donations has come and gone. For one thing, in today's context the requirement raises the appearance of a conflict of interest, as if power over the organization or access to leaders were somehow for sale. Let generous donors give freely, without the shadow of an explicit requirement.

It goes without saying that many of your highest donors will find their way to the board. It also goes without saying that you also need the perspective of some members who cannot afford to give as much. Your board needs at least a few teachers and students, social workers and janitors, health-care workers and unemployed people, in addition to the bankers, lawyers and real-estate tycoons, in order to see the issues from all sides.

A spot on the board is a demanding job, a personal sacrifice of service. Board members take on a significant time commitment as well as the personal liability of a fiduciary. The board is for hard workers who understand fiduciary duty. That undoubtedly includes a rotating subset of your highest donors along with a number of leaders who don't offer such personal financial resources.

Nothing requires that nonprofit boards be elected by general membership. The board is the decision-making authority for the organization: remember, board members are those at personal liability so decisions are ethically and legally theirs. Some nonprofit boards choose to seat successors by a vote of the board itself, which is certainly appropriate in organizations without a general membership structure, or those in which membership implies a general endorsement without decision-making power (think public radio). Subject to law and internal regulations, boards are free to choose the terms of their succession. For synagogues, let us sidestep other models in favor of a simple recommendation: Synagogue boards should be elected to limited terms by a general vote of synagogue members in a democratic process.

Even under that recommendation, boards have a lot of leeway to structure themselves. Between fully at-large and partly *ex officio* boards, there is a wide range of flexibility for what a board needs at a given time. These structures are defined in your organization's bylaws; see Chapter 4 for a discussion of how they should be adopted and changed. Whatever your board structure, I believe it should meet the following criteria:

- Board members serve no more than 4 to 6 years total. There may be an exception for the presidential line of succession.

- The board enjoys diversity of experience and viewpoint.

And in synagogues and other general-membership organizations:

- At least one-third of board members are elected at large by a democratic vote of the full membership.
- Every member has a realistic chance to have input on who serves on the board.
- Every member has a realistic chance to be considered for board service if they distinguish themselves appropriately in leadership.

Let's review those criteria. We've already spoken about limited terms, diversity, and the importance of at-large members. The last two criteria guard against insularity and detachment from the needs of any part of the community. They also support the organization's legitimacy by guaranteeing every member the chance to participate fully. Direct at-large election of the full board by staggered terms certainly fulfills these criteria. So does a board largely composed of *ex officio* committee chairs, in which the committee chairs are democratically elected by the committee membership, which in turn is suitably defined to serve democratic principles.

Because board members make decisions authoritatively, legitimacy requires wide participation in selecting them. That leaves a pretty broad range of workable structures. But inordinate barriers to participation, cliquishness, and overly long terms of service interfere with that feeling of participation. And in addition to legitimacy, democratic, inclusive processes do the best job ensuring we get a range of ideas on our boards. You never know where the next great idea will come from, so—like in our *shiur*—it's best to let ideas sprout from the ground up.

3.5 SYNAGOGUE MEMBERSHIP

This essay focuses on synagogue members, although much of it is applicable to other membership organizations.

Members of a synagogue are people who are eligible for membership, who choose to take on membership, and who are approved—often "elected"—to membership by the organization. The entire process is defined in the bylaws (see Chapter 4), together with the privileges that membership may entail. An organization is free to adopt any membership scheme it chooses, although as we'll see there are advantages and disadvantages to several common membership schemes.

The board is the legal authority of the organization, but the board is free to delegate its authority. Synagogue boards usually delegate to membership the ability to select board members through an accessible democratic process. Some boards delegate to a periodic *congregational meeting* their supreme decision-making authority, whose decisions the board binds itself to uphold until changed by a future congregational meeting. The specifics are defined in the organization's bylaws.

These decisions are too dependent on the details of each community for me to make recommendations. In general, greater powers for the general membership mean greater access, greater participation, and a more cautious approach. I say a more cautious approach because congregational decisions are logistically difficult to make and difficult to change.

There are good reasons not to put every decision to a vote of the membership. The membership does not have the board's fiduciary duty to decide solely in the interest of the organization. Relatedly, as excessive power is delegated to membership, the danger increases of members voting with conflicts of interest, which in turn become difficult to police because of the large numbers of people. Finally, the board really is the appropriate place to take the gloves off and duke it out once in a while. I mean rhetorically, of course, and hopefully in a well-moderated environment where shared values and valued friendships prevail (see Chapter 5 for some tips). But conflict cannot be avoided, even heated conflict, when people of goodwill have differing views. That kind of conflict belongs in a board meeting, not in front of a general membership meeting while two-thirds of the room look uncomfortably at their watches.

It's best to approach a congregational meeting with issues that have already been thought through. That doesn't mean members can't disagree, but ideally the major disagreements will already have had a hearing before they come before the general membership, so that outlines of the differing positions are already known.

Membership Eligibility and Rules

One major difference among membership schemes is the decision between individual and household units. There are advantages and disadvantages to each. In their excellent new book *New Membership & Financial Alternatives for the American Synagogue,*[45] Rabbi Kerry Olitzky and Rabbi Avi Olitzky report that one synagogue uses individual member units "to affirm clearly that singles are full and equal members of the congregation." Household member units require some additional thought to who votes: every adult in a household might be reasonable, but that has to be specified. On the other hand, household member units can also be a good way to express that all household arrangements are equally welcome.

Unfortunately, in too many cases this decision has been dictated by a database software package instead of a carefully considered policy chosen to fulfill a strategic goal. My only recommendation is not to let the software cart drive the strategic horse. First choose your membership model, then choose software that enables it.

Synagogues may limit who can join and vote. There is usually a financial commitment, with varying methods of providing special consideration or waivers in cases of need. Members may or may not be required to be Jewish. Such decisions depend on the synagogue's strategic identity. All membership criteria introduce complications, those hinging on Jewish identity the more so because they make governance dependent on interpretating *halakhah* (Jewish law). There is a very broad range of Jewish practice, and different answers will make sense for different communities.

The most important thing is to agree on all such definitions in advance of any procedural question coming up. You do not want to have to decide who gets to vote while a hot-button issue is pending. Take it from me, those are among the worst moments in politics; we don't need them in our holy spaces. Spend the time to settle these issues agreeably in advance of a policy question arising.

Committees

Aside from congregational meetings, boards delegate responsibility to members through *committees*. Usually, these are technically committees of the board. The board may create or dissolve them, although the bylaws may define synagogue committees extensively.

---

[45] Olitzky & Olitzky (2015), p. 10

A committee defined in bylaws is called a *standing committee* or sometimes a *regular committee.* These committees are required to carry out functions defined by the bylaws or assigned by the board. The board can also create temporary committees not specified in the bylaws. These are called all sorts of names: the very formal *select committees*, the rather whimsical *disappearing task forces* (notably used by The Evergreen State College), the Latinate *ad hoc committees*, or anything that implies the committee formed to do a job, and is intended to dissolve when that job is done. In this book we'll call them *task forces*, combining a welcome task orientation with a little harmless militaristic excitement.

Task forces are an excellent tool when something needs to get done and doesn't fit within an existing committee, or when the board needs further deliberation on an issue outside of board meeting time. They can be particularly well suited to situations where a range of different views or experiences are needed. Task-force terms can range from just a month to many years, but they should not be permanent. They should dissolve after their goal has been accomplished. If the Board identifies a permanent need for a new committee, it should be added to the bylaws as a standing committee. For much more on managing *projects*—work directed toward accomplishing specific objectives—see Chapter 8.

If an issue requires more discussion than the board has time for, consider referring the issue to a standing committee, or to a task force. Appoint task-force members with a diversity of viewpoints, and ask the group to report back to the board when it has hashed out the issue. One of the best ways for the board to involve non-fiduciaries in its deliberations is to refer a matter to a task force including some people who are not board members.

Committee chairs are typically either appointed by the board, appointed by the president, or elected from the membership of the committee. Committees may have their own succession structures for the chair. If there is a problem filling committee seats, congregational leadership may try to recruit for the committee among the general membership. A committee that chronically fails to recruit enough members may need to be merged with another committee or dissolved, which may require a change to the bylaws. See Chapter 5 for more thoughts on the life cycle of committees.

The congregation may set criteria for committee membership. Generally, committees are open to congregation members. But there's no reason people who are not synagogue members couldn't serve on committees, unless the bylaws prohibit it. Synagogue staff such as the rabbi and administrator often sit *ex officio* on pertinent committees, usually in nonvoting roles.

Committees are excellent scouting grounds for future leaders. The board and clergy can work together to identify members who may be ready for greater responsibility. This keeps board positions rotating, brings in fresh perspectives, and builds community by deepening members' commitment to the institution. Leadership development also serves donor development, as we will see in Chapter 6. Some volunteers will be happy with their current level of commitment, and leadership development should always validate that while letting everyone know that they will be supported if they decide they'd like to take on more. More on this in Chapter 5.

3.6 BOARD AND MANAGEMENT

Boards delegate responsibility in two major ways: by forming committees and by hiring staff. A large organization may have several entry-level staff positions to help with general tasks, professional positions such as a bookkeeper, and executive positions like an Executive Director. In synagogues, there are also religious professionals such as rabbis, cantors, and educators. Some small organizations have no staff at all, and the board and other volunteers must perform the necessary tasks.

The relationship between board and staff is often a source of confusion. Staff don't "work for" the board in any day-to-day managerial sense. Boards are poor vehicles for managing people, for many reasons. They are not in the office with employees each day to assign, assess, and help them with work. It is not a board's job to help employees develop. Boards do not necessarily consist of experienced managers, although some do. A board is a group of people, and it is unworkable and unfair for staff to be managed by a group. Most importantly, staff management is tactical—getting a job done—and boards need to keep sight of the strategic.

Higher-level policies often require board approval while lower-level policies do not. The placement of this line varies across organizations and may change with time. In small organizations the board may control all or most policy directly. The board typically delegates more authority to managers as the organization grows. In large organizations the board might stick to strategy and to the highest-level tactics that affect major investments, like starting a capital campaign or selling securities. The key is to articulate the authority which the board delegates to staff. This can be done in staff contracts, written into the bylaws, or by a board vote.

What boards do is called *oversight,* which means the relationship between boards and executives who report directly to the board. *Management,* by contrast, means the relationship between an employee and their manager, or between a volunteer and someone responsible for the volunteer work. I love the word *oversight,* which can mean either overseeing or overlooking. Let it be the former!

Oversight in a Robust Organization

Ideally, the board hires a manager to ensure that tasks get done. This position is usually called the *Executive Director.* In synagogues, *Administrator* may be an equivalent title, while larger nonprofits may use *Chief Executive Officer.* This top manager attends board meetings and gives reports on accomplishments and challenges. The board sets the strategy and highest-level policies, and consults with the executive director to ensure that tactical implementation serves the board's strategy. The powers of hiring, firing, and setting the compensation of the executive director rest with the board.

The executive director takes personal responsibility for the organization's management, and is accountable to the board through oversight—including meetings, reports, and being available to answer questions. Because lower-level staff are already being managed, the board does not interfere by directing lower-level staff. The executive director is the board's only appropriate point of staff contact. This system saves staff from the impossibility of working under multiple, potentially conflicting managers, and it keeps board members from tripping over each other's toes or getting distracted with the tactical. At a more basic level, Light puts it best: the board "can't delegate accountability to an executive director but keep the authority to itself. The board must be willing to authorize its delegates to do their jobs and give them necessary authority."[46]

[46] Light (2001), p. 115.

Oversight and Management in Synagogues

In synagogues, it used to be common for the Rabbi (or Senior Rabbi) to fill the top management role, acting as head of the synagogue staff and reporting to the board. However, it is increasingly customary for sufficiently large synagogues to hire an executive director as well. The rabbi manages the spiritual and often educational staff, while the executive director manages staff on the administrative side. There is no set formula for this division of labor; much depends on the congregation and on the preferences of the senior rabbi and executive director who are in place. In this dual-executive scenario, both the senior rabbi and the executive director are overseen directly by the board. It's almost as if there are two cooperating but separately managed staff organizations underneath the same board.

This leads to certain challenges not faced by organizations with a single executive manager. Turf issues happen, which we stand the best chance of resolving optimally when we're on the lookout for them nonjudgmentally. Aside from turf, there can be confusion as to who reports to whom. It is essential to have clear organizational diagrams with no staff member managed by more than one person (although they may support more than one person) because overlapping management is unworkable and unfair. On the other hand, dual-executive arrangements give two great leaders a chance to focus on the areas of their professional excellence, not to mention freeing rabbinic time for the pastoral needs of the community.

Working Boards

In small organizations with minimal or no staff, volunteers pick up the slack of daily tasks. This usually falls to board members; indeed, the board is responsible for the organization and therefore must take on day-to-day tasks if they are to get done. This is called a *working board.* Bridget Clark Whitney and Matthew Downey define a working board as a

> governance structure that appears in nonprofit organizations with smaller budgets (typically $500,000 and less). Due to a lack of financial resources, board members not only perform their fiduciary and strategic duties, but also partner with staff (if any are present) to fulfill management and technical functions.

The presentation by Whitney and Downey is well worth viewing for its helpful analysis and suggestions for working boards.[47]

There is nothing wrong with board members taking on extra responsibilities. But working boards must not leave the captain's wheel unattended while they go to swab the deck. The principal dangers of working boards are burnout and becoming overly tactical. I recommend to them a particular study of Chapter 2, and of the resources in this book on burnout prevention and keeping a volunteer pipeline. Don't let a year go by without a strategic review, and don't let a single meeting go by with only tactical content discussed (like how a synagogue will plan for the High Holidays).

To preserve strategic leadership, a working board needs to set aside time for strategy more stringently than a board in a traditional oversight role with staff taking care of the nitty-gritty. That's because the tactical tends to encroach. Working boards must be self-aware and intentional about their strategic responsibilities.

The best way to balance strategic and tactical roles in a working board is to understand that they are separate jobs. They are both important, of course, but they are separate; indeed, they are done by entirely different people in an ideally staffed organization. It is laudable for working boards to take on task work, and it sets a good example for others. But I would make time for it outside the board meeting—even if that means having a shorter fiduciary board meeting immediately followed by a task session consisting of the same people. When these separate jobs are kept separate, the board makes time for its strategic job while also collaborating to get task work done.

A tiny organization's working board looks very different from a large organization's highly formalized oversight board. But in growing organizations it can sometimes be difficult for boards to know where to draw the line. Here are my recommendations, which are so important that I'll let them be the last word in this chapter:

- Realize that although task accomplishment the board's responsibility, it is not ideally the board's work. Understand that it's preferable for the board to concentrate on oversight.
- If your organization is too small to afford staff, think about ideal staff job descriptions anyway. That way, you'll be

[47] Whitney & Downey (2013), presentation slide 6.

ready to go when you have the funds available, and the job descriptions will help you keep board members' fiduciary duties separate from their filling in as volunteers at jobs.

- As soon as possible, hire an executive director (rabbi, administrator, CEO, or other equivalent title appropriate to the organization, signifying full responsibility for managing the organization). The board should never, ever attempt to give direction to anyone except this person. Let them manage all lower-level staff.
- If your first hire is a lower-level staff person who requires management, such as an administrative assistant, this can create serious challenges distinguishing management from oversight, which can lead to bad habits later, not to mention driving the poor assistant crazy with multiple managers. Your best bet is to designate a volunteer for the managerial role, if possible not a board member, and try your level best to separate that managerial role from the board. Sometimes the president does this job, but it isn't ideally a board president's job. Review Chapter 7 for some management tips. Above all, whoever does the managing, it must be only one person. Board members must defer to the designated manager to do the managing.
- As you hire staff, board members accustomed to the working-board environment will need to understand that staff will often make different tactical decisions than they would have made, and that this is actually a good thing. Refer to Chapter 7 to see why.
- As the organization outgrows its need for a working board, board members may find themselves still filling in at some staff roles while having already delegated others. That can be a challenge to keep straight. Job descriptions will help, as will simply keeping the issue in mind. If it's difficult to find the right answer, a board development consultant with experience in small organizations may be able to help.
- The cardinal rule for working boards is: If you've hired someone to do a job, let them do the job.

Chapter 4

GOVERNING DOCUMENTS

4.1 SHIUR

> *Moses received the Torah at Sinai, and transmitted it to Joshua, Joshua to the Elders, the Elders to the Prophets, and the Prophets to the Members of the Great Synagogue. The latter used to say three things: Be patient with justice, raise many disciples, and build a fence around the Torah.*
>
> Pirkei Avot 1:1[48]

Thus begins the Mishnaic tractate *Pirkei Avot* (Chapters of the Ancestors), one of the oldest parts of the Talmud. The first chapter of *Pirkei Avot* continues in this vein, tracing the transmission of Torah down through the generations of scholars right through the generations of the Mishnaic authors themselves. The text asserts an unbroken chain of tradition between the original Torah of Moses and the Talmud of the Rabbis many centuries later.

In Judaism, the chain of tradition is represented in documents. Each receiver of the Torah adhered to its law while implementing it for their time. Especially by the time of the Talmud, after the destruction of the Temple in Jerusalem around which so much of the written Torah revolves, Jewish law had become less about following precise directions from Heaven and more about deciding how to apply the law in new situations. To record and justify those decisions for future generations, the Rabbis adopted a written system of discourse.

In our mishnah,[49] the Elders are the leaders of the generations who come between Joshua and the Prophets. The Great Synagogue was said to have been founded by Ezra the Scribe. The text goes on to say that the Great Synagogue passed the

[48] Translation from the Soncino.

[49] A verse of Mishnah is called a *mishnah*.

Torah along to the first Rabbis. (It is noteworthy that the Rabbis trace their spiritual lineage through the prophets and not the priests, but that's for another time.) To establish their legitimacy, the Rabbis claim their place in the chain of Torah transmission.

Our mishnah leaves us with the three principles most important to the Great Synagogue—what those leaders wanted to accomplish. Today we would call them strategic values and goals. They guide the Rabbis in all future decisions. They can also guide us, as we seek to create documents that carry the torch of our organization's legitimacy and give voice to its strategic values and goals.

Be patient with justice. The Sages knew that almost every decision is a contest of competing good values. In our quest to codify our high principles into consistent policies and organizational structures, the Sages advise us to be patient. Let every point of view have a chance to be heard, making special room in our minds and hearts for views with which we disagree.

Raise many disciples. The Rabbis' strategy was to save a decimated Judaism, after the Romans destroyed the Temple, by attracting as many students as possible. In many ways, this is our project too. Between the terrible memory of the Shoah and the asphyxiating hug of assimilation, our generation also faces the need to raise many disciples. This implies an imperative to be inclusive. Surely there is a place at the Jewish table for everyone who sincerely wishes to sit there. Within the boundaries of our Jewish identity and conscience, let us always try to find it.

Build a fence around the Torah. One of the bedrock principles of Jewish law, this is an excellent example of a strategic principle driving policy decisions. The idea is that it's so important to avoid breaking a Torah law that we make regulations for everyday life that are stricter than the Torah law, so as to give ourselves a safety margin if we should inadvertently violate one of those regulations.

I'm not talking about your community's norms of observance or your beliefs about the Talmud here. I'm at home in Jewish Renewal and Reform Judaism myself. But as heirs to the rabbinic tradition, we do build fences around our laws in more ways than we may realize, especially in our organizations. The idea of holding our core principles so dear that we take precautions not to break them, and codifying those precautions into written regulations for daily life, can be traced as far back as there were rabbis and even farther, to the legendary Great Synagogue.

The ethical guidelines we discussed in Chapter 3 are an excellent example of how "building a fence around the law" can keep an organization healthy. In this chapter, we will discuss many other ways written decisions can implement an organization's strategic direction. Once we've decided which strategic values we hold most dear, we codify written regulations to reflect them and to ensure we keep them. Those regulations will ensure we live by our values, in the chain of Jewish tradition—in the tradition of the Jewish chain.

4.2 BYLAWS AND CONTRACTS

We spoke in Chapter 2 about strategic documents, which are the result of strategic planning and strategic review sessions. Just as a quick refresher, an organization's *purpose* is the formal, legal reason is exists, the *mission* extends the purpose to give a fuller account of the activities the organization exists to do, and a *vision* explains what life will be like when the organization does its mission well.

Remember, our definition of *policy* is a written tactical decision by an organization. Policies can encompass a wide scope, from a preferred office-supplies vendor or a snack schedule for kids to the process of electing the organization's president.

Bylaws regulate the ongoing life of our organizations. They are tactical: they tell us what to do in a given situation. However, they are (or should be) for general permanent application as opposed to addressing particular incidents. In that sense, they can be called *high-level tactical* decisions because they are designed to apply to categories of situations. *Contracts* are also high-level tactical decisions, because they bind the organization to agreements with another party. Bylaws and contracts, therefore, are special types of policy that are particularly high-level and difficult to change.

The many lower-level tactical decisions bound by bylaws and contracts in our organizations are just called *policies*. When we talk about "bylaws, contracts and policies," as we often do, we're using the term *policies* in a narrow sense. Strictly speaking, bylaws and contracts are high-level policies themselves. Ideally, aside from any confidentiality issues in contracts, bylaws and contracts should go into a policy handbook along with the organization's other policies.

There is a tension in organizational policy between consistency and adaptiveness to circumstances. Often, this tension manifests as an individual request, in response to which decision-makers must weigh fairness against leniency: fairness on the side of consistency (would others be treated the same way?) and leniency on the side of adaptiveness (the request is reasonable, there might not be other situations like it). Suppose a child requests to miss two months of synagogue Bat Mitzvah preparation because of a long-planned family trip. Or, the bookkeeper wishes to become a synagogue member. Or, a non-Jewish parent wishes to participate in a Bar Mitzvah ceremony.

Situations like these will be uncomfortable if our policies have not anticipated them and we are caught without having done any forethought. Under such circumstances, any decision can appear as if it were taking sides personally. The legitimacy of organizational policy depends, therefore, on its having been adopted prior to a crisis situation. This was the approach of the Talmudic sages: they investigated many hypothetical situations in order to arrive at a universally applicable policy—which for them was a decision about Jewish law—that would be available when a real situation arose.

Recall that the legitimacy of decisions also depends on their not being changed too often. A personal request or interpersonal situation lends emotional weight to this underlying reason our decisions can appear less legitimate when they are responsive to events. Sometimes exceptions need to be made, and sometimes policies need to change, but when we consider situations in advance as much as our experience permits us, we protect our legitimacy by limiting those necessary exceptions to a tolerable few. This is why it is important that policies direct our actions categorically, not situationally, whenever possible.

Policies help accomplish this by being written and available for future application. There is also something about the process of writing and maintaining policies that lends itself to research, comparing our policies with those of other organizations, and updating them intentionally. On the other hand, when we "wing it" with spur-of-the-moment decisions by individual staff or volunteer leaders, we risk inconsistency and the perception of bias.

In order from highest- to lowest-level decisions, organizational governing documents include the purpose, mission and vision, strategic goals, bylaws, contracts, and (other) policies. Let this order be a guide to the frequency with which it's a good idea to change these decisions. Our strategic decisions should serve us for years or decades; annual strategic reviews are to ensure that our policies conform to our strategy, not the other way around. On the other hand, when we need to prescribe the way something should be done, it is advantageous to do so at the lowest level possible, in order to leave maximum leeway to set policy according to unforeseen needs. Don't pass a bylaw when a simple vote of the board would do.

Bylaws

Bylaws are written rules, adopted through a formal process, that describe how an organization governs itself. (Depending on the jurisdiction, the word *constitution* may also be used. Because this may be misconstrued to refer to the articles of incorporation, we will use *bylaws* in this book.) Because governance systems affect every other aspect of organizational life, bylaws have a special status apart from other policies. Bylaw changes require a vote of the board or membership, sometimes a supermajority, and sometimes a filing with the state's public-records agency. Those details depend on the organization and the jurisdiction, but the principle of predictable governance safeguards people's right to participate as they expect.

Bylaws generally state the organization's name and purpose, how the board is organized, the officers and their duties, how all of these are elected, terms of office and procedures for removal from office, the terms of membership including dues or other financial obligations, the privileges of membership in good standing such as clergy access and committee service in a synagogue, the duties of key staff including clergy, the functions of standing committees, and terms of adoption and amendment of the bylaws. Synagogue bylaws may additionally stipulate movement affiliation including terms recommended or required by that movement, as well as the role of the rabbi in setting congregational policy, which depends on the synagogue's stream of Jewish tradition. On *npgovernance.org* I have listed several good resources for sample bylaws, for synagogues and for other organizations. Your state may also provide a helpful template for bylaws.

Bylaws are one of only a few devices available to constrain the board's authority by formally delegating issues to other decision-makers on the board's behalf. This should be done sparingly because the board remains responsible for all that happens. For example, in Conservative and Orthodox synagogues the rabbi's authority to make decisions on issues of Jewish law may be central to the community's Jewish identity; it therefore belongs in the bylaws to prevent it from being changed without advance notice and formal deliberation.

The board may also choose to assign topical areas to committees and staff. The *annual budget* is an excellent example: instead of approving every little expenditure by separate vote, the Board preapproves a block of money to be spent by designated staff or officers for preapproved purposes, requiring additional approval only if operations should need to deviate from the budget.

It can be tempting to use bylaws to enshrine decisions about which people feel very strongly, but it is often advantageous not to do so. I recommend that bylaws be kept to matters of organizational structure. Define standing committees with a very broad, one- or two-sentence statement of their purpose, but avoid using bylaws to specify exactly what tasks or programs a committee will do, or to delineate staff roles too precisely. Why? Because bylaws are difficult to change. The less we say in bylaws, the more room we leave ourselves to make policy. Certainly staff and committee roles should have clear direction. But the best place for that direction may be in the lower-level policies of the organization, not in the bylaws.

Policymaking always involves a tension between foreseeing too little and prescribing too much. My advice: be more predictive, but less prescriptive. By all means brainstorm and try to foresee as many possible situations as you can, guided by strategic decisions about what you value as an organization. Then, record the resulting policy decisions at the lowest level where they make sense, so as not to constrain the options of future decision-makers unnecessarily. I would keep bylaws to describing governance structures, along with any language required for 501(c)(3) or other nonprofit status and movement affiliation as applicable to synagogues, while keeping all other issues to the policy handbook. Elections and terms of officers belong in the bylaws. Meeting schedules and detailed committee descriptions, detailed executive job descriptions and any mention of non-executive staff, gala plans and school curricula belong in the policy handbook.

Contracts

A contract is a *meeting of minds* between the congregation and some other person or organization; it has (at least) two signatures to show that there is an agreement binding both parties. A contract may be the most difficult policy to change in an organization, because it cannot be changed without the assent of the other party. Therefore, be careful in making contracts, and never sign a major contract without running it by a lawyer.

All staff should have contracts. It is common to hire staff informally, especially in small organizations, but a good contract protects all parties. A detailed discussion of staff contracts is beyond my expertise; my recommendation is only to have them. Please consult a lawyer for help with staff contracts.

Contracts with executive staff—including clergy—deserve special attention because they may bind the organization to high-level policies, or may cede policymaking authority to these key staff. For example, rabbinical contracts should and generally do specify freedom of the pulpit, meaning that the rabbi is free to say whatever she or he wishes without taking direction from lay leadership as to the content of those teachings. Likewise, an executive director may negotiate for a contract that she feels gives her the authority she needs to be an effective leader.

Thus contracts often delegate policymaking. In a synagogue or other close-knit membership organization, legitimacy requires that the relevant terms of any contract be made available to members, including the fact that they were agreed to contractually and therefore cannot be changed unilaterally. Legitimacy also requires that the procedure for adopting those contracts be transparent and accessible to any member wishing to have input. However, not all terms of staff contracts should be public. Compensation issues are often personal and private. My rule of thumb is that issues affecting membership decision-making processes, if applicable, be available to and fully understood by the membership.

Other types of contracts may bind the organization to policies. An agreement to co-host a homeless shelter with the church down the street, an agreement to rent space, an agreement with a publisher, a software provider, a governance consultant, an architect, a neighborhood association—all are contracts that bind the organization. Contracts are an essential part of business. The key is to recognize them as policymaking instruments, to ensure they conform to existing policies, and to respect transparency and the right of stakeholders to participate, as applicable, when considering contracts that set new policy, or that limit future policymaking options.

4.3 THE POLICY HANDBOOK

Building on the bylaws and contracts that create binding policy, the policy handbook fills out the portrait of organizational life and facilitates continuous introspection and improvement.

The board can delegate responsibility for certain areas of work while retaining ultimate authority over them. For example, a synagogue board could theoretically decide to overrule the School Committee and buy one textbook instead of another, or to overrule the Social Action Committee and nix official participation in a march. This is sometimes necessary but should be done very sparingly, for two reasons: it can distract the board with tactical details that committees were appointed in the first place to handle, and if overused it can damage legitimacy by making people wonder if decisions made by the advertised process will be honored. Absent a very good reason not to, boards should allow those tasked with making decisions to make them.

That principle gives rise to multiple sources of policy in our organizations. The board is always able to make policy. So are committees, staff, and local chapters, depending on the organization, within their delegated areas. A synagogue Social Action Committee can make policy for charitable projects within its budget and authority to endorse. An Executive Director can make policy for parking and employee management. A rabbi can make policy for sermon content. A local chapter in a national organization can make certain official statements to the media. There are always questions around the margins, and if they can't be decided informally based on current policy, they may need the board's deliberation, giving rise to a new general policy. It is always better to try to foresee as many of these situations as possible, so that policy will be available to guide ambiguous or contentious situations when they occur.

I recommend that boards delegate low-level policies while retaining control over high-level ones. That is to say, policies that are about a particular area assigned to a committee are best decided in committee. Wise boards will be skeptical about temptations to intervene, even if a board member individually disagrees with a lower-level decision. Delegation helps us get more done, as we will discuss in Chapter 7. On the other hand, committees may discuss issues and then treat a committee vote as a recommendation to the board for final ratification. When this is done, a wise board will ask not whether board members personally agree with the committee's recommendation, but whether the recommendation's implications were accounted for within the committee's process.

It is wise to make decisions at the lowest level whose scope includes the major implications of the decision. For example, a synagogue board need not spend time legislating the scheduling of services. An Executive Director shouldn't bother ordering office supplies if a lower-level staffer can handle it.

Organizational policies are relatively easy to change, compared to binding documents, but that still doesn't mean they ought to be changed too often. The point of policies is for longer-term decisions to guide shorter-term decisions. Policies lose their legitimacy to do that if they are always being changed. Change them when necessary, but a good high-level policy could last for decades.

Good policies define the *who, what, when* and *where* of what happens in the organization. Who should be at the meeting, what's on the agenda, when and where it takes place, are the sort of information a person needs in order to participate effectively in a meeting. Who teaches the children (what kind of qualifications are needed, how many teachers, etc.), what they teach, when and where classes are held, are the sorts of information needed to run a school. These policies are highly practical. They are the nuts and bolts of organizational life.

Why and *how* questions are less suitable for policy. *Why* questions are matters of strategy; these overarching decisions guide policymaking. Always know why you're doing something before you do it. *How* questions, on the other hand, ought to be left to the individuals doing the work. There is no sense making synagogue policies on how to make latkes.

How questions are the stuff of *procedures:* how best to accomplish a task based on previous experience. These are great to have, and many organizations combine them with policy right into a Policies & Procedures Manual. Policies and procedures both need to be available when something needs to be looked up.

But policies and procedures are quite different, despite the tempting alliteration. For one thing, I am not at all convinced that procedures represent decisions. When there is a need for an institutional decision on a step-by-step protocol—for example, what steps to take in an emergency, may one not occur—that ought to be adopted as a policy, to signify the weight of communal decision-making behind it. On the other hand, if a smart employee comes up with a highly efficient way of entering data, that may be well worth preserving but it does not need to be a policy. I don't think it's an organizational decision. It's simply a helpful observation of what worked well; it's advice from a past to a future worker. Perhaps against the conventional wisdom, I say it's good to be clear about those distinctions. We'll come back to procedures in Chapter 10.

Policy Handbooks in the Twenty-First Century

Organizational policies can cover a broad range of topics, come from different policymakers, and guide the actions of different people within the organization. Many organizations create *policy handbooks* to keep their policies easily available for reference. A policy handbook should state who created each policy, the date it went into effect, who is required or advised to follow it, and what the policy is. If the policy is more than a couple sentences, there should be a summary and then a full statement. There could be separate policy handbooks for different roles: in a synagogue, for example, there might be handbooks specifically for board members, committee members, committee chairs, rabbis, executive or managerial staff, employees, religious-school teachers, religious-school parents, congregation members, and others.

The value of policies is clear: they support the organization's legitimacy, record decisions, manage expectations, pre-empt arguments and misunderstandings, and minimize appearances of partiality or having to reinvent the wheel. This leads to high legitimacy and is a hallmark of good governance.

If your organization does not yet have an organized list of policies, you will want them, but you don't have to do all the work at once. Ask staff and board members to write down draft policies anytime they come up. This drafting should be done in loose, informal language. Scan minutes of previous board meetings for decisions. Standing committees could be asked to do the same thing. And from now on, whenever a decision is made, record it in the right place in the policy handbook.

Finally, ask your local Jewish Federation, national movement organization if applicable, and a couple other Jewish organizations (or maybe even a church for a fresh perspective) if they would share their policy manuals with you. That kind of collaboration forges local ties and is an ancient Jewish form of peer-to-peer learning.

When examining another organization's policies, don't just copy them. Rather, use them as food for thought about what you might need to address. If you find yourself starting a policy manual afresh with a treasure trove of sample policies, it may be helpful to use a KJ diagram to categorize the policy options along with further brainstorming, then, taking each category individually, decide which policies you'd like to enact. The board, committees, clergy and staff can all do this activity, and may refer issues back and forth to each other, or they may do it together. Reviewing or especially starting a policy handbook is a lot of work, so take it one step at a time, taking on an amount of the work each month that feels comfortable.

I'm a fan of laying sidewalks where people are walking. A story is told about a college campus renovation, a few decades ago, in which planners did not build sidewalks across the quad for the first year, instead letting students tread down pathways through the grass. Then they laid the sidewalks where people had been walking. This is either a good urban myth or a rather common practice, because I've heard versions of it at the State University of New York at Stony Brook, the University of California at Berkeley, and elsewhere. In any case, it's an excellent model for policy. We can't possibly predict all of our organization's future needs, so we're better off making the policies we need.

There are two factors to remember when making policies this way. First, we should not allow policy to become reactive, being careful in particular to avoid exaggerated emotional snap-backs from bad experiences. Experience should inform our policies, but we need to consider it with some remove. For example, if you received bad publicity after co-sponsoring a social-action march, don't let the emotional tide lurch the organization all the way in the other direction by ramming through a board vote to ban all marches forever. Instead, take some time to deal with what happened and set policy when people are calm and able to hear different viewpoints. The same is true of good experiences: if a program worked well, that doesn't necessarily mean you must always do every future program exactly the same way, ossifying something that had been fresh and engaging into a stultifying stolidity. Policy made reactively tends to be made overreactively, so I recommend building reflection time into the policymaking process.

By a similar token, problems of an interpersonal nature are not likely to be solved or helped by adopting clever new rules. We are not computer programs; our interpersonal problems are generally not caused by errors or omissions in our rules. Interpersonal problems ought to be solved interpersonally. Much of the remainder of this book will focus on interpersonal challenges from a variety of different angles.

Policies explain and policies constrain, but they should explain as much as possible while constraining as little as possible to protect people's safety and rights, and to serve the strategic goals of the organization.

Second, even when we lay the sidewalks where people have walked, legitimacy still demands that policies be already in place at the time they're called upon. So it pays to predict our future needs to the extent we reasonably can. Here again is our policymaking tension—predicting too little versus prescribing too much. Every organization makes its own path between those extremes.

Consider putting your policy handbook online. Online policy handbooks are searchable, and can be organized in multiple ways at once (for instance, by policymaker, by date adopted, by who is affected, by content). They can be password-protected if necessary. They make editing by multiple policymakers much easier, without the need for a staff member or volunteer to be in charge of officially reformatting a central document. They make it possible to jot down a policy when it's decided and have it immediately become searchable and available to all. Online policy handbooks can always be printed as needed, annually or on demand. Chief among the advantages of online policy handbooks is their savings in labor, which could make the difference for a small, busy organization between keeping well-maintained written policies or not.

If you don't already have an online policy technology, consider a free password-protected blog package. A policy handbook may sound different from a blog, but the structure of posts (policies), categories and password-protection options can make everything easier to organize and find.

Abraham Lincoln, who knew all about accomplishing major goals, is said to have remarked that if he had eight hours to cut down a tree, he would spend six of them sharpening his ax.[50] The idea is similar to that of Kohelet (Ecclesiastes) 10:10, which has it, "If an axe is blunt, and a man does not sharpen it beforehand, then he must exert all his strength to wield it, but it is an advantage to prepare one's skill in advance."[51]

Today we are more likely to be planting and preserving trees than chopping them down, so we need policies instead of ax sharpeners, but we need them for the same reason. Good policies make every future decision easier.

Good policies are well-engineered tools that are available for us when we need them. They prepare us for tasks ahead by making distinctions and rules in advance, which can then be applied. They cut down on surprises. They protect us from being caught unawares in an unforeseen situation. They allow us to document lessons learned from experience and reuse them in new situations (see Chapter 10 for more about that).

Policies take effort to develop, but the work can be done in small pieces. If your policy handbook needs to be started or refreshed, why wait?

---

[50] As is often the case with important quotations, Lincoln does not seem to have actually said this. It's an important idea anyway. The reason it was attributed to Lincoln, apparently no earlier than 1960 according to QuoteInvestigator.com, is tangential to our discussion but is an interesting excursion into how spiritually important textual traditions develop.

[51] Translation by Gordis (1968), p. 192; quoted in Pinker (2011), p. 175. Pinker gives a totally different perspective on the meaning of Kohelet 10:10.

Chapter 5
VOLUNTEER LEADERSHIP

5.1 SHIUR

> *Seven marks characterize the clod and seven the wise person. The wise person does not speak before one who is greater in wisdom and does not break in upon the speech of a fellow. She is not hasty to answer. She asks what is relevant and answers according to the* halakhah *[Jewish law]. She speaks on the first point first and on the last point last. Where she has heard no tradition she says, "I have not heard." She concedes to what is true. With the clod, the opposite of all of these is the case.*
>
> Pirkei Avot 5:10[52]

Leadership is largely about eliciting the opinions and cultivating the capabilities of others. The leader's life is full of discussions, negotiations and meetings. In this *mishnah*, the Rabbis seem to understand the challenges of discussion. A wise person listens before speaking, because they might learn something they had not thought of. They think before speaking, because haste makes waste. The wisest person in a meeting might be the one who waits patiently until everyone else has held forth, then slowly speaks the three or four most important words of the day.

It amazes me that the *Tannaim* (sages of the Mishnah) already shared my personal pet peeve: interrupting. A clod cannot wait to be heard and does not listen to others, barging in at full volume in the middle of someone else's sentence. A wise person knows that the best ideas come from a calm, respectful environment in which interruptions do not occur. How basic to human communication this rule must be, if the rabbinic sages already recognized it almost 2,000 years ago.

[52] Translation from the Soncino except that I modified the gender pronouns.

The *mishnah*'s fourth and fifth points show the ability to categorize information, not speaking willy-nilly or in the order of personal emotional urgency, but in a logically organized way that others can follow. The ability to answer according to the *halakhah* (Jewish law) can be taken at face value for traditional congregations, but it has additional meaning for all of us. The wise person does not answer merely according to personal feeling, but bases her answer on something available and agreeable to everyone. There is no expectation of unanimity in any Jewish discussion, but there is an expectation that contributions to discussion will be rooted in study and careful respect for the views of others.

The sixth point is a gem of the Talmud, perhaps the most important of the seven: "Where she has heard no tradition, she says, 'I have not heard.'" How simple and how difficult this is for us! The Talmud also says: "Accustom your tongue to say, 'I do not know,' lest you become entangled in a web of deceit."[53] We are to resist the temptation to present as Jewish tradition that which we may personally favor, but do not know to be the tradition. It is very tempting for leaders to claim unearned justification for their views. The *gemara* quote (the latter one) shows the consequences of inflating our opinions into laws: we get pulled into a web of lies, constantly faking it with no chance of ever making it. There is no shame in not knowing something, but there is shame in pretending to know what we do not. It is so tempting that we need to practice saying "I do not know" until it rolls off our tongue instinctively, instead of whatever else would otherwise have fallen out of our mouths. Accustom your tongue to say, "I do not know."

Finally, we need to admit when an opposing view has bested our own at argument. It happens to everyone. Civility and cordiality depend on our ability to gracefully concede, and this makes group decisions bearable. When clergy, senior staff and volunteer leaders set the example of conceding, others feel more comfortable doing so themselves. Even God concedes an argument elsewhere in the Talmud, notwithstanding that the human rabbis in the story had the proverbial Wrong Answer.[54] If God can do it, so can we.

---

[53] b. *Berakhot* 4a. Translation from Steinsaltz (2012), p. 18.

[54] There is not space in this book to do justice to the "Oven of Akhnai" story (b. *Bava Metzia* 59), but an exposition of it is available on *npgovernance.org*.

5.2 COMMITTEES AND LEADERSHIP

Almost all organizations make use of committees from time to time. This essay will use a synagogue example, but it will be equally applicable to any organization with standing volunteer committees. Some organizations do not use standing committees, but may use task forces commissioned by the board for specific projects.

For whatever purpose a committee is formed, it shares certain characteristics with any other deliberative group. As we saw in Chapter 4, standing committees are created by boards to address particular areas of interest or need. Commonly used synagogue committees include Adult Education, Beautification, Building, Cemetery, Communications, Community Concerns or Bikkur Cholim (helping members in need), Endowment, Executive, Finance, holiday- or event-preparation committees, Israel, LGBTQ, Library, Membership, a men's group, Nominating, Outreach, Parent-Teacher Association, Personnel, Ritual or Religious Practices, School, Security, Social, Social Action or Tikkun Olam, Ushers, a volunteer gift shop, a women's group, Youth, and many more, often under different names. (Our committees are an alphabet of *whoa!*) Your synagogue does not necessarily need all these committees, and I have undoubtedly forgotten many good ones. They are listed only to jog your thinking.

To review from Chapter 3, *standing committees* handle ongoing work and exist permanently, while *task forces* are designed to accomplish a specific project and then disband. This essay is mainly about standing committees, while Chapter 8 is devoted entirely to projects. However, a few task forces' time periods are so long that they function practically like standing committees over many years. For example, a capital campaign will take several years, but its steering committee is likely to be technically a task force.

Committees can set their own internal policies, as long as they don't conflict with higher-level policies. Policies can be set by the chairperson or by a vote of committee members. The latter is preferable because it confers greater legitimacy and remains in effect from one chairperson to the next, but a policy from the chair may help if it is noncontroversial *or* if it is firmly within the chair's prerogative to act. I've done both. In 2006, I mediated a very emotional debate about *kashrut* policy while serving as the Religious Practices Chair of a Reform synagogue. I announced the policies we would use months in advance, hoping they would prove acceptable to all. I stated that we would devote our May meeting to discussion and hold a vote in June, and that we would alternate speakers between the two major sides (both relatively noncontroversial policies; both also firmly within my prerogative). I further stated that I would recognize votes only from synagogue members who attended both meetings. Nothing gave me the specific power to do that, but the bylaws did not prevent it, either, and with no other guidance I asserted my prerogative to decide who could vote at my meeting. The congregation did not have to let me get away with that, but they did, probably because they felt my policies were unbiased and likely to save everyone trouble, and because they were announced so far in advance that any procedural concerns could be addressed separately from the policy debate. Just the same, those policies would have had no legitimate weight if I'd announced them right before the vote in June. What tenuous legitimacy they had came from the advance notice and lack of opposition over time.

War stories aside, it's better to adopt policies by vote, even if they are within the prerogative of the chair. The same Religious Practices Committee often voted on policies. We adopted policies such as granting ushers the individual discretion to act with congregational authority in services. We voted on the times services would be held, and we voted to spend money within our budget on refurbishing ritual objects and books.

Although committees and staff are free to adopt policies, and indeed often do so in the course of their work, the board necessarily has final say. This can lead to confusion over when a policy needs board approval. As with operating authority granted to staff, every organization draws this line in a different place. A good rule of thumb is to submit a policy to the board if there's any question that it might need their approval, if it affects the organization's strategy in any way, if it affects areas outside the committee's purview, *or* if it is so controversial that it impacts the harmony of the group.

Board approval is not needed for an announcement that organized visits to chronically ill members will occur on Thursdays and Sundays. It might be needed for a major change to the website. It is definitely needed for a change to *kashrut* policy. The board may also initiate its own review of any committee policy at any time, although it behooves the board to delegate policymaking to committees. Policies adopted by committee, announced to all, and not immediately challenged should be regarded as being in effect. It is possible to support this with a clause in the bylaws, for example, stating that committee votes take effect after the following board meeting if the board takes no action. Subject to the bylaws, the board is free to create, modify or remove committees as needed.

Indeed, no committee lasts forever, so let our last general remark on committees be not to fear the natural committee life cycle. Even standing committees see interest periodically wax and wane, and while certain standing committees will always be needed, the board should not fear to expand or consolidate them according to the ebb and flow of enthusiasm for them.

We can model the committee life cycle in terms of the seasons. Committees may start or get reinvigorated in a springtime of enthusiasm, often with a persuasive internal leader who rallies people to the cause. They enter a summer growing season of productivity and harvest, which may last many years. They naturally wane over time, as people get bored or pursue other interests, longtime leaders depart, unsolved frustration gets the better of morale, or there doesn't seem to be as much to do as before. They enter a wintertime of introspection and planning, pruning back to the most cherished ideas and letting others die off, until, usually with the help of outside gardeners, winter eventually gives way to another enthusiastic spring.

Every synagogue would like to do far more social action, holiday preparation, building beautification, children's education, visits to the sick, and so many other activities than they could ever possibly have time for. As long as it can't all be done, don't be afraid to let people plug in where they're most enthusiastic, and at their own pace. If you're moving toward winter in the ritual department, try consolidating holiday committees, *halakhah* and ushering into one group, and cut back on expectations to match the volunteer interest available. Or, if interest in the physical space is hurtling through springtime, maybe a new Beautification Committee could split off from the Building Committee to allow one group to focus on construction while the other focuses on design. My purpose is not to offer such steps as better than the alternatives, but to illustrate the menu of options available to fit your committees into the breathing rhythm of your community.

Restricted-Membership Committees

Boards of larger organizations often need standing committees or task forces which are only open only to board members, or only to people appointed according to the bylaws or board policies. These are generally for handling intensive, deliberative or confidential fiduciary work that does not need to take the full board's time. These are good reasons for restricted membership, and it's important to note, neither such committees' existence nor their membership are secret at all. If restricted-membership committees exist to address a specific need for confidentiality countervailing against the generally positive value of disclosure, boards should meet in *executive session* (without taking minutes and without guests present) when hearing and discussing reports from them.

I caution against overusing restricted-membership committees. I have seen organizations get into trouble by keeping information from fiduciary boards in this way. These committees are not vehicles to avoid disclosure or to bypass the board. Having said that, the most common restricted-membership standing committees include a Personnel Committee, a Nominating Committee, and (sometimes) a Finance Committee and an Executive Committee.

Personnel committees exist because performance evaluations of individual staff ought not to be public. While I still believe there is no information to which a board member should not be privy if they need it for their fiduciary deliberations, it is advisable to keep highly sensitive personnel information to a group as small as possible, and to avoid distributing printed records of that information and of deliberations on it. A board member with a bona fide need to know someone's salary, for example, can always ask for that information and should be given it in confidence. Otherwise, a Personnel Committee might consist of just the President and a couple other people, charged to oversee contracts and negotiations with specific personnel. A synagogue Personnel Committee might also handle the nitty-gritty of rabbinic contract negotiations and renewals, reporting to the board on progress made between meetings.

One very important caution: *the Personnel Committee does not manage the staff.* We spoke in Chapter 3 about the difference between staff management and board oversight. The Personnel Committee may be the point of contact for top executives (Rabbi, Executive Director, etc.) in terms of their individual performance and compensation, while those executives continue to discuss the substance of synagogue business with the full board. Lower-level staff should not have to deal with the Personnel Committee at all; they already report to a manager within the office. However, a Personnel Committee might hear appeals of staff grievances according to a governing policy on employee disputes.

Nominating Committees identify and nominate a slate of future officers and Board members prior to an election. They do much of the leadership recruitment work, often in collaboration with clergy who have that "special touch" which might convince a great volunteer to become a board member. While organizations may permit nominations from the membership floor during general elections, this is rare unless a serious dispute is going on, or unless there has been trouble filling the position. (A contested election is sometimes but not always the best way to deal with a disagreement over policy.) Therefore, Nominating Committees enjoy significant power to select future leaders, although this may involve more cajoling and begging for applicants than selecting among an overplus of applications.

Finance Committees are often chaired by the elected Treasurer, and may include the Executive Director or equivalent staff position *ex officio*. They serve a variety of roles. They usually assist the Treasurer to monitor the accounts, perhaps dividing financial oversight work among committee members. They may draft, and they certainly review, the annual budget before submitting it to the board for approval. They make projections and try to keep board members informed of the organization's financial position and direction. They may be involved in fundraising as well, although fundraising and accounting are entirely different jobs (see Chapter 6). Aside from fundraising, most of these functions fall within the Treasurer's job description, which is often far too much work for one person to do well. Therefore, much of a Finance Committee's work may be framed as assisting the Treasurer.

An Executive Committee is a subset of the board that meets more frequently and acts with power between board meetings. In organizations with an Executive Committee, the bylaws may state that Executive Committee actions must be ratified at the next board meeting in order to take effect permanently.

Executive committees come with pros and cons. They can make board deliberation more efficient, saving precious board time for the highest-level issues while allowing the nitty-gritty to be handled elsewhere. They can also enable faster response times in cases demanding action before the next board meeting.

On the other hand, Executive Committees can create the temptation to keep information and decision-making hidden from the board. In all but the largest organizations, the appearance of an Executive Committee might be a red flag that the board is too large. The board should be the seat of deliberation, and it should be the right size to do that. Individual board members are the ones responsible for the place, after all.

Executive Committees work best for handling nondeliberative, day-to-day business that falls to officers, like check signing and building inspections, with the power to make spot decisions when those decisions are unlikely to be controversial.

Boards may appoint other restricted-membership committees, especially task forces. Sometimes the task is to deliberate on an issue and report back to the full board, in order to save board time by generating ideas elsewhere. I was on one such committee to consider changes to the dues policy at Temple Beth Am in Seattle. The committee was small, five members if memory serves, and was appointed by the synagogue president from board members and experienced volunteer leaders to include a diversity of viewpoints. We met for several months, after which we referred our ideas back to the board. This mechanism gave us extra time to deliberate among ourselves and saved board time, while the small size of our group made discussions more collaborative as we got to know each other better. No decisions were taken away from the board. Restricted membership was necessary in order to keep the group small, to ensure the desired diversity and balance of viewpoints, and to avoid the misimpression that the committee was the place to be for deciding on a hot-button issue.

Whether or not they are limited to board members, restricted-membership committees tend to deal with issues internal to the board's proper purview. Issues which are too low-level to be pressing fiduciary concerns—like the subject matter of standing committees—generally do not justify the use of restricted membership. It is difficult to imagine a reason why regular synagogue committees should not be open to any member who wishes to serve. If there is too much interest in a committee, as mentioned above, I would look for ways to plug in additional volunteers, instead of turning anyone away.

Open-Membership Committees

The remainder of our committees are open-membership. People usually join by showing up, though as I found on my Religious Practices Committee, it can be helpful to have policies defining voting membership in advance, either from bylaws or internal committee policies.

This book does not have space for a compendium of common open-membership committee definitions and work; besides, that information is readily enough available. I've compiled several noteworthy links on *npgovernance.org*.

The structure of committee meetings and work between meetings is up to, and often a reflection of, the chair—so much so that it's important for the chair to avoid becoming a one-person show with members cast in a spectator role. People will get bored if the committee doesn't meaningfully engage them. Volunteers approach committees wanting to help. They can rise to the occasion, but often don't have a specific idea how. They wait in limbo until they either become genuinely engaged or choose to disengage.

5.3 KEEPING A VOLUNTEER PIPELINE

A volunteer-run organization needs a volunteer pipeline, carrying people as high into organizational commitment as they are willing to go. It's not a contest: some volunteers are happiest just doing tasks, which is absolutely essential to the group getting anything at all done. Others might have the potential to lead. Identifying new leaders is the key to moving the organization forward and avoiding the specter of stagnation; it is a key part of how boards, clergy and top lay leaders can guide the development of committees.

Volunteers come in two main types: worker bees and leaders. Both are essential, and both can and should be encouraged to stretch themselves into the other role. An individual may change back and forth over time, or may play different roles in different situations.

Worker bees don't want continuing responsibility, but are happy to spend time they have on tasks requested. They may have only a little time or they may be extremely generous with their time, but they typically are not interested in taking on a lot of risk or stress.

Leaders want to make decisions and influence policies, directing others to get their vision accomplished. They thrive on achievement and can be bored by lower-level work. Leaders also may have less or more time to give, but they tend to go all in once engaged.

Worker bees and leaders are highly symbiotic, so a robust organization has plenty of both. They are not personality types, but ways of volunteering. Some people are worker bees or leaders in everything they take on. But often a leader in one organization (work, the home, your organization, another organization) is happy to be a lower-stress worker bee in a different organization. An ideal relationship between leaders and worker bees is cordial and mutually grateful, not hierarchical. They are both volunteers and they need each other to do their own volunteer work well.

One of the most valuable aspects of my time in politics was the chance to learn surprising lessons from these two volunteer types. Politics is a highly stressful, competitive field with an endless need for volunteer worker bees and very few paying staff positions. You might think that everyone wishing to get hired would want to distinguish themselves as a leader. But actually, volunteer leaders in politics are a dime a dozen. Everyone and their sister knows best how to run a campaign and will stop at nothing to blare their ideas as loudly as possible. Far fewer are willing to work a phone bank or walk door to door, doing that nitty-gritty work on which the whole operation depends. So, the key to recognition and advancement in these organizations was distinguishing yourself as a worker bee. If you could take direction, do repetitive work professionally and cheerfully, leaving voters with a consistently good impression, well, you might understand enough to lead.

I remembered the lesson as my political career advanced. As a manager, I never permitted my staff to work longer hours than I did. If they were not being paid adequately, I would not let them stay more than 8 hours. I made it a point every year to spend some time phonebanking and doorbelling, even though I was by then a senior staffer. It kept me sane and connected to realities on the ground. (When you have me to speak at your organization, remind me to tell you the story of the woman in the white sweater.) Nobody is too important for worker-bee work—but, to be frank, some of us have jobs too important *not* to spend some time doing worker-bee work. Why not grab a pile of envelopes to stuff?

Worker bees are perfectly happy stuffing envelopes, or doing other work that may bore leaders. A wise leader, therefore, will spare no opportunity to let worker bees know how much they are appreciated. Carefully not to overtax their generosity, increase your requests of them little by little. Some worker bees may be willing to take on small leadership roles, such as organizing other volunteers to complete task work that they have come to know well. It's important to check in with worker bees about what they enjoy, so as not to take advantage of them and—more importantly—because their focus tends to be so tactical that they may not be thinking of their own enjoyment or wishes. An important part of thanking these crucial volunteers is working to understand what they want to get out of their work, and steering them toward more of that.

There might be too few worker bees in an organization, but there is no such thing as too many. Never get caught without an answer to the question "How can I help?" This is a key concept in efficient volunteer management. We will revisit it in more detail in Chapter 7, where I also offer advice to organizations wishing their volunteer pool were larger.

Leaders may have a personal agenda, and they may have ambition. It is laudable to wish to lead an organization you believe in. When there are more leader volunteers than leadership slots, leaders may find themselves in competition. But there is never a lack of volunteer positions in a nonprofit organization; there is only a lack of creativity how to fit people in.

The best way to deal with emerging leaders is to steer them toward progressively responsible roles. Start them on a relatively mundane task, and if they distinguish themselves, steer them toward a larger project, or a subcommittee or committee chair. If they prove capable and wise, they should not escape the Nominating Committee's notice.

Leaders need training in leadership—in the person-to-person, bookkeeping and ethical mechanics of helping other people be their best. And unfortunately, there are many leader volunteer types whose ambition exceeds their skill. Some just want to boss others around, while others are crusaders so intent on a personal goal that they run roughshod over organizational priorities and strategy, not to mention other people's rights and feelings. Volunteers not suitable for leadership may need to be gently redirected, or creatively placed in roles where they are harmless. Others may have a high aptitude but need to develop skills. This book largely consists of what I wish I had been taught when I was new to leadership.

The need to guide volunteers toward greater responsibility is not for the volunteer's benefit alone. An organization needs a steady flow of people up the ladder, knowing that many will be comfortable staying where they are. Boards need rotating membership, and the only way to get that is by developing volunteers. Board service generally requires a leader's level of commitment, but in a pinch experienced worker bees can become great board members too, cheerfully carrying the weight of tasks like taking minutes.

To get a worker bee to stretch, you may need to clearly delineate the extent of responsibilities and provide them a pretty firm portrait of what daily life will be like in a new role. Leaders may more readily take on additional obligations, and may need help to avoid taking on too much. I say take a risk. Rabbi Chanina ben Dosa says, "He whose works exceed his wisdom, his wisdom endures; but he whose wisdom exceeds his works, his wisdom does not endure."[55] Our aptitude amounts to nothing if we are afraid to give it a whirl.

Most synagogues and many other organizations have a Nominating Committee, which we introduced above. It is usually populated by leaders not running for other office, such as past presidents, board members in their final year in office, or experienced members not otherwise serving in leadership. It's a good idea to place one or two promising newer members on it too, as a way to gain a diversity of perspectives and to give them a taste of leadership. Stewardship of the organization's leadership pipeline might be a fine job for the Nominating Committee when they're not busy with the annual board slate. Committee chairs and staff people with high member interaction could also be asked to help identify potential new leaders.

---

[55] M. *Pirkei Avot* 3:10. This line could frame a great text-study lesson.

5.4 HOW TO RUN A GOOD MEETING

I love meetings. I don't love every meeting, but I love meetings as a craft, as a skill to improve. Meetings can be crisp, efficient and cheerful, leaving everyone with a sense of accomplishment—even if they deal with difficult issues. If I could leave most organizations with only one gift, it would be better meetings.

Good meetings have ground rules, understood by everyone and enforced by the chair. I call these *Talking about Talking*. These ground rules can be part of your group's policy development. There don't need to be too many, but group participation in suggesting them is a good way to build the group's assent.

Above all, maintain an atmosphere of respect. Distinguish respect for individual colleagues from agreement with their ideas: show people how to argue without making it personal. In questioning each other's ideas, group members are not to question each other's motivations or ability to speak. Everyone wants what is best for the organization. An atmosphere of respect will decrease defensive behavior, which can also inappropriately personalize the agenda. The chair may be challenged to balance diversity and tradition, depending on the organization's strategic identity.

I strongly recommend prohibiting interruptions. This may be a challenging cultural shift, but no single rule is more essential. A good meeting considers everyone's ideas and decides which are best through deliberation and reasonable argument. Interruptions skew that focus toward whichever ideas happen to be spoken by those most willing to interrupt. That would not be more than an etiquette problem if there were a correlation between willingness to interrupt and having the best ideas, but, as you may have noticed, there is not.

Interruptions also undermine the chair's control of the meeting, preventing any of the rest of this essay from being of value. Remember, our God speaks with a still, small voice.[56] If that voice spoke in our meetings, could it be heard?

Meetings are for making decisions. They can also be for providing information and getting feedback, but if that's all the meeting is about, it can be accomplished more efficiently *offline* (outside of meeting time). Meetings are excellent

[56] I Kings 19:12.

places to assign responsibilities to people, and to answer questions that are before the organization. Meetings can be good places to plan and control projects, especially if the whole group's feedback is needed or if the meeting environment helps enforce accountability for progress. But progress reports in meetings should be crisp and brief, minimizing the use of meeting time merely to announce information. Meetings can be good places to provide a sense of group unity, but only as much as needed and not more.

Do not spend meeting time on issues that do not involve every member of the group. Handle these offline or appoint a subgroup if necessary.

In a meeting, it is always appropriate to:

- Make decisions *as a group*.
- Have participants report on progress and get feedback.
- Bring new ideas to the group's attention.

In a meeting, it is sometimes appropriate to:

- Have fun and relax as a group.
- "Workshop" policy ideas or event plans.
- Leave extra time for comments and/or announcements.

In a meeting, it is never appropriate to:

- Discuss issues that do not involve every member of the group.
- Chastise any individual from the chair.

Good meetings begin with a clear opening, and end with a sense of closure and accomplishment. Begin with a clear announcement that meeting time has begun. Meeting time is a shared, scarce resource in which everyone agrees to self-conduct which helps the group; it is therefore important to distinguish between meeting time and offline time. A cheerful, firmly articulated welcome works well, as does a traditional call to order. After welcoming participants, distribute the agenda on paper so that members can refer to it.

End with a clear sense of closure. Review very briefly the meeting's accomplishments, decisions made and responsibilities assigned; then pronounce the meeting over. People should not be getting up and leaving one by one. When the chair provides a clear sense of closure, members will leave with a sense that their time was worthwhile. Enforcing these boundaries helps to keep meeting time in order by emphasizing its difference from offline rules of conduct

—a principle we borrow from Jewish distinctions between holy and undedicated time. There is a certain ceremony to meetings, however informal: a sense that we intentionally join together for a shared purpose to behave in ways intended to accomplish that purpose. We therefore set clear boundaries around it.

Good meetings start and end on time. Start your meeting as soon as possible after the scheduled time. If there is a quorum requirement, start as soon as the quorum is present; if not, I would start as soon as there are three people. Watch your first impression: if the first few meetings you run start on time, people will know to arrive on time—but the reverse is also the case.[57] (Correcting a bad pattern mid-course is sometimes possible but never easy.) The same goes for the end of the meeting, except that this time the chair is entirely responsible for a punctual end. Steering the meeting to a precisely timed conclusion takes skill.

Punctuality shows that you are in control of the meeting, that you take the group's business seriously, and that you respect people's schedules. Punctuality is your first opportunity to show your skill as a chairperson.

Setting the Agenda

Meetings need agendas like cars need roads. We do not have to wander aimlessly in the wilderness for a 40-year meeting. The agenda is a road and a roadmap, complete with signs and waypoints. It helps the meeting run efficiently, and provides the sense of accomplishment that comes from reaching goals.

The agenda is provided in writing. To give members a chance to review it prior to the meeting, it is distributed at least 24 hours in advance. If it isn't possible to fix the agenda 24 hours in advance, distribute at least a draft agenda. Soliciting agenda items from the group can be a great idea, but it's entirely up to the chair.

When setting the agenda, think about group members' interest level and attention span. If you have a full agenda, intersperse long discussions with quick items in order to maintain a feeling of movement. Put the majority of quick items earlier in the meeting: people get anxious if you're halfway through the meeting and still working on Item 1. And let's face it, some items are more interesting

[57] "One *mitzvah* leads to another *mitzvah*; one transgression leads to another transgression." M. *Pirkei Avot* 4:2.

than others, so I would put most of the boring items toward the beginning when there's a bit of a honeymoon effect. Leave more interesting items for later, when interest levels might otherwise flag. Plan for as much as you think you can reasonably accomplish, but not more: your goal is to accomplish your agenda. Be sure to end the meeting on a positive note.

Agenda setting involves deciding how much time each item is likely to take. These time estimates can, but do not have to, appear with their items on the agenda. The chair should always be aware of them and stick to them during the meeting. Give extra time to items of greater consequence to ensure they're thoroughly explored, to those likely to be controversial, and to those needing a safety margin because they are difficult to predict. Controversy can be especially challenging to manage on a schedule; you can make the job easier by allocating extra time in advance. However, you might allocate *less* time for a controversial item, if you feel the arguments have already been aired and you plan to ask the group for a decision.

Agenda setting is about planning to accomplish the right amount for the time available. It's sort of like bidding in bridge: the idea is to take on as much as we think we can get done. Sometimes we take on too little in agenda setting, but most of the time we take on too much. If this happens, there are some ways to manage it while still accomplishing as much as possible:

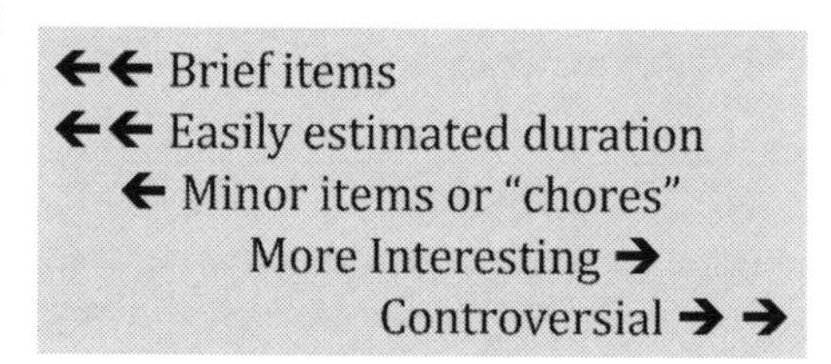

Figure 2. Ordering the Agenda.

- *Set and adhere to strict time limits for each item.* This is a skill that you will acquire with practice.
- *Plan to continue some items at a future meeting.* Try to make at least some progress at this meeting. Break a large task into subtasks, and accomplish at least one subtask.
- *Postpone some items.* Perhaps some of your work could be "pushed" to the next meeting.
- *Insist on business.* Maintain an especially businesslike tone. The more you use this tactic, the less it works. Overusing it is like crying wolf: people will comply occasionally, but when

overused it begins to sound like customer-service centers that always seem to have an unusually high volume of calls.

The chair is responsible for keeping the meeting within the scheduled time. If it should happen that the agenda does not require the full scheduled time, my recommendations for volunteer and staff meetings differ. In an office, by all means end early. Meeting time is expensive, and staff have other work to do. With volunteers, however, I tend to think the value of scheduled regularity takes precedence. Extra time could be a great opportunity for a strategic review or tactical brainstorming exercise. I'd worry that ending early might subtly communicate that the group is unable to use the time contribution that volunteers had been prepared to give—somewhat like returning $20 from a $100 donation. I tend to think we're better off filling the scheduled time in a volunteer meeting.

Agenda setting is a significant prerogative of the chair. Even if your group uses Robert's Rules of Order and a clever participant knows how to modify the agenda from the floor (which usually leads to no good) setting the initial agenda is still a significant prerogative. The chair decides what will be discussed, in what order, presented by whom. A wise chairperson will combine restraint with creativity in using this powerful tool.

Facilitating Discussion

The chair recognizes people to speak; this can be done formally or informally. At the formal extreme, for example at government hearings, speakers may sign up in advance or undergo a special procedure to be recognized. At the informal extreme, closer to our usual experience, recognition may not be much more than the chairperson turning their body to face the speaker and projecting interest. For three reasons, some form of speaker recognition is practiced in every well-run meeting:

- It establishes that one speaker has the floor, and may not be interrupted;
- It is essential to the chair's ability to maintain control of the meeting; and
- It helps shy or quieter members feel more comfortable speaking up.

The degree of formality is entirely up to the chair, unless it happens to be set by a governing document or other authority. *Formal recognition* here means that people raise their hands, and do not speak until the chair recognizes them by name. *Informal recognition* may take a number of other forms. Factors to consider include the size of the group, the stature of the group, the usual decision-making method, and the expected level of controversy. Informal recognition works best in groups smaller than 10, while formal recognition can prevent chaos when there are more than 12 members. Stature and gravitas play a role: formal recognition might make more sense on a national board than within a loosely organized get-together. If the group always makes decisions by formal vote, formal recognition can support the legitimacy of a fair process; the same is true when the discussion is expected to be controversial. Formal recognition gives the chair greater ability to control who speaks when, while informal recognition can feel less pressured and be more time-efficient. Some factors will probably weigh one way, while others weigh the other.

Unless governing documents require a certain recognition style, you are free to vary the degree of formality, even between meetings. If you expect more controversy than usual, it is entirely appropriate to announce when opening the meeting: "I know there are different views on agenda item 4, so to be extra sure we give everyone a chance, we will use formal, hand-raising recognition on that item."

Informal recognition attempts to retain the benefits of formal recognition while adapting it for a less formal environment. But there should be no mistake that the chair is actively recognizing speakers. To use informal recognition, generally call people by name, even without strict rules. Keep a queue in mind, and even announce it: "Mike, then Sarah, then Ann, then Moshe." It is okay to let people speak one after another as long as only one person wishes to speak at a time. Use hand gestures and face the speaker, making it clear with your body language that you have recognized someone. Keep close tabs on the discussion. Do not hesitate to cut right in if the discussion needs to be steered back on topic, or if there are too many people wishing to speak at once. (Only the chair can ever interrupt, and only for these reasons.) You can always go back to recognition by name without making it too formal: "Okay, hold on, we have a lot of people wanting to speak. Mike, I think you were first; then Sarah, then Ann, then Moshe."

Usually, recognize people in the order they signal their wish to speak. There are a couple exceptions. First, in contentious debates it is traditional to alternate between speakers for and against a proposal, to ensure roughly equal time for both sides. Formal recognition can make this simpler to manage. Second, the chair is free to *entertain* a particular viewpoint—that is, to recognize that viewpoint before others may speak. This can be done formally or informally. It is appropriate to entertain a viewpoint if a minority view is not being considered or heard: "Does anyone have a different take on this?" It is not appropriate merely if the chair personally disagrees with the group's emerging consensus.

The chair never speaks personally nor takes sides on any issue, because the chair's responsibility is to run the meeting fairly. Ideas will come from the group. Because the chair serves the group as a whole, and because the chair has power to decide who is heard and when, it is very much a conflict of interest for the chairperson to give a personal opinion. Chairpersons do so at their own peril as legitimate chairpersons.

A chairperson who feels they absolutely must take sides on an issue may formally yield the chair to a vice-chair, if one exists, and then speak individually as a group member. This is done as discussion begins, not in the middle, and lasts for the duration of the discussion item. This option is not available if there is no vice-chair: there is no legitimate way for the chair to elevate a group member who has not been legitimately elected or appointed to take over in a contingency. But as laudable as it is to distinguish the chair's office from the role of a participant, it doesn't solve the problem fully. Even if kept to a rare occurrence, it still undermines the chair's impartiality by drawing attention to the spectacle of the chair laying down their cards. Conversely, an individual who often feels they must speak persuasively is not a suitable chairperson. The chair is a service position, a facilitator first and last. That means making room for all members during discussion, and afterwards being able to represent the group's decision faithfully even if the chairperson happens to personally disagree with it.

This is no less true in professional meetings run by an executive who makes decisions personally. Meetings are very expensive time. There is no reason to hold one if you don't intend to elicit people's views. Manager or volunteer chairperson, the less you say about your own views during the meeting, the more participants will say about theirs. I offer more about manager-run staff meetings below in this section, and more about staff management in Chapter 7.

Be aware of cultural issues, which affect people's behavior in meetings. In particular, Jewish organizations are more culturally diverse than people may realize. Culture also impacts our ideas about gender. Good ideas come from people in all walks of life, so if you're only hearing from a culturally dominant subset of people, you're not getting the best ideas. Here are some things to watch:

- *Volume of people's voices:* Are only the loudest voices being heard?
- *Willingness to interrupt:* Can non-interrupters get a word in edgewise? I feel strongly that interrupting is incompatible with a well-facilitated meeting.
- *Waiting time before speaking:* People may wait to begin speaking anywhere from a quarter-second to a full second or longer after someone else has finished. (Interrupters don't even bother to wait for the previous speaker to finish.) Notice participants' differing habits and make sure everyone has a chance to be heard. With informal recognition, sometimes people will wait the entire meeting to speak because others always seem to cut in just when they're about to say something. If this is a problem in your group, try recognizing speakers by name. If you're not sure, ask your members.

Many formal groups make a commitment to Robert's Rules of Order, on which a whole book could be written, and many have. Some organizations stipulate in their bylaws that the board must use Robert's Rules of Order, and some jurisdictions assume that corporation boards will use Robert's Rules if their bylaws do not specify otherwise. Robert's Rules are no less appropriate in Jewish environments merely because Henry Martyn Robert served in the American military during the Pig War.[58] Unfortunately, their formality and complexity tend to scare people.

---

[58] The last military confrontation between the U.S. and U.K., the Pig War is my favorite military-history story because it involves fascinating characters and has a happy, nonviolent ending arrived at through alternative dispute resolution. See *npgovernance.org* for a very entertaining digression.

If you don't use Robert's Rules, you can still use their fundamental principles, which include equal time for opposing views, decorum and respect for all, and the requirement that comments be germane to the topic at hand. Decorum is incompatible with *ad hominem* remarks, which impugn a person or their motivations instead of engaging with their ideas, so put a quick stop to these. It is possible to run Robert's Rules "in the background" even if they are not being enforced formally. They can be treated as the governing authority in case of procedural questions, and their spirit of fairness and restraining personal opinion in favor of general order should pervade the meeting.

This book cannot come close to a full treatment of Robert's Rules, but I will share one good secret: the decision of the chair can be overruled only by a majority vote after a properly made motion. The chair should hew to Robert's Rules in a group operating under them, but the chair remains entirely free to interpret them, unless and until someone raises a procedural challenge in a procedurally proper way. I don't recommend abusing this power, certainly not for the chair's personal agenda, but I do think a good chair is unafraid, when necessary, to state the way things are going to be.

Mastery of Robert's Rules is a wise skill-building investment for a chairperson, especially in more formal groups. In any case, when the chair's procedure is clear, crisp, cheerful, and confident, it goes a long way toward group members' comfort complying. Except in the very most contentious situations, most people just want to be told the way we're going to do things, so they can get on to doing them. And in those exceptionally contentious situations, the chair's confident and cheerful command of procedure will move things right along, even through a heated debate or procedural challenge.

Informality makes things easier for participants but harder for the chair. I recommend giving at least some reference and at least some deference to Robert's Rules. Robert's Rules might be set as the official reference point when one is needed. Otherwise, bear in mind the wide latitude Robert's Rules give the chair, and—one of the few times I'll say this—wing it with confidence. With fairness always in view, I always prefer crisp, cheerful procedure, even if occasionally mistaken, to the chaos of an unguided meeting.

Do not, therefore, cast about unsure of what to do in a case of procedural challenge or discord. Do not let the meeting get away from you. At worst, if you can't wing it convincingly, apologize and say the committee has work to do deciding how to handle this issue fairly. Call a recess if you need time to think. People of goodwill will respect you for putting in every effort to ensure a fair meeting.

The Usefulness of Progress Reports

I have said that meetings are for making decisions. Progress reports are often useful at meetings, but I think we tend to spend too much time on them. Most progress reports don't really require as much of everyone's undivided attention as they get. Boring meetings lead to low morale and are a red flag that time is not being used efficiently. Consider, therefore, the many alternatives to traditional round-robin reports. Consider sending announcements by e-mail rather than intoning them before an assembled group. Refer issues that do not require everyone's participation to be dealt with in smaller groups. Consider doing more business in subgroups that meet more frequently, leaving full committee or staff meetings to hear just the summaries they need to make the decisions they need to make.

Having said that, well-facilitated progress reports help groups accomplish work. They're great for enforcing accountability for work done between meetings. Nobody wants to be caught before a group without anything to report. The beauty of this approach is that it does not need to take a lot of time (see Chapter 9).

When all or most participants are in a position to give useful feedback, the accumulated feedback represents a group decision and justifies the use of meeting time. Progress reports are also helpful when everyone at the meeting needs to know about the status of each project and written announcements are not sufficient.

Keep progress reports succinct; avoid unscheduled discussion. Also avoid reports that lack a meaningful reason for group feedback. I can tell you from experience on both sides: sometimes the boss or chairperson is the worst offender. Beware of lectures. Use the home video test: if the monologue could just as well be recorded in a video for people to watch at home, then I wouldn't necessarily do that, but it would make more sense than using meeting time for it. When detailed progress reports or other reports do not require group feedback, they might be better handled in subgroups or by e-mail.

Managing Disagreement

First, don't be afraid of disagreement. Your group may be doing its best deliberative work! Just keep it cordial and fair. Articulate and follow rules for discussion, being especially careful to ensure the group understands the rules in advance of a contentious discussion. Emphasize civility, put a quick stop to problematic behavior (more below) and try to make sure everyone can at least live with any decision. Entertain a minority view if necessary: "Sue, you look really uncomfortable with this. Everyone, I see a clear majority but we need to hear from Sue before we move forward." Strong feelings present a challenge; much of the chair's job outside meetings may be to assuage those emotions and make sure a group member feels valued even if a contentious decision did not go their way.

Brainstorming can loosen people's ideological commitments and open them to new possibilities. You can set brainstorming time on the agenda, or—if the group lets you get away with it—even modify the agenda midcourse if necessary to take time out of debate for brainstorming. A modified KJ diagram can help here. Hand out sticky notes and pens—*always* carry sticky notes and pens—and ask each member to brainstorm different ways to handle the issue at hand, including at least one they disagree with (they can even mark it). This can be a useful check to make sure participants are listening to each other, and it can be mind-opening to see the multiplicity of options. As you would with a KJ diagram, place the notes on the board, positioning like with like, and see which categories emerge. There might be something new there. If not, at least you know you're facing a decision between two or three clear options.

(I like sticky-note exercises better than traditional marker-and-board brainstorming in which a facilitator dutifully copies ideas onto the board as they are stated by members. Sticky notes take less time to generate more content, and they prevent wasting time on wordsmithing the facilitator's ways of summarizing the comments.)

In negotiation theory, we learn to distinguish between people's *positions* and their *interests.* Many books have been written on this topic; see *npgovernance.org* for some helpful references. A *position* is what a person wants, or demands, to have happen. An *interest* is why the person wants that. A widely told parable[59] illustrates the difference. A brother and a sister were making a special family brunch, and fought over the last orange in the house. Their Ima

[59] So many versions of this parable abound that it was difficult for me to tell who originated it. It appears in Fisher, Ury and Patton's classic *Getting to Yes* (1991, pp. 56–57) but they call it "proverbial," suggesting they did not create it.

suggested they split it in half, but their Mama thought to ask what they were planning to do with it. It turned out that the sister was making a special orange-juice drink, while the brother was making a special tea with orange rind. They didn't need to be in conflict at all! Instead of splitting the orange in half and giving each child half of what they wanted, the family split the pulp from the rind, and each child got all of what they wanted. This is called an *integrative solution*, and *integrative negotiation* is the collaborative search for integrative solutions. The children's *positions* were that they both wanted the whole orange, but when their *interests* were uncovered, it turned out an integrative solution was available.

Now, none of our real-world negotiations are 100% integrative like the case of the orange. Real-world cases call for a mixture of integrative and *distributive* (zero-sum) negotiation. But the parable illustrates the value of uncovering the interests behind people's strongly stated positions. Interests allow you to ask if an integrative solution can be found, which might give people results they'd be even happier with than the positions they're insisting on. Nobody loses anything by spending some time looking for integrative solutions. If the search doesn't work, the parties can always go back to distributive negotiation.

Because integrative negotiation is creative, it also lends itself to brainstorming. To get at interests, try giving participants a couple sticky notes or pieces of paper, and ask them to sketch out (not write in beautiful language, it's just for their reference) what goals or values their positions serve. It can help to look back at the organization's strategic values, because most contentious disputes are clashes of competing good values.

Or, give participants sticky notes, perhaps in different colors signifying pro, con, and undecided positions. Ask them to write not what policy they prefer (everyone can see that from the color) but what values lead them to prefer it. Categorize these once again into a KJ diagram, and see what it looks like. You might be surprised. If there are two big clusters, with diversity (let's say) only mentioned by the pro side and tradition (let's say) only mentioned by the con side, that can be at least a useful visual display as to where the discussion is. If on the other hand some of the same values are prized by both sides, or particularly by the undecideds, those might be fruitful areas to explore. Areas of agreement or even integrative opportunities might lie there.

Managing disagreement is largely about helping members out of fixed thinking patterns. But if that doesn't work, the bottom line is fairness, consistency, procedural predictability, and impartiality. If you conduct your meetings in these ways, you need not fear contention or even high emotions. Sometimes heated, emotional debate is the sound of free people making decisions together. Keep it respectful, and you will get through it.

Dealing with Problematic Behavior

Stressful situations can give rise to problematic behavior. Also, some people will behave problematically anyhow. Part of the chair's job is to help people grow, but first to prevent problematic behavior from derailing the group. In a meeting, problematic behavior is anything that infringes on the ability of other group members to participate effectively. It goes without saying that *ad hominem* remarks are incompatible with the mutual respect a decent group demands. Interrupting derails the basic assumptions of respect and cannot be permitted. There is also unacceptable performance in assigned work. Finally, there are two conversational behavior types that I call *Dominators* and *Silent Shadows*. Dominators monopolize the floor, insist on speaking too frequently, or act in a domineering or inappropriately loud or physical way. Silent Shadows sit there sullenly, checking their phone or e-mail, dragging spirits down through the boredom they project. When problematic behavior annoys other group members, it can undermine the legitimacy of the chair, whose job it is to guarantee everyone a pleasant and fruitful experience in exchange for their attention.

A manager of staff may have more authority than a volunteer chairperson to deal with problematic behavior, but that doesn't make it any easier. It is probably the least pleasant part of the chair's job to get the behavior out on the table and handled. In many cases, problematic behavior can arise from emotional baggage or unmet interests; in these cases the techniques of Active Listening may help. That's another topic much too big for this book, but I have links to useful resources on *npgovernance.org*.

Never, never, never, never, never, never, never chastise a person from the chair during a meeting. This is a very common mistake, and it is a very big mistake. Publicly chastising a group member, however much they may deserve it, violates the Jewish imperative not to embarrass our fellow;[60] it violates the rule not to use meeting time for issues that do not involve everyone present; it undermines the chair by setting up a personal conflict between the chair and the individual, with the rest of the group as spectators. It sets an unpleasant tone. Never do this. Talk to the member offline. You might even announce that the two of you need to talk offline, if their behavior gets too serious, but that is absolutely the farthest the chair can ever go toward calling out a member publicly. If you can't stop the problematic behavior within the meeting, you might need to live with it until the end of the meeting, taking the ordeal as an incentive to get a difficult conversation done before the next meeting.

Within the meeting, watch your tone of voice and word choice. You can communicate the same idea in many different ways. Tone of voice can completely change the meaning of a remark. Try saying "Let's give someone else a chance" without and then with a heavy, sneering overemphasis on the word *else*. Or, compare saying "So far, your project is a failure" against "Your project has not yet met its objectives": even though the literal meaning of those two sentences is precisely the same, the tone and implication could not be more different. It takes effort to keep your tone constructive, open and welcoming, impersonal and impartial. It takes practice to master the quick self-check necessary to say things in the moment in the ways you intend. The effort pays off in easier handling of problems, and in minimizing our own problematic behavior.

Consider that a Dominator may feel unheard or insecure, while a Silent Shadow may feel useless, incompetent, or uninterested. With Dominators, do not tolerate interrupting, and try phrases that show the effects of their behavior, like "Let's give someone else a chance" (delivered nicely). Don't set a bad example by dominating the conversation yourself. With Silent Shadows, offer praise and encouragement, especially offline. Try to find out if their problem is a feeling of uselessness or incompetence. It's amazing how far a kind word from the chairperson can go toward developing a member who is unsure of himself. In private, ask them about their interests, maybe take them out for coffee. Once in a while, using discretion, you might try cold-calling on a Silent Shadow in a meeting if you think they'll rise to the occasion. With both Dominators and Silent Shadows, try listening carefully to them in an offline conversation if

[60] See b. *Bava Metzia* 58b–59a.

you think they may feel unheard. Silent Shadows can be easier to reassure if you think they may be insecure, while Dominators may react more defensively to your probing their emotions.

At worst, it is usually within a committee chair's prerogative to remove a member from the group. On boards, members generally serve out their terms, although no rule prevents asking for a resignation if it comes to that. It probably won't. Most problematic behavior occurs because people are emotional, or because they have not considered that their behavior inconveniences others. A skilled chairperson can deal with those issues. Clergy, if available, might be enlisted for help.

Making Decisions

The most important thing is that formal decisions be accepted as legitimate. This means that decisions must be made *by the group* and *by the rules.*

Your group's legitimacy builds on itself from one well-managed decision to another, while a poorly managed decision can fritter it all away. Nothing guarantees it. Adhering to agreed-upon policies builds legitimacy every time. Doing the work to make sure everyone can live with every legitimate decision also builds legitimacy, including the all-important cleanup work of soothing hurt feelings after a difficult meeting. The best you can do is follow impartial rules, be willing to represent legitimate decisions even if you personally disagree with them, and model a firm respect for the legitimacy of decisions duly made. In a synagogue, clergy can help build or rebuild legitimacy if they are seen as legitimate themselves.

There are three common types of groups, according to how they make decisions: voting groups, consensus groups, and groups where a single individual (usually but not necessarily the one running the meeting) makes decisions personally. The latter are more common in staff meetings than volunteer meetings, but they can happen in some synagogues; for example, in discussions about ritual or Jewish law when the rabbi is empowered to make the final decision.

Even in groups with a personal decision-maker, legitimacy does not reduce to fiat. (Remember from Chapter 2: there is no such thing as fiat; there is only legitimacy.) Legitimacy is still a matter of how the decision-making process is perceived by stakeholders. If you will be making a decision personally, take the opportunity to hear and evaluate the different views expressed in the meeting.

Participate lightly in the discussion, without dominating it. Your personal decision-making authority removes the conflict of interest against your biasing the meeting, and the opportunity for group members to converse with you countervails against the value of letting them decide by themselves. However, with a personal decision-maker it is often still possible to frame the meeting as an open invitation for legitimate group advice. From there, the group can function very similarly to a consensus or voting group.

Nothing is more important to the legitimacy of decisions than adhering to the adopted decision-making process. Most committees, and I believe all boards, should operate by voting. Voting is most appropriate when the group must take formal policy positions, when the group is larger than 8 to 10 participants, or when decisions may need to be made quickly. Consensus—meaning every member must agree to a decision—makes sense in groups that have a specific common goal, that are fairly small, and that desire a more cautious approach. Consensus is sometimes seen as politically progressive, but it is not morally superior to voting, nor is it necessarily more fair. Consensus supports high group cohesion and also high caution, because it gives every member a veto.

If all or most participants seem to agree, or if the group is at an impasse with arguments getting rehashed on all sides, it is time to move toward a decision. These are signs that continued discussion is no longer productive. If you see consensus or near-consensus in a voting group, hold a quick vote and be done with the issue. In a consensus group, getting a decision is as easy as stating it and having everyone agree.

If you see an impasse, with discussion generating few new ideas, try to reach some agreement if possible, or at least make sure everyone understands the minority's view. The suggestions under "Managing Disagreement" above may be helpful. In a voting group, within the requirements of any rules, it is entirely appropriate for the chair to hold a vote (or, formally, to entertain a motion to vote). It is time to vote when discussion becomes unproductive.

In a consensus group, decision-making is harder, and you may have to accept indecision. While remaining impartial on the issue, make sure everyone understands the consequences of indecision. A consensus group may not resort to voting; even if there is only one holdout, there is no consensus. If someone is blocking consensus for horse-trading reasons, end the discussion and postpone the decision until you have had a chance to talk with them about their conduct.

After a contentious decision, resist the minority's temptation to reopen it. This is hardly ever a good idea. To recap from Chapter 2, do not permit a decision to be reopened unless you are *surprised* by a strong negative stakeholder reaction, unless it becomes clear to *you* that *you* made a consequential procedural mistake, or unless your group's rules require you to reopen discussion. You may have wide latitude even in the latter case. Everyone needs to practice living with decisions they disagree with, from the chair on down.

I was once running a committee where a member objected to the need to vote. She thought it would be easier if we avoided the whole formality of voting. But it is so much faster and easier to vote on noncontroversial items than to sit there figuring out how else to signify that there has been a decision. When an issue is not controversial, getting a fully legitimate decision can be as quick as saying the magic incantation "those-in-favor-those-opposed-thank-you." My advice? Say the magic words and get the decision done.

Records and Confidentiality

As chairperson, it is your job to ensure the group keeps *minutes*. Minutes remind you what happened at the meeting, and they help members who were absent get up to speed. They may provide information to outside stakeholders about your process, and they will be a model for future groups like yours. Good minutes include:

- A list of decisions made, with vote records as applicable;
- Individual members' responsibilities for the next meeting;
- A *concise* summary of any progress reports; and
- Only if needed, a *brief* list of key ideas from discussion.

These are best presented in bullet form. Contrary to common practice, good minutes *do not* include verbatim, paraphrased, or chronological records of discussions. These are almost always useless, and they make important material difficult to find.

Sometimes rules about confidentiality may need to be created or followed. When a meeting enters *executive session*, non-members leave the room and minutes are not taken. Boards may meet in executive session to deliberate on extremely sensitive issues. The overuse of executive session is a red flag that transparency is being avoided, which should invite scrutiny. On quasi-juridical groups like personnel committees and disciplinary boards, deliberation may be done in secret, but the group is still required to give a public verdict, often with some justifying reasoning. Non-fiduciary groups do not generally encounter appropriate reasons to use executive session.

In regular session, there may still be times when certain material must be discussed confidentially within the group. Minutes may be redacted for public consumption, or occasionally kept secret. But they should always be distributed to group members. If a person was privy to the meeting, they are privy to the minutes. Often, decisions on confidentiality are up to the chair, so if you make confidentiality rules, be certain everyone understands them.

Some groups are fortunate enough to have staff who take minutes. Others elect a recording secretary or similar officer to take minutes. If your group doesn't have a permanent person in this role, try rotating "recorder" responsibilities among group members. I recommend against taking minutes from the chair. Minutes are important, but in a pinch, running the meeting is more important.

Summary

This essay has presented concepts and techniques that everyone can use to run a good meeting. A good meeting:

- Has clear ground rules.
- Begins, ends, and proceeds punctually.
- Emphasizes respect.
- Is well planned, with a clear agenda.
- Is guided by an active chairperson.
- Does not enable problematic behavior.
- Makes decisions—explicitly, legitimately, and fairly.
- Is recorded, with minutes that are easy to skim.
- Leaves everyone with a sense of accomplishment.

5.5 YOUR JOB AS THE CHAIRPERSON

We've talked about running meetings. This essay is about running a group between meetings.

My advice to chairpersons is to set clear expectations, model an example, and expect no less and no more from your members. Expect no less: don't ignore issues of poor performance, but deal with them promptly, respectfully and privately. Expect no more: resist temptations to have extra meetings, and keep extra work optional and specifically appreciated. Don't make decisions at optional or unscheduled meetings, as this is not fair to members who attend properly scheduled meetings. My basic expectations of every group include proper decorum and the idea that work will be done between meetings; that last point applies to the chairperson especially. Between meetings the chairperson's job includes:

- Being a resource and problem-solver for members.
- Tactical and strategic planning for the group.
- Maintaining morale.
- Keeping tabs on the group's projects.
- Conflict resolution and discipline.
- Ensuring confidentiality when necessary.
- Reporting and organizational learning
- Representing the group externally.

Providing Resources and Accountability

I've had good luck framing nonfiduciary committees I've chaired as working groups for projects. If possible, I assign every member to a project. If someone is enthusiastic about leading a particular subject, I'll ask them to be in charge of that area. If they're a worker bee looking for ways to help, I'll try to match them with an enthusiastic visionary. I present myself as a facilitator and resource for members' projects. I spend my time supporting members exploring what they'd like to do, identifying talent and suggesting ways people might help, cultivating volunteers, helping them solve problems, ensuring they obtain legitimacy from the committee as their work requires it, and standing behind them to the extent they've obtained that legitimacy. Committee members then act with significant autonomy, taking initiative to accomplish goals that everyone has agreed upon together. Members take pride in accomplishing their own goals between meetings, so we make the most of our time together checking in and making decisions. There are many ways to structure a committee, but I think this one is a great model to consider. It might be called a *working committee.*

On the other hand, this model is not appropriate for boards, for all the reasons working boards are not ideal (see Chapter 3).

Working committees lend themselves easily to expansion or contraction with the times, as we discussed in Chapter 3. In the years I chaired the Religious Practices Committee at Temple Beth Am (Seattle), I found our scope increased because issues needed to be dealt with, and we seemed able to deal with them. For example, security, not obviously a Religious Practices issue, came under our purview because we organized volunteer ushers, and the ushers were thinking more about security in the years after 9/11.

There started to be a lot to discuss, but that led to tension. Some of our best ushers did not want to spend time discussing music, and some of our most generous volunteers caring for our ritual objects did not want to debate the synagogue's *kashrut* policy. A year into my service as chair, I built members' support for appointing subcommittees, one for ushers and security, and one for ritual objects and books. Those topics seemed to need particular interpersonal collaboration and took a lot of meeting time, while members most interested in those areas were just as happy to be excused from full committee meetings. We made time at each full committee meeting for a report and feedback from each of the two subcommittee chairs. This allowed the full committee to set policy if necessary, while taking less meeting time for everyone. If in the future one of those subcommittees should start to flag, it might then make sense to reabsorb it into the full committee. To a very great extent, management of a working committee goes with the flow, creating ways for strong volunteer energy to be useful, and reabsorbing groups that do not appear to be useful any longer.

On a working committee, the chair plays an accountability role. (Someone else may do this, especially on large projects where accountability tracking may be a major task, but the chairperson retains responsibility for it.) It could be as simple as checking in between meetings to make sure a member's project is moving along, and to see if they need any help. Verification of assigned *action items* (to-dos) from meeting to meeting can be crucial to agenda planning.

Or the committee could use productivity-management methods such as those discussed in Chapter 9.

The chairperson is always a point of contact for members who need help. The chairperson is like the hub of a wheel: ideally not bustling about too much herself, but rather serving as a central facilitator for everyone else to get their jobs done. Group members should always feel free to approach the chairperson for help.

Tactical and Strategic Planning for Committees

A committee is like an organization within the organization. Just as the organization needs a strategy and tactical plans, so does your committee. Tactical planning to accomplish specific goals is the subject of Chapter 8, whose methods are applicable to all projects regardless of size. Within a committee, you can use project planning and tracking techniques to ensure you meet your goals, just as the larger organization would.

Strategic planning for committees shares many characteristics with strategic planning for the organization, but its standpoint is the committee's position and role within the organization. It may be appropriate for the board to assist committees to develop strategic plans, and then subsume those into part of the organization's strategic plan; or, committee strategic plans might stand on their own. Committees may have a mission and vision of their role within the organization, as well as strategic goals to get there.

For example, a synagogue School Committee may wish to increase the diversity of its members and cultivate an approachable, friendly, competent and trustworthy image among congregation members. A Social Action Committee may wish to ensure that it addresses issues important to a broad base of congregants, and educates congregants about issues they might not have considered. These are committee strategic goals, from the standpoint of the committee's position within the larger organization. All committees should work to serve the organization's strategic goals, aligning their own goals to strategic decisions made by the larger group.

Both strategic and tactical planning require awareness of external and internal issues. By external issues, I primarily mean issues affecting the whole organization as opposed to the committee itself, while also including issues affecting the public sphere outside the organization. Are there pending issues, controversies or decisions that may affect your projects? Organizational needs, priorities, budgets and politics can generate goals, opportunities and limitations for the committee.

Many committees use surveys to help with planning; some use focus groups. Surveys are a very passive way to relate, and I would not overrely on them. They take little effort compared to individual conversations, but as often as not, I think you get what you pay for. Surveys often do a poor job measuring opinion due to low response rates. It can be difficult to avoid asking questions in ways that bias the results. Most problematically, surveys about policy questions can create the misimpression that the survey is the organization's decision-making process. Surveys work best for open-ended brainstorming questions where nothing is being quantitatively measured. They also work for simple, precise questions, like whether congregants would prefer Shabbat evening services to be held at 7:00 or 8:00. In the broad middle ground between those extremes, consider whether you might be better served by offering people opportunities to participate in legitimate processes.

Focus groups are probably too much effort for too little return in a small nonprofit, but sometimes a consultant will facilitate them in order to help with strategic planning. Further resources about surveys and focus groups can be found on *npgovernance.org*.

External needs and issues require your active engagement. People not on the committee will not offer their opinion unless asked. Committee chairs need an ear to the ground in the broader organization, taking opportunities to talk with people about the committee, making sure they know that you are available. A newsletter column may help. I like the idea of devoting periodic meeting time to an informal "meet and greet": you might get new interest in committee membership in addition to the feedback you need! Consult with experts within the community: clergy, staff, fellow committee chairs, old-timers, elected leadership, anyone who knows more than most about your topic areas. They can provide useful guidance and experience as you plan.

Morale, Conflict Resolution and Discipline

The chairperson works to maintain positive feelings, making sure all members have a sense of accomplishment and are contributing constructively. To that end, it is important to give frequent praise. Tell members you appreciate what they do. Find something good to say about every person.[61] Be sensitive to members' feelings. When a group member says something emotional, in or out of a meeting, ask yourself what emotion may be driving their speech and manage the conversation accordingly. I recommend that chairpersons learn and practice techniques such as Active Listening, about which I offer more information on *npgovernance.org*.

Giving credit generously builds morale. The chairperson may be asked to take credit for the group, either in a formal ceremony or in informal conversations. If you scrupulously deflect credit to your group's members, it will pay off many times over. Credit for accomplishment is not a zero-sum pie to divide. In fact, the more credit you publicly give your members, the better it all reflects on you. If your group is so good that members are being recognized for their accomplishments, then you must be doing a pretty good job leading it. It is in your personal interest as much as the members', therefore, to give lavish praise to them, and to ensure they get personal recognition for their accomplishments.

Committees are places where conflicts arise. In fact, the absence of conflict is a red flag that the committee is not taking on substantial work, or (more likely) unarticulated conflicts are simmering below the surface. Within meetings, conflict should be topical, specific and impersonal. Between meetings, the chairperson needs to guide conflicts toward constructive resolution. Integrative negotiation and mediation skills will come in very handy; again, I've offered some helpful resources and links on *npgovernance.org*. Remember, integrative negotiation is about identifying the interests behind people's stated positions, then looking for ways to resolve the conflict that satisfy everyone's interests.

Resist the temptation to judge between two group members who complain about each other. That drags you into the conflict personally; moreover, you do not have any particular legitimacy as a committee chairperson to adjudicate an interpersonal conflict. Rather, ensure that each member knows you care about them and are happy they are part of the group, and that your role is to help them. If the conflict is about group policy and you find that you must decide (instead of, for instance, putting it to a group decision, which would allow you to depersonalize your own role) then you will need

[61] "Who is the person who delights in life? Lover of days, seeing good things always." Psalm 34:13.

to take special care to ensure that the members involved understand that you respect and care about them personally, and that your personal preferences play no role in your decision.

Any effort toward conflict resolution, even if unsuccessful, will probably improve your group's morale when the dust settles. Everyone knows conflict resolution is challenging, and noninvolved members will appreciate your honest effort. Conversely, though, do not permit a conflict to fester unarticulated an inch beneath the surface. Nobody enjoys being in such an environment.

You may have heard of the "Forming, Storming, Norming, Performing" model of cooperative group development, which was introduced by organizational psychologist Bruce Tuckman[62] in 1965 and has since become ubiquitous. Tuckman observed that after an initial phase of moderate productivity, every group enters a period of conflict as a phase in its maturation. The group gets through this "storming" phase by establishing ways of working together and new understandings—"norms"—that give that group confidence going forward. With those norms in place, the group can "perform."

My experience says Tuckman was onto something. That "storming" stage can look very different in different groups, but groups are always stronger after getting through their first conflict. There is something tentative about pre-conflict groups, while an unarticulated, simmering conflict can be deadly. In any case, conflict cannot be avoided. Fear of conflict hardens into fear of change, as conflict prevention takes priority over strategic thinking. This feels like walking on eggshells, even if relations remain cordial. Fear of conflict can also lead to stagnation or to cold, snarky behavior. As in romantic relationships, a total lack of conflict becomes a red flag.

Therefore, in groups stuck in the "forming" stage, I've sometimes tried to move things right along into "storming." I don't mean picking a fight, of course, but such a group may need introspection and brainstorming to identify issues that need deliberation. A skillful chairperson can elicit these conflicts into the open while keeping deliberations cordial, or at least professional. When interpersonal conflicts are the source of a "storm," the chairperson may wish to use *shuttle diplomacy*: private conversations with one party, then the other, back and forth.

---

[62] Tuckman (1965).

A less pleasant and—fortunately—less common concern is unacceptable performance: someone consistently not pulling their weight, breaking promises, speaking inappropriately about others or the group, or behaving problematically within meetings.

I believe in finding every possible way to accommodate a person.[63] An underperforming member may need help. Emotions or misunderstandings may be getting in the way, or the member may need you to engage them. They may be in personal difficulty. People may be feeling guilty about underperformance on volunteer obligations when they are balancing part-time jobs, illness, caring for an ill relative, or other life demands. An approach of caring in a time of need can go a long way toward building community.

Nevertheless, some behaviors are disruptive, even with the best intentions or reasons. If people cannot commit to consistent work, perhaps you could find one-off jobs for them. If someone has a problem with self-conduct, it can take a lot of personal commitment on their part to get over that, but the chairperson owes it to the rest of the group to insist on it. You can't let an overbearing Dominator or sullen Silent Shadow refashion meetings in his[64] own image.

At worst, the chairperson usually has leeway over committee membership, unless it is formally defined in bylaws or written policies. (Don't write definitions of committee membership without also including provisions for removal and term limits if applicable. My quick advice: if term limits don't make sense for your group, you're better off leaving membership undefined.) Most of the time in committee work, if "firing" a member becomes necessary it will come as a relief to the person. They may have long wanted to end their commitment, but were embarrassed to say so. A gentle conversation can save the day for both of you. You might initiate such a conversation by asking the person if they wish to continue on the committee. They could breathe a huge sigh of relief and say they do not; then the two of you can have a pleasant conversation from there about how much you appreciate the contribution they made.

---

[63] "Despise no one, and call nothing useless, for there is no one whose hour does not come, and there is no thing that does not have its place." M. *Pirkei Avot* 4:3, translation from Stern (1975), p. 23.

[64] Verbal domination is a stereotypically male gender role in our society, in conformance with which, Dominators tend to be male. This is a consistent remark of female executives. However, there are certainly female Dominators.

If they don't want to leave, you may have the authority to inform them firmly but gently that they will not be continuing. If you do not have this authority, you might get help from someone who does (the president?)—or perhaps from a clergy member who could at least be persuasive. If all else fails, you may have to live with the situation, resolving conflicts as they continue to arise.

When you must give negative feedback, bracket it with praise, placing positive feedback before and after the negative. "Brad, I loved your idea about the rabbis' robes. . . . Yeah, that was a great way to handle it. . . . Hey, I've got to ask you something. I really want everyone to wait till other people are finished speaking before starting with a new thought. . . . Yeah. Thanks, Brad, that would be great. I used to do it all the time myself. . . . Great, and look, we're so blessed to have you with us on the committee, you're a very valuable part of the group. Thank you so much for everything you do here." It's not magic. It gets the job done. In this day and age, it's probably a good sight better than, "Brad, gevalt, shush already!"—although it communicates the same meaning.

Phrase negative feedback constructively. Don't use the phrase "you always." If you find it very hard to avoid phrasing feedback that way, practice substituting "you sometimes" for "you always" in the moment. "Hey Brad"—*after* the positive praise above—"you sometimes interrupt people in our meetings." Believe me, Brad knows that "you sometimes" is a euphemism for "you always." Brad therefore also knows, consciously or not, that your words have intentionally left room for him to improve. The phrasing in the previous paragraph is better because it avoids the accusatory *you* entirely. The goal is not to state how bad a person Brad is, but to give him a chance to improve. And he probably will improve, sooner or later, if given room to do it. On the other hand, trapping Brad into an identity as a problem person will only prolong his misbehavior by making it difficult for him to change.

Try stating facts and asking (fair) questions. "Sara, I missed you at the meeting yesterday. Do you have any concerns?" Facts are not accusatory; they are just facts. The person will react to them and the conversation will go from there.

Do not blame, and do not use sarcasm or an ungracious tone of voice when giving criticism. Make it simple, unemotional, and as cordial as possible. Criticism can be a collaborative problem-solving effort.

If you are upset, handle your own emotions before dealing with others. You may wish to seek pastoral care or psychotherapy if your emotions are getting in the way of your leadership. This is very common for leaders, and it shows inner strength and good personal hygiene to seek counseling when it occurs.

Discipline is the least pleasant aspect of leadership, but it is part of guaranteeing a wholesome, safe and fulfilling experience for all. Discipline and kindness are both important expressions of God—and they may, with skill, be expressed at the same time. Therefore, do not fear discipline. Treat problems as they arise. With respect for all and with shared commitment to ethical principles, we will reach Tuckman's fourth stage, "performing."

Reporting and Organizational Learning

I recommend every group produce a brief written annual report, and brief after-action reports on projects and events. Reports enable future incarnations of your group to know what you've done. If you lead a group, don't you wish you had good records from the past—or aren't you glad you have them? As with meeting minutes, reports are best written in bullet form for easy scanning later.

In a report, include successes and lessons learned. These are solid gold for future similar efforts. Someone will have an easier time planning the High Holidays five years from now if they know that your parking configuration saved everyone from a traffic jam. If your group was given specific *charges* (things to do), state what you did and where you ran into difficulty on each. Reports ought to be formally adopted by vote. If they are at all controversial, the vote becomes important to their legitimacy, but the chair will need to steer the group away from wordsmithing. If a report is not controversial, just hold a vote and make it legitimate.

Representing the Group Externally

Being chairperson empowers you to speak for the committee, but be aware that your public behavior reflects on the group. Representing your group involves holding events, being there to fulfill community needs, letting people know about your group, weighing in on issues before the community, and building a strong membership base within your group in order to assist these activities.

Do not confuse your own opinions with those of the group. The chairperson's job is to represent the committee's decisions, not the other way around. If you wish to express your personal view on an issue, you need to make it clear that the view is your own and not that of the group. But it is usually wiser to keep mum. Don't risk undermining the legitimacy of your committee and leadership.

I mentioned above that I once facilitated a difficult argument about a Reform synagogue's *kashrut* observance. Some folks thought I was a crusading young Turk (three Abrahamic religions in one!) charging forward to implement a stricter policy. I took it as a mark of my fairness in umpiring the debate, because my personal view was actually in favor of a looser policy. For the record, we ended up finding a partially integrative solution everyone was able to live with. But if I hadn't kept my personal preference on the issue to myself, my legitimacy as a leader would have been shot, and we'd have accomplished nothing. (A series of columns I wrote for the newsletter about this issue appear on *npgovernance.org*.)

I've said it before but it's important: use every opportunity to give committee members credit and recognition. A great way to express confidence in your members is to refer inquiries to them, showing that you trust them. When appropriate, allow them to speak for the group. Help the leaders among them gain the experience they would like to have.

A lot of responsibilities come with group leadership, both in and out of the meeting room. Don't feel overwhelmed. We've covered these topics in significant detail. In practice, if you have the right attitudes, much of it will come naturally.

On the other hand, it's usually not a good idea for the chairperson to take on additional work. It can be tempting to roll up your sleeves and join your members in the trenches, but leadership is a big enough job in itself, especially when you're new to it. Delegate the tasks that need to be done, while you focus on your job as the chairperson.

Chapter 6
FINANCE

6.1 SHIUR

> *Samuel and Ablat were sitting, while certain people were going to a lake. Said Ablat to Samuel: "That man is going but will not return, for a snake will bite him and he will die." "If he is an Israelite," replied Samuel, "he will go and return." While they were sitting he went and returned. Thereupon Ablat arose and threw off the man's knapsack, and found a snake therein cut up and lying in two pieces. Said Samuel to him, "What did you do?" "Every day we pooled our bread and ate it; but today one of us had no bread, and he was ashamed. Said I to them, 'I will go and collect the bread'. When I came to him, I pretended to take from him, so that he should not be ashamed." "You have done a good deed," said he [Samuel] to him. Then Samuel went out and lectured:* But tzedakah delivereth from death;[65] *and this does not mean from an unnatural death, but from death itself.*
>
> b. *Shabbat* 156b[66]

In this story, the Talmud makes a powerful point about the value of *tzedakah*. The Jewish idea of *tzedakah* means much more than charity, a gift from the affluent to the needy. *Tzedakah* is a way of life, an attitude toward ownership, a set of assumptions about right and wrong, an overarching concern for the whole experience of those who struggle financially.

Ablat, a non-Jewish astrologer, has identified a certain man as being marked for death. But in recognition of an especially meritorious act of *tzedakah*, divine intervention saved the man's life. It seems the man was involved in a regular potluck,

[65] Proverbs 10:2.
[66] Translation from the Soncino.

in which each member contributed something to the overall welfare of the group. But the man knew of a member who was poor and did not have bread to contribute that day. He asked permission to take the day's collection himself, and when he got to his poor comrade, he pretended to take bread from him and put it in the communal basket, but in fact he took nothing. In this way, he saved the poor man from being embarrassed about his poverty: others in the group would not have known that the poor member did not contribute.

You don't have to subscribe to the Rabbis' views about the supernatural power of *tzedakah* in order to understand their point, but it may be helpful to put this story in context. The Rabbis have been discussing the predictive power of astrology. They seem to think astrology is real: Ablat accurately predicts the snake entering the picture. But the power of God overcomes that of the stars: God is able to make intentional exceptions to astrology's predictive rules.

In this story, heavenly powers seem to manifest in the small, unexplainable coincidences of life: the snake's sudden appearance, and its accidental killing inside the bag. The would-be victim and the snake both met their date with destiny. The snake showed up on schedule, but because of the man's unusual merit the plot suddenly swerved away from what the astrologer predicted.

For the purposes of this book, we need not worry about stars and snakes. The point is that the man's particular "good deed" had so much merit that his life was saved. Why does the Talmud hold this particular act of *tzedakah* in such high regard?

In his book *The Culture of the Babylonian Talmud*, Rabbi Jeffrey Rubenstein shows how important the issue of social shame was for the Rabbis.[67] He demonstrates that the Rabbis were especially concerned about the poor man's feelings of shame. He contrasts our story above with a corresponding story from the Palestinian Talmud that does not mention shame, and he gives several other examples of passages in the Babylonian Talmud that are concerned with shame.[68] Because the *halakhah* follows the Babylonian Talmud, we may use its counterpoint with the Palestinian Talmud's approach to underscore how important it was to the *halakhic* Sages to emphasize the need to avoid putting others to shame.

---

[67] Rubenstein (2003), pp. 68ff.

[68] Another such example is my exposition of the Oven of Akhnai story, available on *npgovernance.org*.

Today we tend to be less honest, I think, in dealing with shame and its connection to the financial support of the community. Shame is as much a factor today for Jews struggling financially as it was in Talmudic times, but the Rabbis' frank treatment of it can make us uncomfortable. If it had not been written in or before Talmudic times, we would probably not choose to pray:

> *And please, O God, let us depend not on the open hands or loans of others who may offer us, but only on Your full hand, which is open and holy and wide, so that we may not have to feel embarrassed as long as we live.*[69]

The Rabbis see what we too often refuse to see: that it is necessary for everyone to contribute, but at the same time, it hurts to be unable to provide the level of contribution that other, more fortunate members of a community are providing.

6.2 ACCOUNTING

There are three reasons to do accounting: to know how much money you have, to be able to answer questions about that money, and to prevent fraud.

To know how much money you have is the most basic reason, and we will see soon why it isn't enough just to look at your bank-account balance. Beyond that, the board needs to be able to ask and answer questions about money in order to deliberate effectively. If someone asks how much was spent last year on office supplies, or how non-dues revenue has tracked over the past five years, or whether a religious school contributes or costs money—accounting answers those questions. Finally, as we discussed in Chapter 3, no organization is immune from the possibility of fraud. Accounting provides safeguards against such occurrences, safeguards that every responsible organization takes.

For very good reasons, accounting is a professional field requiring specialized training to practice. I am not qualified to give you advice on how to manage your organization's accounts; this

---

[69] Birkat Hamazon (Grace after Meals). Translation original: it is from my full singable English translation. See *npgovernance.org* for a link to more.

book does not do so. The goal of this essay is simply to pass on a bit of vocabulary, strictly from one amateur to another, with enough knowledge to enable you to ask your treasurer or accountant meaningful questions. Let me underscore this whole chapter with a strong encouragement to do so.

Understanding the Terminology: Double-Entry, Accrual Basis

Double-entry accounting is the universally recognized best practice for organizations; it differs from what we may be familiar with from our home budget. In home accounting, we might add up income and expenses, and balance our checkbook every month. This is called *single-entry accounting*: every transaction is recorded once, as either a debit or a credit to the bottom line. But for even the smallest organizations, this practice is not sufficient. It is time-consuming or impossible to sift through all those receipts for answers to the kinds of questions I gave above—questions organizations need to ask.

Most importantly, with many rapid transactions against the operating account, it becomes impossible to know how much money is available just by looking at the bank-account balance. Single-entry accounting typically deals with the cash balance at any given time; transactions are recorded whenever they happen to hit the central bank account. When the organization is not very complex, like a home, balancing the checkbook monthly and keeping a minimum account balance can take care of any worry about bouncing checks. This is called accounting on a *cash basis*.

But in most organizations, there is simply too much going on for that to be possible. An organization could have just written many checks that have not yet cleared, or it could be expecting a million dollars in annual contributions to arrive next week. Organizations need to show information like that on their books, to provide a full financial picture of themselves. Therefore, we need to record transactions not when they happen to hit the books, but rather, *at the time a decision is made*. For instance, when a check is printed, we need the books to show a decrease in available funds, even if the money hasn't really left the central bank account yet. This is called accounting on an *accrual basis*. The organization is said to *accrue* an expense when they receive a bill or write a check.

If you're new to organizational accounting, it might be best to forget what you know from home accounting. Instead, think of your organization's money like water in a large lake. Many tributary streams deliver water into the lake, and the lake also has several streams flowing out. Money, like the water, doesn't just pop into or out of existence all of a sudden. Money only moves around. Income comes from somewhere; expenses go somewhere. The streams that bring new money in are called *income accounts*. Those that draw money away are called *expense accounts*. Our lake itself—to keep things simple for a moment—is called an *asset account*.

Asset accounts hold money (or nonmoney value) that you own. Income accounts are sources of money, and expense accounts are places money goes, never to be seen again. When you get a donation, you are transferring the money *from* an income account (let's call it Donations) *to* an asset account (let's call it the Operating Bank Account). Think of the water coming *out of* a tributary stream and *into* the lake. When you spend money on salaries, it gets transferred *from* an asset account (the Operating Bank Account) *into* an expense account (let's call it Salaries). Think of the water coming *out of* the lake and *into* an outflowing river.

No water appears or vanishes in this lake without explanation. Just the same, everything that happens in accounting is a transfer of money, *from* one place, *to* another place. All transfers balance: if $300 came from the income account "Donations" and went straight to the "Main Operating Bank Account" asset account, then the record of the transfer (called a *journal entry*) shows $300 out of the income account and $300 into the asset account: a balanced transaction. This practice is called double-entry accounting because two sides are recorded for every transaction: where money is *coming from*, and where money is *going to*. Those two sides are always in balance, to show that all of the money involved is accounted for.

The words *debit* and *credit* are often used to denote the two sides of a transaction like this. *AccountingCoach.com* says that these words have been in use for over 500 years, and are more traditional than descriptive. To tell you the truth, I am wholly unqualified to explain which side is the debit and which is the credit. What I have done is created a place on *npgovernance.org* to poll accountant friends who can help us.[70] I will avoid those terms here. Let's concentrate on what's going on, on money out and money in.

---

[70] To be perfectly honest, sometimes I enter transactions backwards by mistake and correct them after seeing QuickBooks change balances the wrong way. That's another reason to hire a professional accountant. I enjoy learning about

In a simple double-entry transaction, money goes out of one account and into another. Many accountants prefer ledger diagrams with two columns; I like to use arrows to illustrate transactions for myself visually. Let's say a $300 donation comes in, and the money goes straight to the operating account. I would mark it like this:

The circle shows the money came from the income account, and the arrow shows it went into the asset account. The transaction balances. Remember, income accounts are sources of money, so we're always taking money *out of* them. Their counterparts, however, expense accounts, do nothing but swallow money up, so we're always putting money *into* them.

Now let's complicate matters a bit. Suppose the $300 came in via the website, and the credit-card processor took a 3% fee. Now $9 has gone to a fundraising expense, so we need an expense account; let's call it "Payment Processing Fees." And we have a more complex transaction, involving three accounts this time: the income account, the asset (bank) account, and the expense account.

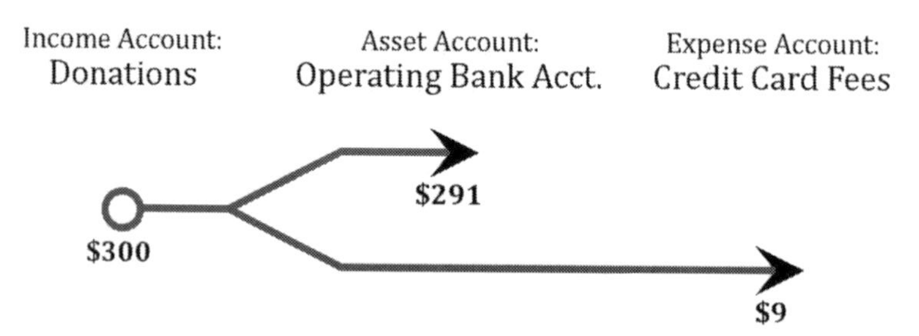

The diagram shows $300 coming *from* the "Donations" income account, and then splitting off two ways. Of that $300, $9 goes to "Payment Processing Fees"—an expense account—without even

---

accounting but I, perhaps like you, am an amateur at this. It is good for accounting amateurs to be on a board, because we each bring a different expertise to the table. We need to know enough to ask questions, and we need to hire professionals to ensure we've got this stuff right.

going through the "Operating Bank Account" asset account. This reflects reality exactly: we never saw that $9, so we shouldn't record it as having gone into our bank account. But we thank the donor for $300, not for $291, so the "Donations" income account should show $300. We as an organization incurred the credit-card fee as a fundraising expense, so we show $9 going into that expense account. Like the simpler transaction earlier, this three-way transaction also balances: the total of funds taken out of all accounts ($300) equals the total put into all accounts ($291 + $9).

This three-way transaction tells the right story. We might have only ever seen $291 cash income, but we *accrued* a $300 donation. We might never have written a check for the fee, but we *accrued* a $9 expense. If a board member were to ask about our payment-processing expenses over time, we could never answer that question by poring over our bank statements and check register. Nor could a bank statement help us avoid the embarrassing mistake of sending an automated thank-you to a donor for their generous gift of $291. Double-entry accounting on an accrual basis helps us tell the right story of what happened with the money.

Again, accrual-basis accounting records expenses as soon as checks are written, not when they are cashed. It also records income as soon as it is owed, not when it comes in. That may seem strange, but it reflects the organization's true financial position, separating logistical issues of debt collection from keeping records of the organization's assets. Being owed money is an asset: I'd rather be owed money than not. However, to reflect the fact that the money is not yet available in cash, an accountant will not record it going into the main operating account, but rather into a different asset account: let's call that account "IOUs" for now. This is an excellent example of why organizations have multiple asset accounts.

Suppose a synagogue was expecting to receive the Silberstein family's dues on Sept. 1, but now it's Oct. 1 and they have not paid. We record the situation by moving funds from the income account "Dues" to the asset account "IOUs" on Sept. 1. The dues were properly charged, and now it's just a matter of logistics to move them into the operating bank account—that is, to collect them.

If the family pays on Nov. 1, we would record a separate transaction on that date. That transaction would move the funds out of the "IOUs" asset account into the operating bank account. The funds sit in the "IOUs" account for two months, reflecting the time they are legitimately owed to the synagogue but not yet collected. By the way, the accepted accounting name for this "IOUs" account is *Accounts Receivable*, which is abbreviated A/R.

The organization got richer on Sept. 1: its bottom line gained $300, in the form of an IOU in Accounts Receivable. But the funds entered the operating bank account on Nov. 1. The two separate transactions in the diagram below tell the proper story of exactly what happened, and when it happened, with the money:

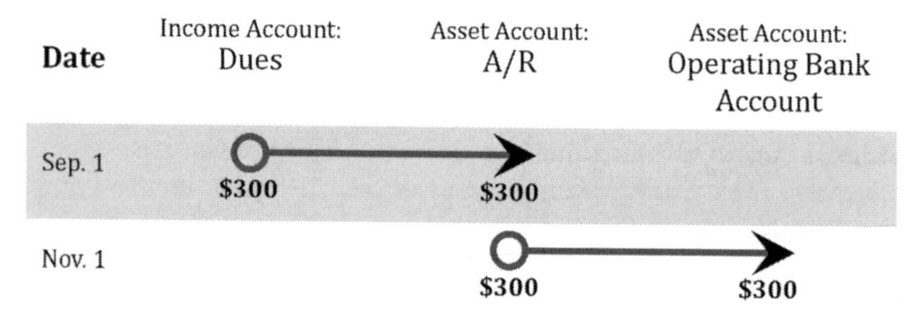

Now suppose that instead of paying dues, the Silbersteins send a letter dated Nov. 1 that they've decided to leave membership, and will not be paying. The dues will never be collected. We can't go back into the September books and erase their bill; that would improperly hide the earlier part of the story. It's not as though we erred by charging them the dues on Sept. 1, but we became officially unable to collect the debt on Nov. 1. That sometimes happens. What we need is an expense account to reflect the fact that we lost money on Nov. 1 by writing off the debt. We could call this account "Bad Debts," but let's be kinder to the family and just call it "Resigned without Paying." This expense account will record all funds written off in instances when this situation happened.

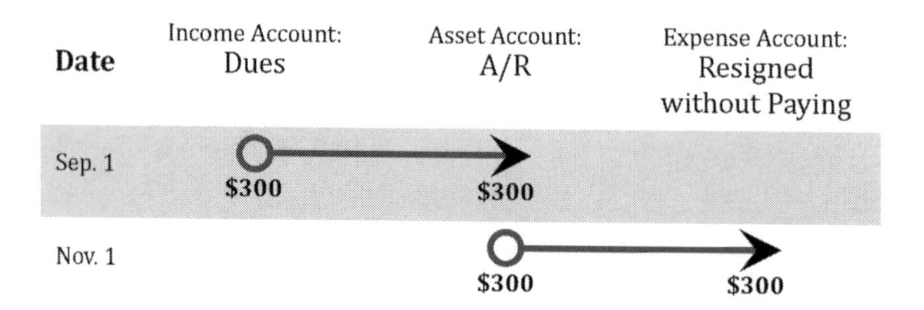

This diagram looks almost like the previous one, except that now the funds went into an expense account. The organization got richer by $300 on Sept. 1 by *accruing* the Silbersteins' dues: nothing about the family's eventual failure to pay changes the fact that the dues were properly charged on Sept. 1. But this time, the organization got poorer on Nov. 1 by officially admitting that the bill could not be collected, which is reflected by the use of an expense account. The organization *accrued* $300 revenue on Sept. 1, in the form of the Silbersteins' IOU. Then it *accrued* a $300 expense on Nov. 1, in the act of writing off the Silbersteins' IOU.

No money ever actually changed hands, yet the accrued revenue and accrued expense tell the right story. You might wonder why we should bother with these theoretical accrued transactions if nothing really happened. But something did happen. If we were to simply erase the September transaction, we'd be telling the wrong story. Double-entry accounting on an accrual basis helps us tell what happened. With it, we can correctly report the amount of dues that were owed on Sept. 1, and of that total, the amount that was never collected because people resigned without paying. We can track those "resigned without paying" amounts over time. If this year's was higher than usual, we can ask whether anything happened to cause that. We can see if special outreach efforts are effective at reducing next year's amount. All of these policy choices are made possible by our use of double-entry accounting to tell the right story.

Liability Accounts

In addition to income, expense, and asset accounts, there are also liability accounts. A liability account means the organization owes money to someone else: it's an IOU from us to outside parties. Such IOUs arising from day-to-day commerce—such as when we receive a utility bill and need to pay it—are called *Accounts Payable* and abbreviated A/P. So A/P is a liability account, while A/R (Accounts Receivable, which we saw above in the case of the Silbersteins' dues) is an asset account . There are all sorts of common liability accounts. A/P may have many subaccounts for salaries, wages, vendors, taxes and more. Funds held but intended to be returned, such as security deposits, may also be recorded in liability accounts because the organization owes the money back.

Suppose we receive an electric bill for $2,000 on Jan. 1. We book the expense the same day. We legitimately owe the money: it is no longer available for other expenses, so the books need to show that we are $2,000 poorer. Money needs to go into an expense account—let's call it "Utilities: Electricity"—because that's the reason we are now $2,000 poorer. Out of which account does that money come? It comes out of Accounts Payable, whose function is to record IOUs we've written to outside expenses. Very much like an accounting credit card, A/P then carries a balance that *we owe*.

Suppose we then pay the bill on Jan. 15. We move money *into* A/P from the operating account on that date. But when we move money *into* a liability account like A/P, the account balance goes *down*, like paying off a credit-card balance.[71]

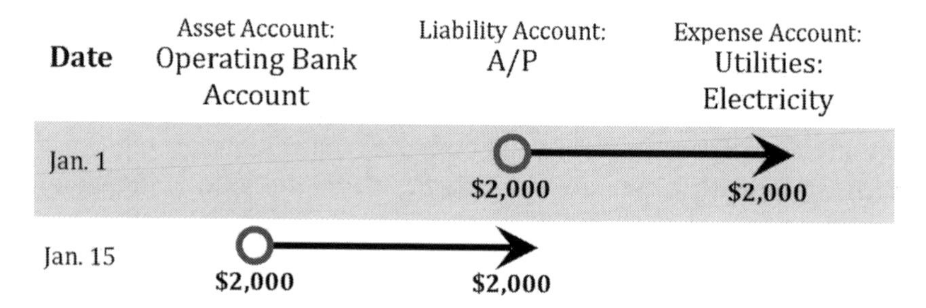

Organizations do a full accounting review annually to paint a clear picture of the organization's status, resolve pending issues, and figure any annual fees or taxes owed. This is called *closing the year*. In the process of filing their governing documents, organizations are free to choose their own *fiscal year*—that is, the schedule on which they close the year. Many organizations use a calendar year, while others find that a start date other than Jan. 1 is more natural to their annual rhythms. For example, many synagogues and schools use a July 1 or other summer start date for their fiscal year, because the rhythm of life in those organizations lends itself more naturally to an academic year, or to a Jewish year starting in the fall with major dues collection, than to a calendar year.

Asset and liability accounts are categorized as *current* or *long-term*, according to whether the transactions they record are intended to be resolved within the current fiscal year. There should

[71] For my math friends: a liability account is exactly the same thing as an asset account with a negative balance. We call it a liability account only because it's usually clearer to show balances without negative numbers all over the place.

ideally be no current assets or current liabilities when the books are closed for the year. That often means a special effort to collect debts and to pay accounts payable so the books can be closed with as accurate a picture of the year as possible. Questions about that process should be addressed to your treasurer or accountant.

One final word about A/P and A/R: they are the site of a lot of tricks, some occasionally helpful and others harmful. This is because managers, fiduciaries and reviewers are seen as less likely to probe these accounts, on the idea that they are mere operational details of a large organization. One of the most common tricks to make an organization look better for fiduciaries or for outside accreditors, or to conserve scarce funds at the cost of sustainability, is to hold payables for 60 to 90 days while aggressively collecting receivables. But it is easy to see through this trick: the books will show a high balance in A/P with a low balance in A/R. On the other hand, the wide variability of balances in A/P and A/R makes it possible to hide questionable transactions in them.

Always ask questions if you have any. Payables or receivables sitting for more than 60 days, or more than a few older than 30 days, are red flags, as are unusual balances, or custom-entered or unusual A/P or A/R transactions. I would ask about such numbers if I were a board member and saw them. Such numbers do not (usually) mean there has been wrongdoing, but they do mean it's time to ask a question. Ask for detail if you are not provided breakdowns of A/P and A/R by time outstanding (current, 30+, 60+, and 90+ days are standard categories), and ask for detail by vendor if you aren't certain what's happening in those accounts. Do not be intimidated to ask, just because you lack accounting experience. The point of your reviewing your organization's reports is to provide a fresh pair of eyes. I can't overemphasize that board members are individually responsible for understanding their organization's accounts.

The Chart of Accounts

Organizations typically have many accounts. They are arranged hierarchically, so that an overarching "Expenses" account might include, for a synagogue, subaccounts for the school, each holiday, office supplies, etc.; many of these might have their own structure of subaccounts. The same is true on the income side: there might be many different types of donations and income. Asset accounts will not be limited to the main operating bank account; they might be all sorts of subaccounts of IOUs, not to mention the value of real estate, securities, and all kinds of other assets.

A higher level of account organization, widely used, is to give each account a number, usually four digits, with the accountant free to use the numbers to denote the hierarchies needed. So you might see Account 4131: Discounted Seniors Family Dues, under Account 4130: Family Dues, under Account 4100: Dues, while every account number starting with 4 is an income account. If you see numbered accounts on statements provided to you, ask your treasurer or accountant to help you understand the structure.

The hierarchical list of an organization's accounts is called the *chart of accounts.* It can be useful to see the chart of accounts when interpreting financial reports, if it isn't clear which account comes under which. Organizations are free to name and organize their accounts in ways that make sense for them. If you are building a new organization or newly moving to professional accounting software, it may be useful to ask a similar organization if they'd share their chart of accounts as a model to help you get started.

A good chart of accounts helps you tell the story of your money. You want understandable labels that reflect reality in your daily operations, so your chart of accounts depends on how you operate. So, if you're a synagogue, your chart of accounts could include various kinds of income from dues, donations, school fees, etc., probably several asset accounts, and expense accounts for things like prayerbooks, *tallit* cleaning, school supplies, and food. If you're a service organization, your chart of accounts might include income from donations and grants, and expense accounts for things like direct grants, goods and services purchased for clients, food, etc., perhaps subdivided by program. Every organization has assets, liabilities, revenue, and expenses, but given those high-level similarities, the chart of accounts for a chapter-based organization, an independent synagogue, a university and a gas station will look totally different. There is no one right way to structure a chart of accounts. It depends on what categories you need to tell the right story of what's happening with your organization's money.

Endowments and Restricted Funds

Not all of an organization's financial accounts are intended to fund general operations. Instead, they may serve special purposes in the organization. A *restricted fund* is money set aside for predetermined purposes, often with specific rules agreed to by contract with donors or grantmakers. An *endowment* is an account whose principal is invested rather than spent down, allowing the dividends or interest to become a permanent source of income. Organizations may protect the endowment principal from being spent down through board resolutions, bylaws, or even contracts with donors.

Endowments are often invested in low-risk securities for the purpose of paying predictable returns. A professional investor will place the money where it will perform best financially. Ask your treasurer, accountant or investment professional for details on your organization's endowment, if you have one.

With a 4% annual return—a rule of thumb used in one of my organizations—you need 25 times as much money in the principal as you would like to receive each year in dividends. In other words, an endowment would need $2.5 million principal in order to pay $100,000 a year. Endowments do not need to be large: a $1,000-a-year initiative can be endowed in perpetuity for $25,000 using the same rule of thumb. Endowments are a great way for high donors to leave a lasting legacy. They can also be funded over time from the grassroots as an ongoing effort to improve financial stability. The more your organization is funded through endowments, the less you have to worry about raising the funds for each year's budget.

Ethical quandaries over the investment of endowment funds are common. Investment in companies or industries seen to be at odds with the organization's mission may nevertheless be the best way to gain funds for operations. There is no universal right answer to these dilemmas. The board may decide to forgo some income in order to place funds with mission-oriented investments, or they may decide to keep the endowment's focus on maximizing funding for mission-driven operations. The organization that finds mission-oriented investments that perform at the highest level is a happy organization. There are investment funds, firms, and advisors specializing in these issues.

There may be many restricted funds aside from endowments. Restricted donations may be used in the general budget, but only for their restricted purpose. Organizations funded by grants often find most of their budget comes from restricted funds, whose rules they must juggle to ensure everything gets funded. Named funds or programs may be given by donors for a variety of purposes, funded by endowment or by recurring or even one-time donations.

Acceptance of a restricted gift is a binding contract with the donor. Therefore, while organizations generally welcome restricted gifts, boards should ensure these gifts do not create a high cost of participation. An accountant and a lawyer need to be part of any conversation involving the acceptance of restricted donations. As for restricted grants, I advise organizations to think twice. It's great to get money, but if a grantmaker wants an application and required custom report that could take a total of 40 hours for a $3,000 grant, is that really worth it? Sometimes it is, sometimes it isn't. Donors and grantmakers dealing in restricted funds may benefit from reading Chapter 10, where I suggest replacing onerous and inefficient applications and reports with simpler, more realistic assessments of their grantees' operational efficiency. On the receiving end of restricted funds, boards need to make sure their organizations are pursuing good deals while rejecting those whose cost of participation exceeds their value.

Reading Financial Reports

The two main financial reports given to fiduciaries are the *balance sheet* and *income statement*. You may also see a *cash flow statement*. In a well-run organization, these reports are provided in writing to board members every month at meetings, and upon request. You may see a summary version, but you can always ask for more detail if you have a question. The basic annual report is a more detailed version of these same reports, often with clarifying comments.

A *balance sheet* is a statement of the organization's assets and liabilities at a snapshot in time. It will have a column for assets and a column for liabilities, and it is nice for there to be more assets than liabilities. The value of assets minus liabilities is called *equity* and represents a measure of the net worth of the organization's property (remember, the legal value of a nonprofit corporation itself is zero). Equity is often shown at the bottom of the liabilities column, to show that the value of the assets balances the value of the liabilities plus equity. Equity may be negative, but that is not as nice a situation.

In nonprofit governance, concerns about equity differ from what you might expect from home budgeting or for-profit experience. Negative equity is not necessarily bad, if it's something like a mortgage the organization is progressing each year in an organized way toward paying off. Very high negative equity raises concerns about the solvency of the organization, as with for-profits; however, nonprofits need to ask whether corrective actions like membership assessments or dues hikes could damage the organization's mission.

Moderate positive equity is perhaps an ideal situation, if the organization's finances are sound and include a reasonable rainy-day fund. But in nonprofits, very high positive equity can be a red flag: is that money being used to support the organization's mission? If the organization maintains endowments to finance operations, hats off (or if you prefer, hats on) to you: that is a great reason to maintain high positive equity. But money collected for operations should generally be spent on operations during the fiscal year in which it was collected. The accumulation of money may be the goal of a for-profit, but it is not a legally acceptable nonprofit purpose.

Nonprofit financial oversight, therefore, is about more than making sure the organization is well provided for. It is also about using money to advance the organization's mission. There is a natural tension between these two goals. A rainy-day fund, for example, is a good idea, but it has to enable your mission in some acceptably defined way while not preventing the right amount of money from actually being spent on your mission. If you have questions in this area, ask a professional accountant, tax advisor, or attorney for help. These issues are far too involved and professional for me to offer specific advice. I just want you to know enough about these issues to raise a question on your board if necessary.

When looking at a balance sheet, remember that it only reflects a moment in time. Make sure you understand the liabilities, and if there seem to be a lot of uncollected receivables month after month, that suggests a good question to raise about operations.

The *income statement* summarizes the organization's income and expenditures over the period of time indicated—usually, the previous month or year. You will see a list of sources of income (income accounts) and a list of expenses (expense accounts). As you might expect, it's good when income exceeds expenses. However, as above, it's best for income to exceed expenses moderately. If expenses exceed income, that raises questions about sustainability because no organization can keep that up forever. If income greatly exceeds expenses, that raises questions about whether enough money was spent to advance the organization's mission.

The income statement is very often called a *profit and loss (P&L) statement*. The names are used for historical and legal reasons, as well as simple convenience: your accounting software may call an income statement a P&L. However, although nonprofits certainly have income, they do not have profit, by definition. On the other hand, the term *income statement* doesn't capture the fact that it also includes expenses. Just be aware of these two names.

The *cash-flow statement* is a report of cash on hand over a period of time. The income statement reports on an accrual basis, but you may need to know your bank-account balance in order to make it through a month. Reliance on cash-flow statements is a red flag: organizations should not fly so close to the ground that they constantly worry about bouncing checks. However, in grant-funded organizations this may be a reality of life. Such organizations may live hand-to-mouth for operational expenses while cobbling small grants together. In such cases, the cash-flow statement keeps the board informed so that the board may help keep the organization afloat. Tight cash-flow situations may call for additional donations, or the organization may try to collect receivables (debts) and delay payables. Such policies are not sustainable, of course, so they require careful management as well as oversight.

Ask Questions

You will encounter many other specialized terms and techniques of accounting during your fiduciary service. This has only been an amateur introduction to the basics. As a board member, you are not required to be an accounting expert. But you *are* required to satisfy yourself individually—not taking anybody else's word for it, but based on your own independent understanding—that the accounts are correct, well managed, and in keeping with your organization's mission and policy as you independently understand them.

Your colleagues are there to help you in this task, and to some extent you them. If you are new to accounting, your treasurer, executive director, outside contracted accountant, outside advisors, nonprofit-leadership volunteers or fellow board members with greater accounting experience can help you understand things.

If you don't understand part of a financial report or need help with terminology, ask for clarification. You may not be the only one. If a new cohort of board members has just taken office, consider scheduling a primer on reading financials during a board meeting. This is also a good topic for an annual board training program.

The quality and readability of financial reports varies greatly among organizations. Most of my fiduciary boards have provided reports from automated software such as QuickBooks. One provided handmade reports in Excel that were difficult to interpret (and, I think, probably harder to create that way than they would have been in QuickBooks), while another did not provide reports on a regular schedule—a definite problem. If your organization is large enough to have the fiduciary board separate from operations (i.e. not a working board) then it is large enough to need monthly written financial reports in order to keep board members informed. If your organization does not yet have the capability to do this, help is available. See *npgovernance.org* for some ideas.

Above all, don't be afraid or embarrassed to ask any financial question. Don't assume other, more knowledgeable board members will handle the financial issues. They may, but satisfying yourself independently is how you pull your weight as a board member. The only dumb financial question is the unasked financial question.

6.3 FINANCIAL SECURITY

I remember the scene like yesterday. My boss, the head of the organization, called me into his office. "Jeremy," he asked, "did you spend any money on computer networking?"

"Not other than a box of cable," I replied. "I did all the work myself. Why?"

"What would you say," he continued, "if I told you they spent $60,000 on computer networking?"

Something had seemed wrong, but now it was obvious. "Listen," I replied, "if I told you I went out to buy a loaf of bread, and it cost $100, and you really wanted to give me every last benefit of the doubt, you might say that must have been one fancy gourmet loaf of bread. Now if I told you I spent $1,000 on a loaf of bread—"

I didn't need to finish the sentence. My boss and I both knew the financial statement he had been given was false.

The third motivation I gave for accounting was to prevent fraud.[72] I've seen three confirmed cases of embezzlement, for one of

[72] Actually, accounting just provides financial information, while it's internal controls on accounting that prevent fraud. But I'm talking about reasons for

which I was a fiduciary board member. In two other cases I'm pretty sure a trusted leader embezzled, but if so, it could not be proven and they got away with it. In the cases where we caught the embezzler, we caught them because double-entry accounting showed patterns of spending that would otherwise have been missed, buried in a pile of receipts. In both cases where I think an embezzler got away with it, accounting and security practices were loose.

All of the embezzlement cases I've seen were crimes of greed, not crimes of need. These were relatively well-to-do, trusted senior staff or volunteer leaders who had significant unsupervised access to money and were on a personal ego trip.

It is harmful to be overly deferential when reviewing accounts. If you are reading financial reports, then the person who needs to be satisfied with those reports is you. We get into trouble when we assume that if we don't understand something, it must be because we don't know enough jargon, or perhaps we are at too low an organizational level. Always ask questions whenever you don't understand something. It's important to create an organizational climate where those questions are welcomed and answered fully.

Here's how we caught the $60,000 embezzler. A then-junior staff accountant, a friend of mine, was going over the books and thought to ask a question about three large payments of $20,000 to a vendor she didn't recognize. Expenses of that size were not unusual, so the embezzler probably thought he could bury his crime in a large pile of expenditures of similar size. That might have worked if it weren't for double-entry accounting. But something seemed fishy to my friend, and instead of dismissing it as a blip in a huge pile of receipts, she noticed that all three expenditures had been charged to an expense account for computer networking, and that they dwarfed everything else in that account by orders of magnitude. The computer-networking account was part of my department, to my great annoyance, which is how I came to be asked about it. (I'll squeeze in the fabulous story of how we got the money back, if you remind me when you have me for a scholar-in-residence weekend.) Is there someone like my sharp-eyed friend in your organization, who would be careful enough and curious enough to ask questions if something didn't sit right with her?

---

organizations to engage in accounting at all, and reasons for board members to pay attention to it instead of leaving it to others.

Policing by Policy

There are many excellent sources of policy guidance on the handling of funds, some of which I've listed on *npgovernance.org*. Here are a few overarching principles. Again, we adopt these best practices not because there is suspicion of anyone, but in order that there may not be. These are reasonable measures taken by every responsible organization as a matter of course.[73]

- *Two Pairs of Eyes on Every Penny.* No one person should ever be alone with money. If there is a cash box, have two people (whoever they are, staff, volunteers, anyone) go together to count the money and lock it away. For checks, separate the function of writing checks from that of signing them. This goes even for the smallest organizations: when I had a small business with two partners, we signed each other's checks.
- *Clear Written Procedures.* When individuals handle cash, or enter or alter accounting data, the potential for trouble demands clear written procedures, required by policy, to govern those situations, including specification of exactly how cash transactions are treated on the books.
- *Deterrence.* Crimes are deterred when everyone knows with credibility that they will be reported to the police. We may not be able to eradicate such crimes, but we can make our organizations bad choices of place to commit them, and that means a culture of reporting. Sometimes organizations choose not to report crime, but I say you're generally better off reporting. Refer to Chapter 3 for more on this issue.
- *Open Books.* A membership organization's basic financial statements should always be available to all members. These are the same reports that would be given to the board. Making them available to general membership supports transparency and is educational. Some organizations may choose to make them public. Transparency demonstrates a squeaky-clean commitment and helps everyone.

---

[73] For in-depth further reading on best practices, see *coso.org*, the website of the Committee of Sponsoring Organizations of the Treadway Commission. The Treadway Commission, formally the National Commission on Fraudulent Financial Reporting, was formed in 1985 to develop and disseminate best practices for internal financial controls in organizations.

6.4 REVENUE

In most North American synagogues, operations are primarily paid for by the financial gifts of members. That includes dues, religious-school and other fees, and income from endowments, among others. In community organizations, income may come largely from grants and professional fundraising, as well as membership payments if applicable. There are many high-quality resources available on all of these issues, and I've done my best to curate a few of the best links on *npgovernance.org*. This essay will focus on higher-level issues that all of these revenue streams have in common.

My perspective is informed by my experience in social-media fundraising, including as the CEO of a software team that processed $85 million in political donations in 2008. Despite today's trends challenging North American Jewish affiliation, I believe synagogues and Jewish advocacy, community and charitable organizations have the potential to raise a lot more money than they now do.

I've given very little space in this book to perhaps the largest emerging issue in synagogue governance: the structure of dues, including alternatives to required membership donations. It is not for lack of an opinion that I've glossed over that discussion. I want this section to be an introduction to the basics of revenue for people new to the field, and I can't do that in a highly opinionated way. I do recommend the excellent new book by Rabbi Kerry Olitzky and Rabbi Avi Olitzky, *New Membership & Financial Alternatives for the American Synagogue.*[74] Although I use frequent Jewish examples, the ideas in this essay apply to all nonprofits: Jewish or not, synagogues or not, with dues-paying members or not.

A Culture of Giving and Gratitude

The Torah teaches that giving *tzedakah* is an absolute obligation incumbent on everyone.[75] That being so, does a person deserve moral credit for giving, or are donors merely complying with the rules? This is more than just a theoretical debate, because it impacts how—and whether—we thank our donors.

---

[74] Olitzky & Olitzky (2015).

[75] For example, Deut. 16:17, Proverbs 22:22; "*Tzedakah* is equal to all the other *mitzvot* combined" (b. *Bava Batra* 9a); "*Tzedakah* and acts of kindness are the equivalent of all the *mitzvot* of the Torah" (j. *Peah* 1:1); "Greater is *tzedakah* than all the sacrifices" (b. *Sukkah* 49b). Last two translations from *chabad.org*.

An act of financial support for the Jewish community is *both* a responsibility and a gift. Of course it's a responsibility. But people who give money to our organizations are donors, and the fact that their gifts are Jewishly commanded doesn't mean we can't thank them. They're fulfilling their obligation, *and* we should thank them.

We raise the most money when we instill a culture of giving and gratitude, in which gifts reflect donors' deepest values. On the other hand, transactional, fee-for-service models of interaction are not as successful developing a giving culture. Fee-for-service models enact commercial values, in which parties want to pay as little as possible to gain as much as possible. A culture of giving and gratitude is a statement of values, and it should be a key strategic goal of every organization's revenue program to instill such a culture.

It takes work to build a giving culture rather than a transactional culture, but an easy first step is to thank and recognize every donor—individually and as often as possible. The competition is tough out there. Think about how a major national charity recognizes and thanks a $500 or even $100 annual donor, as opposed to how a synagogue recognizes a member giving several times those amounts in dues. We need to reinvent the experience of giving to infuse it with joy and warmth. Giving should feel like supporting a favorite charity, not like paying a phone bill.

Synagogues are the centers of worship, learning and Jewish community for dues-paying donors; Jewish organizations offer similar ties to our tradition and identity whether they are national or local. All of our organizations enjoy rich opportunities for thanks and recognition. These range from plaques on the wall, to verbal recognition ("Today's lunch was sponsored by Jack and Josephine Jacobs"), to the same sort of notices being printed in the newsletter, to other and more creative ways to telegraph our gratitude. Every member is a donor, and every donor must be thanked.

Thank volunteers, too. Thank them on a par with those who give money. There is no shortage of thanks. Taking time to thank these people could be the start of a deepening relationship.

There should be no shame in thanking high donors. Gratitude is not about creating a competition. People have different amounts of money. If gratitude is simple and gracious, predictable and polite, people of lesser means should not have to feel excluded.

The beautiful thing about gratitude, directed to every part of the income scale, is that it costs very little. It costs the same postage stamp to mail a well-written thank-you letter, signed by the rabbi and president, as it does to mail an updated bill of debt for dues.

Cost-effective, elegant and easy, gratitude is the glue holding every successful organization together. It should be a fundamental community value. It sustains a fundraising program by making everyone feel good about participating in it. Gratitude congratulates donors, assures them that in donating they have made the right decision, and concretely validates their choice by welcoming them into a community of givers who have done the same.

Instead of treating every gift as a transaction, we should be treating every transaction as a gift. There's no such thing as an invoice for a gift. So ban QuickBooks bills for dues or pledges, make your solicitations attractive, and waste no opportunity to thank your donors. Involve the president or rabbi in writing a solicitation letter to donors for inclusion with their pledge statements. Better yet, write a new letter every quarter.

The following table helps reframe common transactional phrases into expressions of gratitude that build a giving culture. These changes of wording require no change in meaning or policy:

Reframing Communications for Gratitude

Paying dues	*becomes*	Giving dues
Dues invoice/bill	*becomes*	Solicitation for a gift
Debt owed	*becomes*	Pledge expected
Account statement	*becomes*	Thank-you note

Expectations and Emotions

Synagogue membership and support for Jewish organizations have been basic cultural expectations of the North American Jewish adult who wishes to maintain the practice of Judaism.

Synagogue membership supports promulgating the Jewish faith to succeeding generations, even if the individual member happens to be without children; therefore, part of membership dues typically help to fund a religious school. Synagogue membership sustains a place of prayer for those who need it—and it follows that people in need must be welcomed without question. Synagogue membership supports the synagogue institution itself, ensuring the continuance of a Jewish religious presence within the larger community. It pays the salaries of staff, enabling their work to continue.

I've provided several links on *npgovernance.org* to various scholars' and practitioners' excellent thinking about synagogue dues policies. There is a wide variety of choice in designing dues, but as I mentioned above, the subject is both too large and too tactical to do it justice here. I have in the past advocated moving away from flat-rate dues, but I think even flat-rate models can work if well presented. These remarks apply to any dues system, as well as the entirety of the synagogue's revenue raised from internal donations. No matter if they're called dues, donations, fees or building-fund assessments: gifts are gifts, are gifts, are gifts, are gifts. The goal of this essay is to help you increase your revenue from gifts.

Here's the bad news. Fifty years ago, I could also have said that synagogue membership and support for Jewish organizations are basic expectations of Jewish adulthood, and that would have been obvious. Today, it is aspirational. We compete with other worthy priorities for people's dollars. Furthermore, dues models have been predicated on a postwar macroeconomic stability that no longer exists and probably will never return. Into that mix come alternative and much less expensive spiritualities, the ability to feel good having given far less money to a variety of charities which thank their donors profusely, and the possibility that today's liberal Jews may be disinclined to make traditional Jewish giving a priority.

Here's the good news. There is a lot—*a lot*—of untapped money in American Jewish communities. I'm a social-network fundraising guy. When I notice that synagogues are behind the times in our fundraising tactics, I'm not primarily talking about technology. I'm talking about managing the emotions of the giving process.

If your synagogue is still sending out dues invoices, it's time for an update. Nobody enjoys paying invoices. But everybody likes supporting organizations about which they care deeply.

Implementing contemporary donor development practices can be expected to yield better results. We tend to assume people don't give because they can't afford it or because they don't care enough, but my experience shows that's not so. When the same member who balks at $1,200 dues raises three times that amount to register for a bike ride, it's not because they despise the synagogue. Rather, it's an invitation to us to improve our game. Whoever sponsored that bike ride created a community around it, making every supporter feel special and wonderful and proud to support a community integral to their values. We can do that. We can do it better.

We have a lot going for us. Jewish organizations are community centers, learning centers, spiritual centers. Our relationships with our donors may be far more intimate than other charities competing for their gifts. But our fundraising tactics are behind the times. We need to update our tactics and compete.

The first principle we discussed was gratitude. The second is to cultivate positive feelings in donors. People give when they feel good giving: this rule explains far more donation behavior I've observed than personal budget or past donation history.

The point of this chapter's *shiur* is that money is a touchy subject. Financial policies cause guilt and shame, and whereas in former times such emotions might have motivated people to cough up, today they are more likely to push donors away. And in today's fickle economy, a person's inability to pay may be quite temporary. When we take special care to make sure the organization is a place free of embarrassment for supporters who may have fallen on tough times, we are likely to be rewarded not only in knowing we've done a *mitzvah*, but also in their loyalty when they finally get that new job. Wealthy members can face discomfort around money too, especially in income-proportionate arrangements where their baseline share is astronomically large. All of these emotions can be dealt with in the context of an intentionally designed revenue program.

The more you engage gratitude, the less room there is for shame and stress. After gratitude, there's engagement with one's cherished ideals, feeling good for doing a good deed, feeling ownership in the community or a part of the community, and feeling that some aspect of the community reflects the donor's values. Make a brainstorming exercise of people's least and most favorite aspects of giving to your organization. Go back to your strategic values: what is most important to you? In your communications and recognitions, make sure donors know how well their gift is working for the priorities you—and they—most deeply value.

People like to give to success. In Chapter 11 I discuss what I call *frowny-face messaging* as opposed to *smiley-face messaging*. For some reason, specifically from Jewish organizations, I see a lot of fundraising messages frantically pleading for urgent help, because the organization is on its deathbed and will perish if I don't donate right this instant. (And then I'll feel guilty!) I don't think such messaging works very well anymore. I don't think it reflects well on the organization.

I recommend portraying your organization as well-managed, responsible, stable and successful. Don't complain that your budget is short; talk about all you've accomplished and how you're going to raise just 10% more to celebrate it all. There's always a way to reframe frowny-face messaging into smiley-face messaging. It might be educational to take a few of those frantic, deathbed solicitations from your recycle bin, and see if you can reframe them.

Fundraising, Development, Advancement

The goal of a revenue program is not only to collect annual payments from members in a predetermined amount, but also, in professional fundraising terms, to develop those donors and help each of them grow into ever more generous supporters of the institution. Three words often heard in these contexts are *fundraising*, *development*, and—mainly in higher-education contexts—*advancement*.

These terms are often used interchangeably, which I think is a mistake. They certainly have a lot to do with one another, but they are different modes of thought. All three have something to offer us. My research found conflicting definitions for these terms, but I'll give you my own definitions. *Fundraising* is getting money in the door. *Development* is working with donors to cultivate them into ever more loyal and generous donors. *Advancement* is moving the organization toward its strategic goals.

Fundraising, as I use the term, is entirely tactical. An annual donation drive is fundraising. A dues program ought to be thought of as fundraising, because that's what it is. Asking a wealthy member to create a named fund is fundraising, as is calling an indigent member about an outstanding balance. Some are better ideas than others; all are fundraising. Fundraising is the set of activities that aim directly to bring money in the door.

Development is about working with individual donors, ensuring they feel wonderful about giving to the organization, and cultivating them over time into donors who gives more. Having coffee with a wealthy member, just to build a relationship, is a good example of development. Buying coffee for an unemployed member while helping with their job search might also be excellent development. Development is about inspiring a sense of ownership in donors so that they are more inclined to give—and inclined to give more—when the time comes. If fundraising is about making asks, development is about relating to the donor between asks. It isn't a contest which is more important, but development accounts for much more of our time than fundraising.

Development can seem like a lot of work. Before the age of databases, individual development officers had to be assigned to each donor to develop a relationship with them. This only occurred with high-dollar donors, because the amount of work involved made development uneconomical with middle- and low-dollar donors.

We now have two major advantages. First, technology now makes it easy to engage donors online, about which I say more throughout Chapter 11. Moderate-level donors don't expect to be showered with personal attention, but it helps to engage online with those who can engage online. Second, especially in synagogues and other local membership organizations, we see these people all the time because they are our members. Saying casually in the hallway, "Hey, Bob, thank you so much for your gift, that was very nice," goes very far toward development—even if the gift was just $50 or was for a scheduled dues payment. If a member pays a large amount once a year for annual dues, then the president, a board member or rabbi ought to call that donor once a year to thank them. That kind of face time can be great development. And it's so much easier for local organizations than it is for national charities with no personal relationship or physical proximity to the donor.

Advancement is the organization's direction of resources to reach its strategic goals. Advancement then informs development and fundraising activities. A good example of advancement might be a strategic-planning session culminating in a high-level tactical decision whether to build a new school building or to build up the endowment. Such a decision directs future development and fundraising activities toward the organization's strategic goals, and so it *advances* the organization toward those goals. This can happen while bringing in no money at all. Research about your members' and the surrounding community's demographics, desires and financial capacity could be great advancement if it helps you develop strategic goals to fit your needs and capabilities.

Talking to potential major donors can be all three: fundraising if it brings in money, development if it builds a relationship with the donor to incline them to give more frequently or more generously, advancement if the conversation is about your strategic goals.

Because fundraising is tactical, it can be tempting to focus on immediate results at the cost of development and advancement. But investing time in higher-level revenue-supporting activities will result in more revenue; this is why the nonprofit fundraising field today has a strong development and advancement focus. When I recommended sending out thank-you notes and solicitations rather than invoices for dues, that was a small example of development. Getting people engaged in a committee could be development too, if it builds ties to the organization. How can your organization develop your donors, so that they give more when you solicit them?

Strategic and Capital Issues

So far, we've mainly discussed supporting the organization's *current* budget and obligations—that is, its income and expenditures from day to day. Organizations also raise longer-term revenue for assets such as buildings, investments, and endowments.

A *capital campaign* is a major revenue drive to increase these restricted long-term assets. Technically, the term is correctly used only for efforts to increase property such as real estate, but it's very common to talk about capital campaigns to generate money for endowments. I will simply call these activities *high-level revenue.* High-level revenue campaigns are closely aligned to strategic goals, and have much more of an advancement focus than revenue for the annual budget. Here are some tips to consider.

Keep Them Separate. High-level revenue is for entirely different purposes than current fundraising. These funds are restricted: you can't just spend them. Don't even think of "borrowing" from these assets to plug a shortfall in the budget. I've been on boards where this has been discussed, but it is a breach of fiduciary ethics and it may be illegal. We need to live within the means of our annual budgets while keeping our high-level funds for high-level projects.

Conversely, funding for capital improvement projects ought to come from a capital campaign raising money for that purpose. A synagogue working on a building addition is confusing capital costs with operational expenses if it is paying the construction company out of dues money.

Make the Right Investment in Facilities. It is a sacred duty of every board to spend the right amount of money—neither too much nor too little—to sustain an organization that is open for business and welcoming to all. Let's do as much as we can to give our future organization the best resources we can afford. On the other hand, spending too much can saddle the organization with too much debt, leading to low operational capacity or high dues, or both. It's a balance between courage and restraint, in which no two organizations will have the same right answer.

If you use dues, adopt dues reduction as a long-term strategic goal. I'm not suggesting the elimination of dues. But Jewish organizations dependent on dues—especially synagogues—increasingly compete with much less expensive options for spiritual fulfillment. Paying off mortgages over time and reducing dues will advance the broader Jewish community's strategic interest in continuity. Every building requires maintenance—the more it ages, the more maintenance. But paying off that mortgage and taking other steps toward dues reduction are strategic goals I recommend to your consideration.

Making Your Ask

There is an entire field of research about how to ask for funds. Here is a quick menu of recommendations to consider.

Don't ask twice when you can ask once. Professional fundraisers know they have a limited audience with a donor. If a person can pay $1,500 in September, do not ask them for $1,000 in September and also say you hope they will come to the annual fundraising gala in February. Ask for as much as the donor can give, at the time you ask.

As a corollary, don't nickel-and-dime your donors. It may be tempting to get on board with the airlines and raise revenue through fees. First it might be late payment fees; next we have activity fees, a $150 mini-assessment just for the new boiler, a field-trip fee, a contribution to Mazon. These little fees focus the donor's attention on small amounts of money, which distracts them from making thoughtfully generous membership gifts. Except for the late fees—which are not a gracious way of communicating with a donor—the other examples were fine causes. There is no reason members' donations shouldn't be funding them. There is also no reason to list them as separate line-items. Provide disclosure and tax statements to donors who request them, but make sure your main monthly financial communications are solicitations, not bills.

People give more to causes to which they feel connected, so barriers to entry make little sense. Membership committees and staff must be careful not to scare potential donors away by coming on too strong with a pitch. Welcome prospective donors in, and nurture them as they deepen their ties to the organization.

Synagogue budgets often include paid High Holiday tickets, but this practice doesn't seem to fit with fundraising best practices. I could make a moral argument against paid ticketing for worship, but strictly from a professional fundraising perspective it strikes me as an ill-conceived practice. The same couple who think $200 tickets are steep might, after being welcomed and developed, happily pay ten times that amount for synagogue membership. How much money does your synagogue make from paid ticket purchases? How many new members would you need to get, or what proportion of new members and new donations would you need to raise, to be able to remove the barrier to entry imposed by paid ticketing?

Fundraisers should make money. It sounds obvious, but many nonprofits lose money or barely break even on their annual fundraising banquets. While there are sometimes justifications for this, I think a good general principle is that it does not make sense. If a fundraiser is performing well, fabulous. If not, stop worrying about it and invest the effort elsewhere.

Asks can take several forms, from the subtle to the bold. One subtle method is to offer information. For example, members might be informed that the average annual cost to run a synagogue works out to about $1,800 per member.[76] This information is minimally threatening because it is just a statement of reality. Members may find it interesting. It gives them a rubric to know how much money must be found from other sources to cover members who are giving less than that average. It also gives members of means an opportunity to self-assess at that amount, even if it is a little higher than what they had been paying. It allows fortunate members to make a very special donation to support memberships for their friends who cannot pay as much. How many ways can you bring up the subject of money without explicitly asking for a check?

Know each donor's contact preferences. Some people are phone people, while others are e-mail people; these preferences tend to be very strong. I recommend every organization keep a field in its database for preferred method of contact. Fundraising needs to get more creative than the phone-a-thon. As for print mail, it has its

[76] The budget should never be secret from members, who are entitled to examine it. But I'm talking here about the format of a solicitation. Most members are not going to read the budget, so the financial information discussed here may be new to them.

place but is not as immediate as the phone or e-mail, and is also quite expensive. Print is useful in counterpoint to the phone and e-mail.

Contemporary Best Practices in Fundraising and Development

Current technology has given rise to new revenue practices, many of which our competitor nonprofits already use effectively. These go far beyond tools, to include entirely new disciplines of expertise. They may require changes in your thinking, but they can make it easier to raise more money. If your organization is new to these practices, treat them like an ice-cream store. Don't jump into all of them at once, but try them one at a time and see if they work for you.

Monthly Giving. Monthly giving is a hot growth area in fundraising. Not only is it friendlier to household budgets than large annual lump sums, but the advent of easy credit-card processing enables donors to put their gifts on plastic as a monthly recurring transaction. Recurring transactions drive poor people crazy (lest they bounce) but for those with credit, automatic monthly gifts are an easy and convenient way to give. If you see political candidates and issue-driven nonprofits frantically trying to sign you up as a recurring monthly donor, that's because this method works.

When I ran ActBlue.com's technology shop in the 2008 election year, a significant part of our $85 million raised came from signing up supporters to give monthly recurring donations of $15. Could they have given more each month? Probably, and some did. But $15 seems like such a low monthly expenditure that many signed up. For us, $15 a month meant $180 a year, no collection problems because the transactions were automatic, and people could give more from there. Add a digit to the dollar amount, and automated monthly giving could make dues a lot easier for all. Some might be willing to give more if they could give monthly. Why not find out?

Finally, while it is certainly understandable to want dues money in advance, having served on several boards, I don't see why it is necessary. Do we not pay major expenses like salary and maintenance monthly or biweekly throughout the year? The main barrier to monthly giving has been the cost of collections, but automated monthly credit-card transactions eliminate that.

E-mail Solicitations. E-mail is an easy and effective tool for outreach as well as fundraising, especially when coupled with online credit-card payment processing. A professional online fundraising consultant—who I think would be kept very busy if hired by umbrella groups to be available for local Jewish organizations—can help small organizations design an e-mail revenue program tailored to their supporters' existing habits and socioeconomic profile. For more on e-mail communications, see Chapter 11.

Online Credit Card Payment Processing. Few technologies are more critical to fundraising in the twenty-first century than online payment processing. While credit-card payments come with a fee, their cost generally pays for itself in better fundraising results and in time saved collecting pledges. Donors now expect to be able to donate online, and credit-card payment processing enables you to receive donations from faraway, unexpected sources. (See below.)

Some organizations have credit-card readers in the office and are able to take credit-card numbers over the phone, often keeping receipts in a filing cabinet. But today's credit-card donors do not want the hassle of dictating a card number by voice, when they could pay online quickly—and quietly. More importantly, from a security perspective, keeping 16-digit credit-card numbers on paper is a terrible idea, and retaining those numbers in your files exposes you to significant liability.

The advantages of online credit-card payment processing are vast. If umbrella organizations pool resources to provide aggregate payment-processing services, they could obtain more favorable rates for everyone. But too much is made of credit-card processing fees, anyway, for the service they provide. Many donors feel just fine paying a surcharge (or a "tip") to cover the credit-card rates, if they want to use a credit card. Donors get rewards for using their credit card, and appreciate that as well as the convenience.

Here's the principle of dealing with busy people: you lose people every step of the way toward making a payment. If a donor can point, click and give, you will get more donations than if their only option is to hunt for their checkbook, find an envelope, find a stamp, copy down your address, write the check, and put it in the mailbox. With online and automated bill paying, many of us no longer use our checkbooks regularly. This is especially true of younger people.

Planned Giving. This is a specialized professional field for which I recommend retaining a professional advisor. This is no place for amateurs: don't risk sounding as if you're waiting for dear old Mrs. Goldenwill to pass on. When professionally done, planned giving does not come off that way at all. It's a beautiful, moving opportunity for the planned donor to think about what matters most to them.

Research and professional experience have established that the best planned gifts come not from the highest-dollar donors, but from those who donated most consistently. What typically happens is that individuals develop lifelong habits of donating to particular causes, and then, with the benefit of a planned-giving program, they remember those causes in their wills.

It would be a windfall to receive a large bequest from a wealthy decedent who loved the community or cause. But often, wealthy members have many charities to support, yours hopefully being one of them. It may be counterintuitive, but professional planned giving officers report that some of the largest bequests come from middle-class people for whom the organization has taken a constant, central place in their lifelong giving habits, and accounts for a significant portion of their will. In planned giving, therefore, it can really pay to give as much attention to that middle tier of donors as possible.

Online Communications. From e-mail to websites, to Facebook, Twitter and even mobile apps, online technology provides rich opportunities to integrate development with the organization's overall communication program. There's more information about online media in Chapter 11.

Write or Raise. One plainspoken nonprofit president said that he recruits board members who have "either affluence or influence." That's completely valid: some people have liquid money, and others have strong networks; both are valuable. Professional development officers know that it is at least as valuable for someone to raise a major gift amount than to give that amount directly. I say more valuable: I would rather have a supporter raise one hundred $50 gifts than give $5,000 directly. Of course I'll take the $5,000 check. But it is hard to get a $5,000 donor to give $10,000, while someone who gives $50 out of the blue might give $100 with a little care and attention. On the other hand, smaller donations are more stable. Many charities found in the Great Recession that their $10,000 donors started giving $1,000 instead—but their $100 donors did not all start giving $10, and their $10 donors did not all start giving $1.

There may be potential for members to raise their annual membership gifts or other gifts. This idea borrows the "a-thon" concept from athletic charity events, where it's proven so successful.

Suppose that 25-year-old Jessica is a low-income synagogue member. She is working at Starbucks and trying to juggle student debt while she searches for elusive job openings in her professional field. It's a common enough scenario. Joe, Jessica's grandpa, lives in a different state and is ecstatic that Jessica has joined a synagogue. If Jessica calls Joe and asks if he will support her project to raise an annual gift to the synagogue, will Joe donate? Probably. Would Joe have given to Jessica's synagogue if she had not asked? No.

From the donor's perspective, there's a motto I use: People give more, and they give more often, when they're asked to give by someone they know and trust. Perhaps friends, *chavurah* leaders or fellow committee or choir members might have better luck asking for annual donations than a stock mail piece from the office. I've got a couple examples of this and other resources on *npgovernance.org*.

In "write or raise," you'll credit donors for raising money as well as for giving it. A member who raises $5,000 should be given the same kind of recognition and attention that would be accorded to someone who had given that same $5,000. A pledge can be fulfilled equally well by writing or raising the money. This principle can be applied to dues, fundraising dinner tickets, or any other case in which a certain amount of money is expected from anyone.

Conclusion

I put accounting and revenue together in this chapter not merely because both involve money. Accounting provides the confidence of accountability, as well as a sense of engagement and ownership among donors. Some donors will engage more than others with financial information. But when we make it a clear organizational value that the organization's finances are everyone's business, that can directly support development.

In our culture it can be embarrassing to talk about money, especially when inequalities of household budget are involved. For the same reason, it can be difficult to ask for a donation. It helps to recognize that the organization's budget is something all who care about the organization are in together. Everyone can take part in stewarding the organization's finances responsibly, and in giving as they are able.

I opened this chapter with a lesson about embarrassment. I'll close it with one about equality. "Each of you shall bring a gift, as your Eternal God has blessed you,"[77] declares the Torah. We are richer in all senses when we benefit from as many gifts as possible.

---

[77] Deut. 16:17.

Chapter 7
PEOPLE MANAGEMENT

7.1 SHIUR

And they came, all whose hearts moved them, and all who had a spirit of generosity, and brought God's offering for the work of the Tent of Meeting, for all its service, and for the holy vestments. And they came, both men and women, as many as were generous-hearted . . . . The children of Israel brought a freewill-offering to God.

Exodus 35:21–22a, 35:29b

And Solomon sent to Hiram, saying: . . . "Now therefore command thou that they hew me cedar-trees out of Lebanon; and my servants shall be with thy servants; and I will give thee hire for thy servants according to all that thou shalt say; for thou knowest that there is not among us any that hath skill to hew timber like unto the Zidonians." . . . And King Solomon raised a levy out of all Israel; and the levy was thirty thousand men. And he sent them to Lebanon, ten thousand a month by courses: a month they were in Lebanon, and two months at home; and Adoniram was over the levy.

I Kings 5:16, 5:20, 5:27–28[78]

I learned this teaching from my friend Penina Weinberg, past president of Congregation Eitz Chayim in Cambridge, Mass., a notable teacher of Jewish text as well as an experienced community leader. This is my own take on it.

Penina points out the difference between the labor Moses used to build the *Mishkan*/Tabernacle in the wilderness in the first text selection above, and the labor Solomon used to build the Temple in Jerusalem in the second text. For space reasons

[78] Translations JPS.

I've skipped a few verses in both texts, but if you look at the Exodus text in a Bible, you will see repetition after repetition stressing that the people built the light, beautiful and portable Tabernacle with lifted hearts, out of their own freely given labor and donations of materials. By contrast, the Temple was built by indentured labor, with a *mas*/"levy" (vv. 27–28), a word that implies the use of kingly authority to compel obedience. Strikingly, the word Solomon uses for "servants" in v. 20 is *avdai*, "my slaves," which the JPS translates as "servants" although it is the same word used for the Israelites' status in Egypt.

The Temple got built, and it was beautiful. It was massive and heavy with gold, metalwork and stone. The Tabernacle was built according to the exact blueprint which God dictated to Moses, whereas Solomon architected the Temple himself. Seen in this light, it's no wonder that God had been unenthusiastic about the people's demand for a king generations earlier.[79]

In his brilliant book *Creation and the Persistence of Evil*, J. D. Levenson sees the Temple culminating creation in Jewish text: "the world, 'heaven and earth,' are not complete until the Jerusalem Temple has gone up."[80] The Temple marks a turning point in Jewish text. The inauguration of the monarchy, beginning with King Saul and culminating in the finished Temple, is the first time—but not the last—that God follows the people's preferences instead of God's own,[81] even while making it clear that the people's preferences are

[79] I Samuel 8:6–21.

[80] Levenson (1994), p. 99.

[81] It is not, of course, the first time things don't go according to God's plan, nor is it the first time God accommodates to mortals' preferences. By Saul's time the instances of human sin have already been too numerous to count, as have the times God has forborne from punishment in response to human pleas. Nor is this the first time God has changed the Law, although I think the incident of Zelophehad's daughters (Numbers 27:1–11) is more a clarification than a change, and in any case, from a religious perspective, the story of Zelophehad's daughters is inextricably part of the Law because it appears in the Torah. It could also be argued that eating meat was a divine accommodation to mortals—that's too big a topic for a footnote—but that argument is complicated and in any case there was no explicit, verbal human request to eat meat.

With the monarchy we see something new. Now God, through Samuel, makes it clear God is displeased with the monarchy idea and warns the people against it (I Samuel 8:4–22), but ultimately goes along with it (I Samuel 8:22–10:24, especially 10:19). Instead of ordering the people to conform to Divine

not a good idea, and even though negative consequences occur just as God predicted. Perhaps not coincidentally, the Temple was the first major accomplishment by humans subject to their king's authority instead of God's direct authority.[82]

If the monarchy and Temple culminate the creation story, they also begin the redemption story. Traditional Jewish sources predict a Messiah descended from the royal line of David.[83] Perhaps the shift from divine to earthly power signifies that humanity will increasingly manage its own affairs, even though it will be painful at times. In particular, the earthly monarchy itself is destined to come crashing down, to be redeemed only at the end of days.

Today, our challenge is to learn from our ancestors' mistakes while building upon their successes. Solomon forced people to do work he assigned them, in accordance with God's prediction[84] but not God's preference. God had preferred the Tabernacle's model, built only on volunteer work and donations joyfully given by people who felt moved to support the cause. Whether we're managing volunteers or staff, joyfully given work is better work, longer lasting, and more spiritually beneficial to all.

Contrary to a persistent misconception, management is not about telling people what to do. Management is a matter of organizing people to accomplish shared goals and to build a joyful, self-sustaining, competent organization. Management is exercising authority without being authoritarian.

7.2 DELEGATING RESPONSIBILITY

This essay introduces four chapters on management—the current one along with chapters 8, 9, and 10—which are intended to apply equally to employment and to volunteer management relationships. There are major differences, of course. However, it turns out that for most of our subject matter the similarities between employment

---

will, this time God warns them of the consequences and allows them to proceed with a path God clearly does not prefer.

[82] I Samuel 8:7 and I Samuel 10:19 make this shift especially clear.

[83] b. *Sanhedrin* 98a.

[84] I Samuel 8:16.

and volunteer management relationships matter more than the differences, so we'll usually consider the two cases together. Some examples will refer to employers while others refer to committee chairs, but I invite the reader to consider how each example might apply to both cases.

Ethics and Skills

Judaism imposes clear ethical requirements on management relationships. My favorite—*A worker's wages shall not remain with you overnight until morning*[85]—is no-nonsense Jewish employment law. Every Jewish organization should follow Rabbi Hillel Gamoran's advice in his excellent book *Talmud for Everyday Living*,[86] in which he carefully explains the guidance of Jewish law in a concise collection of workplace ethics scenarios. I could not hope to do better than Rabbi Gamoran and some of the other excellent resources out there, to which I've linked on *npgovernance.org*. If I don't devote much space in this chapter to Jewish workplace ethics, it's because these and other scholars have already done that job. We also discussed conflicts of interest back in Chapter 3. But let's be clear: the Golden Rule applies to management relationships, and additionally, managers owe a certain fiduciary duty to the well-being of those they manage, according to Jewish text and tradition.

Running an ethical workplace requires not only good intentions but also skills, which will be our focus in this chapter. Have you ever known someone who was better to work *with* than *for*? Sometimes, although a manager means no harm, gaps in managerial skills lead to unnecessary difficulty, or even cause what appear to be ethical lapses. Fortunately, skills can be learned. Therefore, this chapter is intended to support the skills that enable us to live and work according to our highest ethical intentions.

Responsibility vs. Tasks

Do you know the expression, "if you want something done right, you have to do it yourself?" Contemporary management turns that folk wisdom on its head. First of all, there is no such thing as a job being done "right." There is such a thing as a job done to fulfill the criteria, characteristics or functions that the finished job must be able to

[85] Leviticus 19:13.

[86] Gamoran (2001).

fulfill, or which were specified when the job was assigned. Anything else is just a matter of personal preferences.

In management, our goal is never to have a job done exactly our way, because the point of management is precisely *not* to have to do the job ourselves. Other people's work products will never be exactly the same as what you personally would have done. But you can communicate clearly about the characteristics any finished job must have. Often, giving people a sense of how their work fits into your big picture can make the difference in their understanding the job. We need to let go of the illusion of jobs being done "right," and embrace instead a different way of thinking about management.

The verb *to delegate* itself means to empower someone to act on your behalf. A member of a diplomatic delegation, or an elected member of a House of Delegates,[87] represents her constituents. These "delegates" are empowered—delegated—to act on behalf of the people who delegated them. Just the same way, when a leader delegates responsibility to an employee or volunteer, the leader is giving the worker authority to get the job done, using the worker's own best judgment to meet mutually understood standards.

Some people think that traditional management is about telling others what to do, assigning small tasks that the employee then presents to the manager for either approval or rework. But this idea is not traditional at all. Before the Industrial Revolution, most (free) employees were artisans who learned a craft from their manager. Work was structured to provide for both the manager's production and the employee's career and skill development—not out of altruism to workers but because there was no other choice.

Mass production replaced artisans with functionaries doing the same repetitive tasks all day. Hierarchical industrial management models made it possible for corporations to put untold millions of nuts on untold millions of bolts.[88] Today, however, we're returning to delegated management because it works better for our needs. Today's jobs demand attitudes closer to the craft work of 200 years

---

[87] The Legislatures of Maryland, Virginia and West Virginia include a House of Delegates. I found it interesting that the policymaking bodies of several U.S. professional associations also use this term.

[88] See Light (2001), p. 11, and his discussion of Frederick Winslow Taylor's 1911 work *The Principles of Scientific Management.* Contrast Light's critique of "scientific management" with the *standard processes* we discuss in Chapter 10 as part of Capability Maturity Model Level 3.

ago than the factory work of 100 years ago. Delegation also makes more room for respecting workers ethically, but right now I want to be very hard-nosed about this. I'm not talking about relaxing efficiency to accommodate ethics. Delegation leads to higher efficiency *and* higher ethics.

These observations apply particularly to nonprofits, especially Jewish ones, which exist to build communities rather than machines. People feel greater ownership of tasks that they're allowed a measure of freedom to do in their way. That leads to better work, whether done by employees or volunteers.

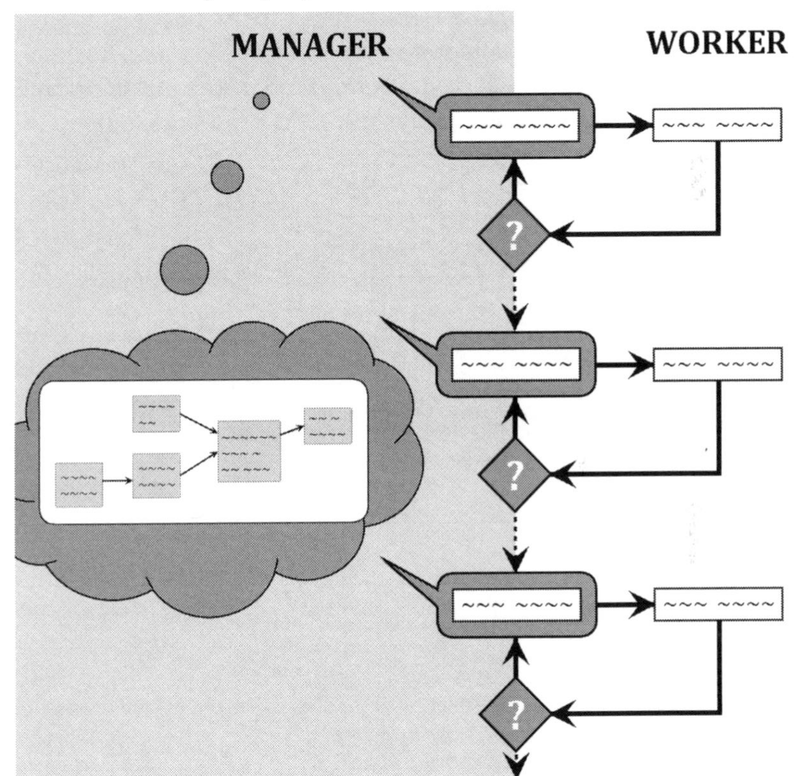

Figure 3. A workflow under the rejection-rework cycle.

Does Figure 3 above look familiar? If so, your organization needs to think about delegation. This diagram depicts a workflow under what I call the *rejection-rework cycle*, typical of ineffectively delegating organizations. The manager may have a plan in mind, but does not share it. Instead, she directs the worker(s) to complete one individual task at a time. The worker then goes off and completes the task. They submit it for approval when they think it's done, but only the manager knows the criteria for when the task is done, or how it fits with the overall plan. If the manager approves the work, she assigns the worker a new task, beginning another phase of the cycle. Otherwise, the manager sends the task back for rework.

The workflow diagram illustrates the enormous inefficiency of the rejection-rework cycle. The rejection-rework cycle keeps the manager quite busy, while the worker, acting like a factory machine, barely uses their mental capacity and is therefore not being utilized effectively, even without rework. But subject to the unpredictability of a manager's whim or of uncommunicated, guessed-at criteria for job completion, even routine projects tend to stretch out over time. If any of this rings a bell, better ways of working are available.

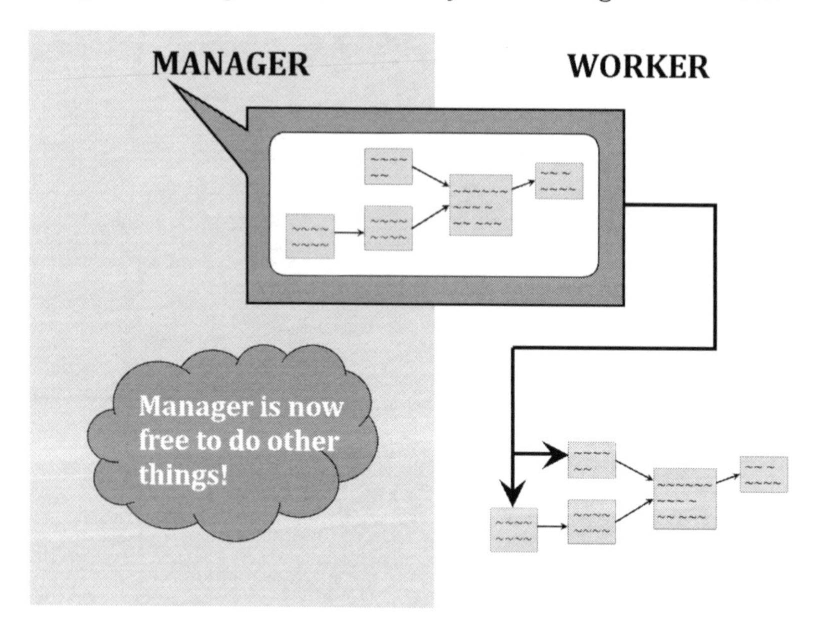

Figure 4. A workflow under effective delegation.

Figure 4 depicts a workflow with effective delegation. A good manager shares with each worker as complete a plan as possible for the work they will be expected to do. Feedback could even improve the plan before work begins. Because the worker now knows all that the manager knows about their assigned work, they can exercise significant self-direction. That, in turn, frees the manager to devote her attention to other things, enabling the organization to delegate and accomplish even more.

Notice, in Figure 3, how little work gets done for the amount of effort everyone puts in. The task cycle is repetitive, the whole work process must often stop and wait for worker-manager meetings or communication, and neither worker nor manager has any guarantee—or even any particular reason to expect—that the work product will be accepted once submitted. The low expectations inherent in the rejection-rework cycle lead to a frustrating and ultimately adversarial work environment. By contrast, just about everything in Figure 4 is directly productive, efficient work.

Most important of all, delegation frees the manager's time to manage other projects and work on higher-level concerns. The organization accomplishes much more with delegation; therefore, a top manager's degree of skill at delegation is a high-level matter of organizational health worthy of board attention. Complaints of insufficient staffing or volunteering may in fact indicate a need for delegation: a much less expensive problem to solve. Ineffective delegation wastes time and makes managers into bottlenecks, while effective delegation frees everyone to accomplish more. Without effective delegation, the organization can never hope to accomplish more than what can fit in the manager's head, while an effectively delegating organization can do many times that amount of work.

Funders and consultants often talk about *capacity*—how much good work an organization can do—and often prefer *capacity-building* programs that make good social investments by enabling grantees to do more. In my opinion, few capacity-building programs offer greater returns than teaching managers to delegate effectively.

Delegation as a Two-Way Bargain

There is no rejection-rework cycle when managers delegate. A delegated work product should fulfill its major goals acceptably when submitted, because the worker has collaborated with management to understand what those goals are.

Imagine hiring a gardener to landscape your yard. In the rejection-rework cycle, representative of poor management, the gardener shows you what he thought you wanted, and you say no, I'd rather the bush be over there and the brick walk be over here. The gardener dutifully digs out the bush and rips out the bricks, lays the brick walk in its new place and replants the bush, and you say no, I think the flowerbed should be closer to the house. Quickly and predictably, the business relationship sours.

It's an extreme example, but I chose it to emphasize the huge expense of rework. With employees, the organization pays directly in cash for all that wasted time. With volunteers, everyone pays in lost morale and productivity. Worse, the rejection-rework cycle is tantamount to a manager constantly changing decisions, which undermines the legitimacy of any decision the manager makes.

A gardening contractor prevents this pitfall with a contract. The *scope of work* (list of what is to be done) is spelled out in words; both parties sign it to indicate their agreement. I've run small businesses doing contracted work (for websites) and I'll tell you this: I'd never do that kind of work without a contract. With a good contract, both the customer and the vendor know how to tell when the job is done.

Within an office or volunteer organization, effective delegation functions almost like an internal contract. The manager acts as the customer, spelling out what is to be done and offering background so that the worker knows the manager's broader priorities. The worker plays the role of the vendor, doing the work to the agreed-upon specifications. Delegation is a matter of managers keeping their word: accepting a task as done when it meets the criteria they asked for, with other details left to the worker's own sense of artisanship. This chart shows the general terms of this "contract":

Manager Agrees:	*Worker Agrees:*
To specify success criteria fully	To accomplish those criteria as efficiently as possible
To accept a work product that meets those criteria	To ask if they have a question
To accept worker autonomy on matters not specified	To notify the manager in case of unforeseen problems
To explain what the worker needs to know, at the beginning of the project	

That's not innovative thinking; it's just good business. Nobody would (or, nobody should) rototill your yard, paint your house, or design your website without a contract. Just the same, no employee or volunteer should work without a clear mutual understanding of what is to be done. It might not be a formal written contract, or it might, but a clear mutual understanding of the criteria for success is what makes Figure 3 into Figure 4.

Problems Solved by Delegation

The rejection-rework cycle can take many forms. Each signifies ineffective management, and can be substantially solved by learning to delegate. There is no rejection-rework cycle in a successfully delegated task. If the rejection-rework cycle appears, it signifies deficient management—not deficient worker aptitude or attitude.

Perfectionism: Perfectionism prevents clear communication due to a domino effect of mistakes. Perfection is impossible to define because it does not exist. Then, because criteria for success under a perfectionist manager are always undefined, the worker returns time and again only to be told to change something else. This happens because the manager's idea of management is wrong.

Delegating a task requires a clear definition of success in words, understood the same way by worker and manager. It is the manager's responsibility to see to this understanding in advance.

Decreasing returns to scale: No vision can ever be realized exactly. A brochure might be better with another paragraph, shorter biographies and more pictures, or a snazzier logo. Let's suppose a brochure is good enough. The difference between *good enough* and *a little bit better* is smaller than the difference between *not good enough* and *good enough*. If staff go ahead and add the photo, now there's an even smaller difference between *a little bit better* and *a little bit better than that*. Eventually, the gain isn't worth the time spent, even if the gain is real. So accept good enough work as good enough, give the worker a sense of accomplishment for doing it, and move on to other tasks whose return is greater.

Moving Targets: Key to morale is to give workers confidence that if they accomplish what they agreed to accomplish, they will be praised, recognized, and (as applicable) paid for the work.

If a work product needs minor review, that's one thing. What managers cannot legitimately do is change the rules in the middle of the game. As with any issue of legitimacy, the benefits of a random brainstorm in the middle of task execution are seldom worth the cost of undermining predictability and trust. Skilled managers have those brilliant brainstorms before, not after, assigning a task.

Dealing with Bad Performance

It will be a valid critique of this book that I've said little about dealing with underperforming employees. In Chapter 5, I presented some ideas regarding volunteers who may not be in the right place. To a great extent, the same suggestions apply in the professional workplace. Listening and setting an example can work in the employment setting as well as they do for volunteers.

Beyond that, there are three reasons I've said little about employee underperformance. First, many other authors have written about that. Second, there are widely disparate schools of thought on that topic, and those divergences are too large for me to resolve in this book. Third and most importantly, over fifteen years of managing small businesses and nonprofits and sitting on eight boards, I honestly haven't seen very much of this problem.

I am of the old-fashioned opinion that hiring the right people and helping them grow once hired are management responsibilities. In cases where employee performance really is bad, managers need to zero in on the problem. Perhaps an employee is facing a challenge they feel unequipped to handle, or perhaps work has become unpleasant for them. Those cases should be rare if everyone has been honest and diligent through the hiring process, and in my experience they have indeed been rare. Better planning (see Chapter 8), more reasonable expectations (see Chapter 9), and the skills we discussed in Chapter 5 are best suited to resolve most conflicts over work performance.

7.3 MANAGING AND MENTORING

Management can be like a jigsaw puzzle: how do you best fit the people you have to the tasks you need? Personnel changes (hiring and firing) are options, but let's talk about the staff you've currently got. Many of these thoughts apply directly to volunteers as well as staff, but we'll use employee management as our example for now.

As you get to know your staff, you will notice that each person has certain strengths and weaknesses, as well as things they love to do and things they do not love to do. Every job, including yours and mine, requires a mix of those. But one way to look at the challenge of management is to give people roles and responsibilities that best fit their strengths and their desired areas of growth.

You might notice that your receptionist happens to be incredible at graphic design. There's a no-brainer: devote more of his staff time to graphic design, if the priorities are at all malleable. If your staff accountant is a neat-freak (and is on salary and not a high hourly rate) let her clean the dishes if she enjoys it, instead of insisting that the most junior staffer do that job. You might find some creative ways to get better work done, cheaper, with a happier staff.

Manager as Mentor, Exemplar, Facilitator, and Boss

We do the most justice to Jewish concepts of individual worth and dignity—and I find we get the best results—when we mentor employees instead of merely demanding task work out of them. I submit that the disappearance of mentorship from management is a product of the Industrial Revolution, in which jobs were suddenly interchangeable and people therefore were seen as interchangeable. It's time to bring mentoring back.

My friend Dedric Carter serves as Associate Provost and Associate Vice Chancellor for Innovation and Entrepreneurship at Washington University in St. Louis. A longtime tech executive, Dedric was one of my first bosses and a model of a manager-mentor. Each week, Dedric would ask everyone how we did on each of his four imperatives: Do excellent work; learn something; have fun; make money. Two were for us and two were for the company. It is a great model, and it translates directly into nonprofit management if you replace "make money" with "advance the mission."

Mentor your staff. Get to know them and find out what they love to do, where they need to grow, and where they desire to grow. Let them know that you wish to help them develop new skills and advance their careers. When employees trust you to mentor them, and you consistently earn that trust, the relationship becomes more than a transaction. Employees do better work when they care about their work, and they care about their work when they are cared for.

As managers, we should always be mentors, but mentoring is not our only role. We are also exemplar, facilitator, and boss.

Have you ever heard any form of "Do as I say, not as I do" in the workplace? I had a funny experience as CEO of ActBlue.com's tech company in 2008. It's not unusual for software employees to manage their own work hours. When I started, I'd come in at 9:30, but few people were in the office and eventually I began coming in at 10. I was glad to see employees there before me, but you know what, I worked so many extra hours as CEO that I began coming in at 10:30 . . . then 11 . . . then 11:30. Everyone seemed fine with it, and I knew my staff were putting in the hours to deliver results. We all saw each other's e-mails at 2:00 a.m.

One fine day, I woke up early and came in at 9:30. Guess what? It was 11:00 before a single staff member arrived. Oops! What had I done? I realized immediately that the staff had been following my example all along.

Work was getting done, but I knew that we needed to work more hours in common with those of our client. I called a staff meeting and apologized, saying I knew this was totally my fault, but we needed to get back on schedule, and I was going to take the first step. From that day forward, the company offered "Hot Breakfast Mondays": omelets or pancakes cooked on-site on a portable electric range by yours truly, served Monday morning at 9:00 sharp, first-come first-served while supplies lasted. It worked. Employees appreciated the humor, the nudge, and the acknowledgment that it was primarily I who had penance to do. We got back on schedule.

My issue was keeping professional hours. For you it might be something else. We as managers set an example. Intentionally or not, staff emulate what they see us doing. If we want to set or change organizational culture, it's up to us personally to model it.

We are also facilitators. As in my model of the working committee (see Chapter 5), much of a manager's work is making sure employees have the information, tools, training, task clarity and resources they need to do their jobs, and that they seek and receive assistance if they get stuck. Senior employees need less supervision and can offer a more equal exchange of ideas, while junior employees may need help developing their abilities and confidence.

Finally, despite all these enlightened notions the manager is still the boss. The workplace is not a democracy, and sometimes we just need people to follow orders. The thing of it is, we can only ask so much of people's capacity to do that. If all we ever do as managers is bark out orders, we are going to have low morale, low legitimacy, a transactional or clockwatching relationship with staff, failure to delegate effectively, and we are going to reap poor results. On the other hand, if we remain the boss without bossing people around, we will bank employees' capacity to just clam up and do as they're told for the very rare occasions when we truly need them to do that.

7.4 MANAGING LOW-PAID STAFF

In most nonprofit jobs, it goes without saying that the salary level does not reflect the quality or value of the work. Although large organizations might be able to offer better pay, it's not unusual in smaller nonprofits for professionals to make half the going rate for their work, while junior staff might be paid close to minimum wage.

Certainly many people agree to work for relatively low wages because they want a rewarding job where their daily work aligns with their values. But I don't overrely on a sense of mission for employee goodwill. It isn't fair to ask staff to give and give and give uncompensated hours even if they really do care about the mission. They're already working hard for below-market pay out of their personal goodwill. So if we want low-paid employees to go the extra mile, we need to go the extra mile for them.

Managing low-paid staff is largely a matter of finding creative ways to recognize their contributions, aside from increasing their pay beyond the budget. Acknowledging and appreciating the generosity of underpaid staff can go a long way toward maintaining morale, just as thanks and recognition benefit donor relationships. That doesn't mean managers should be deferential. But staff already know that the organization can't afford to pay them at the going rate. It's appropriate to let them know they are appreciated.

Underpaid staff have made their peace with their pay, or they wouldn't have taken the job. They need to know they're not being taken advantage of. Therefore, much of our potential comes from intangibles. Many of these ideas cost very little, while some come at a real financial or productivity cost that nevertheless does not come close to the cost of paying a competitive salary. Consider these ideas directly, or as food for thought:

Cultivating Respect. Low-income people face a lot of humiliation in life, so let work be a place where their self-worth is respected. Treat them with gratitude while holding them to high workplace standards. It can be deceptively easy for managers, clients (or synagogue members), and anyone else to assume that just because a person is paid poorly, they must be uneducated or in need of extremely close supervision. Rather, give staff as much latitude and deference as possible within the context of job goals.

Fighting for Raises and Other Benefits. When I had jobs managing low-paid staff, senior management knew that when I came knocking, it would be to talk about increasing my employees' pay. Realistic or not, I saw it as a duty to carry the torch, to keep raising the issue so it could compete with other priorities as new money came in. When employees saw me doing this, they knew I was sincere. I saw it as part of our bargain. This includes salary, healthcare, paid time off, and any other part of an employee's formal compensation package.

Work-Life Boundaries. I've been noted for sending employees home after an eight-hour workday, even though they were committed to our mission and would have been happy to stay (and were on salary, so they wouldn't have been paid to stay). But they had families and lives, and I would not have underpaid employees working overtime on my watch. Jewish organizations are particularly obligated to consider the value of personal and family time, in order to practice what we preach as spiritual organizations.

Liberal leave policies for illness, child care, even vacation, might cause inconvenience to the workplace, but on the scale of what it would cost to pay an industrially competitive salary, these become easy ways to show appreciation and provide what amounts to a raise without a direct budget impact. Not all requests can be granted; not all requests are reasonable. But a bias in favor of granting flextime requests can help.

I am of the opinion that Americans don't enjoy enough vacation anyway. The seasonal nature of much Jewish work lends itself to "free" vacation weeks that need not count against employees' otherwise accrued time. Depending on your situation, that might be an option worth exploring. In any case, leave does not necessarily cut into productivity. Some jobs have no linear relationship of hours spent to work accomplished at all. If an employee takes a personal day to clear their mind after accomplishing a major goal, or if flexible hours allow them to focus on work rather than juggling worries about their child's supervision, those employees might be *more* productive than they would have been under strict leave policies.

Generosity with Titles. A title says a lot about a person, outside the workplace as well as in it. If an able staffer can be called "Communications Manager" and then promoted to "Director of Communications," why not do that rather than saddling them with a low-level title like "Website Specialist" or "Office Assistant"? In a small office, there might not be much practical distinction between the job descriptions for those four titles. In a large nonprofit, there might be, but I recommend giving everyone the highest-sounding title possible. Be creative. A flattering title costs your budget nothing while expressing appreciation and giving the staffer something to be proud of. It may also help them work their way up to a more responsible job; if so, it may have financial value to them.

Teaching Skills. On-the-job training can be an important benefit to employees. If it aligns with task objectives, it could come at minimal cost to the employer. Somebody has got to do mail merges. If the bookkeeper is the only one who knows how to make Excel talk to Word so that properly sorted mailing labels come out of the printer, they might teach that trick to the office manager so that mail merges can happen if the bookkeeper is absent. The office manager learns a marketable skill, the organization's capacity to do mail merges becomes more stable, and everyone benefits. Look for opportunities to teach skills that make employees both more marketable and more effective at their jobs.

Accepting Turnover. Lower-paid jobs are more interchangeable than higher-paid jobs. The marketplace enforces this tendency: if your organization employs someone at low pay for a job nobody else could do, it might be time to think about retaining that person through higher pay, before they drift away to someone who will pay them better for their specific, irreplaceable skill. On the other hand, of course it's entirely reasonable for a low-paid worker to want to move up to a position where they could be more financially secure.

Accept turnover in low-wage jobs as a consequence of the position's low pay. It may not be wrong to employ someone who stays only a short while before moving on and making room for the next hire. We'd all like to minimize the hassle of hiring and training, but turnover in low-paying jobs is just a realistic cost of business.

When we accept turnover, we free ourselves to assist underemployed staff members in working their way up to better employment, without embarrassment. It may seem unusual to think of the workplace as supportive of an employee's outside job search, but if work is getting done, such leniency and active support could be an important benefit for an underemployed staffer. For example, now that an able staffer has proven themselves in a small synagogue office, perhaps a board member knows someone hiring within their professional field. If this still seems counterintuitive, think back to the pre-industrial relationship between master and apprentice artisans. The goal of the apprenticeship always was to build the apprentice's skills in order for them to eventually hang a shingle on their own. I support a return to this way of thinking, especially when a low-paid staffer is underemployed. Let our workplaces be positive places that benefit all who enter them.

Letting People Grow, Letting People Go

No law of nature guarantees any benefit to the organization from advancing staffers' careers. But advancing staffers' careers makes the organization a good place to work, and Jewish organizations ought to be good places to work. My experience does suggest staff see it as an important benefit, which results in better work done.

Not every low-paid employee desires career advancement. Your receptionist might be very happy at the front desk; they might have been there for 20 years and be looking forward to 20 more. That used to be the model of a receptionist job. In many ways it's an ideal situation. That employee still deserves all the respect and intangible compensation I've recommended in this essay, but they might not wish to move into a more senior position.

But in today's economy, underemployment is more the rule than the exception. Young workers have trouble finding first jobs in their field, and must settle for low-paying roles that do not draw on their skills. Older workers get laid off and cannot find new employment at their previous level. Any of these people may turn to nonprofit work for an extra sense of rewarding mission or for the challenge of working in a small organization where they might find a chance to shine beyond their formal job description. A nonprofit job can be a stop on an underemployed staffer's journey toward career recovery.

I've spent significant effort figuring out ways to help employees advance. If I notice a talent in a low-level employee, I try to make it part of their routine. If excellent performance is consistent, I make it part of their job description after a while, offering them a better title and, if possible, a small raise. These gestures matter very much. I always want people to feel that they are advancing, and that I recognize them. People want to work in a place where they are challenged, recognized, and given opportunities for advancement, even though nobody in the office has the salary they would like.

I often used to hire people who were clearly overqualified into entry-level jobs. They might have been down on their luck, or they might never have thought of using a talent I saw in them. They'd work for me for a year or two, during which I'd help them develop their innate talent, advance their title, and accomplish better work. I was very open with them that I thought they were underemployed and that I supported them applying for better-paying jobs, and would give them opportunities to expand their portfolio in the meantime. When they were ready, I'd help them find a better job, with my stellar recommendation about their talent and fast rise in responsibility level. Then I'd do it all over again. As our economy struggles with underemployment and overqualification, this might be a good way to reimagine low-paying jobs.

7.5 ATTRACTING AND MANAGING VOLUNTEERS

Groups of all sizes complain about insufficient volunteer power. But the first step toward volunteer growth is to understand that the complaint of insufficient volunteer power looks at the problem fundamentally backward. You do not have insufficient volunteer power to accomplish your tasks; you are taking on too many tasks for the volunteer power you have. This is true for 100 out of every 100 organizations that make this complaint. Here are some suggestions for everyone who manages volunteers:

Never plan for more work than your volunteers can do cheerfully. If a couple times a year for select volunteers things get heated—right before the High Holidays, for example—that's okay; they signed up for a job known to be challenging. But if you're always pushing your volunteers to work harder and harder, that's a red flag.

Volunteers like to be given things to do. Recall our discussion in Chapter 5 of worker bees and leaders. This principle is true for both. Worker bees like to be given simple tasks in succession, while leaders like to be given more complex jobs to manage. With both, start small and proceed to greater responsibility in order to build a sense of accomplishment and commitment. Never be caught without an answer to the question "How can I help?"

To grow your volunteer capacity, consider these steps:

1. *Pare back your demands.* Even if all your demands are important, pare them back to create space for organizational self-reflection, and until a confident and joyful atmosphere prevails among your volunteers.
2. *Ask if your goals could be accomplished through management improvements rather than additional work.* In addition to this chapter, review Chapter 8 and Chapter 9 to determine if improved project or productivity management practices could assist you in accomplishing the same goals with less work. Try some improvements and see if they help.
3. *Prepare tasks for volunteers who wish to help.* Always have a pile of papers to staple, envelopes to stuff, or database changes to enter, ready for a volunteer who asks to help. Divide your to-do list into as many small, interchangeable, manageable segments as possible. Design office systems around these segments. For example, if you have a steady stream of office volunteers, have a queue of copying or data-entry work for volunteers to come in anytime and do. If you get a lot of social-action volunteers, keep a queue of needs for community projects. Ask employees to do that work only if the queue gets too large or if something is time-sensitive.

   Think in advance how you'd respond to a leader-type volunteer (see Chapter 5) who wants to get engaged. Are there any "nice-to-have" projects on your wish list that are not important enough to take staff time? These can be great first projects to engage and develop a leader. Offices and committees might maintain their own "nice-to-have" wish lists. Almost more importantly than accomplishing work, these jobs bring volunteers in the door, give them a sense of accomplishment, and establish a working relationship that could facilitate more responsible future volunteer work.
4. *Delegate to volunteers according to their interests.* If volunteers come in on a regular schedule, get to know them individually, to the point where you know what activities they enjoy. Match them with work you think they might enjoy doing.[89] If you have so many regular volunteers to

[89] One of my reviewers noted that I gave very similar advice for managing employees earlier in this chapter. That's no accident!

deal with that you can't get to know them all, delegate leadership responsibility (even to volunteers) until every volunteer reports to someone who can get to know them personally.

5. *Develop your volunteers.* Refer to Chapter 5 for tips on developing volunteers toward greater responsibility within the organization. As volunteers take on more commitment, more work gets done, and they will bring in new volunteers from their own networks because they enjoy volunteering.

I've spoken of giving volunteers tasks to do, but the drive should be from the volunteer. Let them make the commitment, and make sure they feel satisfied with their decision to make that commitment. Letting volunteers make their own commitments is the only way to know that the volunteer is doing work they would like to do more of—and are likely to complete. A little cajoling is okay, but a lot of cajoling is not sustainable. Tasks that no volunteer will claim—because they are unfulfilling, or simply because there are more tasks than volunteers—ought to be done by staff for a reasonable wage.

In small organizations, it can be tempting to ask volunteers to fill in staff roles that the organization cannot afford to hire for. This is dangerous. It takes the unpaid worker for granted and is guaranteed to result in burnout and damaged relationships. Still worse, there is no way to exercise management control over a volunteer.[90] Small organizations must not take on so much that they become tempted to misuse volunteers in this way.

The only exception I can think of is the working board as described in Chapter 3: it's still not ideal, but board members are not ordinary volunteers because they are legally responsible for the organization. Especially in organizations small enough to need a working board, the key to growth is paring back enough to make room for strategic thinking.

Too many small nonprofits are chronically stressful places to be, because they've stretched everyone too thin. I have some advice for organizations stuck in this stressful place. First, I repeat because I'm begging you to consider it, please take my advice to pare back. Cut, cut, cut the to-do list. Cut! Next, consider whether the stress might be partially alleviated by matching people better with tasks they

---

[90] As this applies to technology, see Chapter 11's warning about "Uncle Moe."

enjoy. Cutting the to-do list gives you breathing room to suggest people try something different. Try some elements of project planning (see Chapter 8) to get a better sense of your workload and a more organized way to assign and track tasks.

If those steps don't help, you likely have a mismatch between your organization's self-image and its reality. That means it's time for strategic planning, so head to Chapter 2 and try to honestly characterize where you are and where you want to be, strategically. The first step to getting your organization where you want it to be is accepting that you're not yet there. Give yourselves permission not to do everything you'd like to do right now.

When I was in politics, I could always tell a winning campaign office from a losing one, weeks before Election Day. When I visited an office and everything was in disarray, with frantic staff and volunteers scurrying this way and that, shrieking into the telephone, tired and haggard, with crushed potato chips on the floor, angry faces demanding to know why something wasn't different, and a pervading panic in the air, that was going to be a losing campaign. On the other hand, I remember most of my winning campaign offices as neat and cheerful, with people intently focused on work but cordial and organized, everyone from the receptionist to the campaign manager knowing exactly what they were supposed to be doing and doing exactly that. I think a lot of campaign outcomes were caused by the management style as much as indicated by it.

7.6 PASTORAL CARE AND MANAGEMENT: PITFALLS AND OPPORTUNITIES

When rabbis act as managers, there is the potential for a conflict of interest, because the primary fiduciary duty of a pastoral caregiver is to the careseeker, while the primary fiduciary duty of a manager is to the employing organization. This does not mean that rabbis can't play a managerial role, nor does it mean that there's always a conflict or even the appearance of one in this situation. Careful attention to policy can reduce or eliminate the possibility of a conflict arising, and can effectively mitigate conflicts that do arise.

The main principle is that rabbis should not claim to provide pastoral care to people they manage. To whatever extent a rabbi is involved in managerial relationships, the rabbi needs to clarify that while they may care personally for their employees' well-being, as a workplace manager they are not the right person from whom to seek pastoral care. (This is another reason it creates a conflict of interest to hire a synagogue member into the office.) This can go for volunteer relationships, too, if volunteers take on a very task-oriented focus with the rabbi directing the tasks.

Inevitably, every rabbi's managerial repertory will include the spiritual. This is beneficial! By no means should rabbis or the staff reporting to them avoid this rich facet of their relationship. Many bosses have offered me highly beneficial advice that enabled me to grow as a person. I also love to see Jewish organizations infused with a sense of spirituality in all their aspects. Nevertheless, the rabbi-manager cannot simultaneously provide pastoral advice in the fiduciary interest of the employee and manage in the fiduciary interest of the employer. Here are a couple modest suggestions for clergy on navigating this boundary:

Respond but Don't Initiate. If an employee asks a rabbi-manager for spiritual advice, the rabbi should respond to the extent she feels comfortable doing so. The request may have to do with workplace experiences and may thereby draw on the rabbi-manager's unique strengths as such. But a rabbi-manager should not approach an employee with unsolicited spiritual advice—nor, more troublingly, with workplace feedback disguised as spiritual advice. Anything related to workplace tasks or job performance should be put aside from a pastoral discussion.

I'd advise rabbis to be particularly careful when giving negative feedback because of the natural temptation to step into a pastoral relationship mode in order to couch the feedback. It is often beneficial, certainly understandable and normal, for a boss to want more value from a worker. But that is not pastoral care.

Offer to Find Alternative Pastoral Care. If a rabbi-manager feels conflicted by a request, the rabbi might offer to help the employee find alternative pastoral care, with assurances that the conversation will be kept confidential from the rabbi-manager. I am interested in engaging in a "buddy system" with rabbinic peers wherein this might be one of the things we do for each other as a matter of course.

Be Careful with Volunteer Management. We've noted throughout this chapter that volunteer management resembles employee management in many respects. When relationships with synagogue members take on a managerial flavor with the rabbi encouraging members to complete tasks, vigilance becomes necessary to ensure the advertised pastoral relationship comes first.

Management inevitably changes a pastoral relationship. The more senior the volunteer, the more they voluntarily cede some of their rights as pastoral careseekers in favor of quasi-professional collaboration with the rabbi. For example, it isn't possible for a rabbi's pastoral relationship with the synagogue president to be unaffected by the president being the rabbi's counterpart in contract negotiations. These are bona fide conflicts of interest, but they need not be major concerns if properly mitigated. Clear air, open communication, an acknowledgment that the conflict exists and a mutual commitment to work through conflicted situations can go far toward maintaining healthy relationships.

Use Alternatives to Task Management of Volunteers. There is usually a menu of ways to direct volunteers. The more volunteers are empowered to act with responsibility instead of by task-by-task assignment, as we discussed earlier in this chapter, the less room there is for pastoral-managerial conflicts of interest.

Like any conflict of interest, a pastoral-managerial conflict can be mitigated through disclosure, recusal and arm's-length dealing if it can't be avoided. For example, a rabbi-manager who draws a clear boundary around providing pastoral care to employees has recused herself, stepping back from a role she would normally take as part of her profession.

The first step is always disclosure, which means airing the issue out before a problem arises. The rabbi might say: "I'm a rabbi, but as your manager I can't honestly provide pastoral care to you. I'll try to find you appropriate pastoral care if you wish, but I'm drawing this boundary because you deserve a pastoral caregiver who looks after your personal interests exclusively." That kind of statement frames the issue clearly, educates personnel who might not have considered the matter, creates an opportunity to find non-conflicted pastoral care for those who might wish to have it, and sets a tone of frankness that helps build a strong ethics culture.

With volunteers, it is everyone's job to monitor tension between pastoral care and task management. The more a committee or volunteer is focused on a short-term goal, the more everyone should be vigilant for possible encroachment of task orientation onto the pastoral care of individuals. Some degree of tension is inevitable, but disclosure and honest communication can go a long way toward keeping the situation below the level of a conflict of interest, or dealing with it collegially and expeditiously when it is felt to have reached that level due to the volunteer's increasing responsibility. Although this monitoring is everyone's job, in practice it may fall primarily to the rabbi, because she has the professional training and job responsibility to detect and teach about it.

The pastoral-managerial conflict of interest can be a fertile creative tension. It can be a valuable teachable moment, a chance to educate the whole organizational community on ethics. And there are many positive benefits to a spiritual management approach. In particular, as long as both rabbi and employee acknowledge that spiritual communication occurs within a managerial context, it can add greatly to the management relationship. Spiritual management rediscovers the benefits of pre-industrial management models, in which managers were interested and incentivized in the personal and professional development of their staff. The organization benefits when staff members exhibit strength, self-confidence, spiritual health and personal job satisfaction.

Potential ways to build a spiritual edifice from which the Jewish workplace can benefit include creating opportunities for optional group spiritual practice (without the hard sell that would desiccate the experience, let alone become discriminatory), incorporating Jewish text study relevantly into the work week, or even providing spiritual guidance when requested—just as long as workplace spiritual communication is not confused with pastoral care.

Chapter 8
PROJECT MANAGEMENT

8.1 SHIUR

And the fish gate did the sons of Hassenaah build; they laid the beams thereof, and set up the doors thereof, the bolts thereof, and the bars thereof. And next unto them repaired Meremoth the son of Uriah, the son of Hakkoz. And next unto them repaired Meshullam the son of Berechiah, the son of Meshezabel. And next unto them repaired Zadok the son of Baana. And next unto them the Tekoites repaired; and their nobles put not their necks to the work of their lord. And the gate of the old city repaired Joiada the son of Paseah and Meshullam the son of Besodeiah; they laid the beams thereof, and set up the doors thereof, and the bolts thereof, and the bars thereof. And next unto them repaired Melatiah the Gibeonite, and Jadon the Meronothite, the men of Gibeon, and of Mizpah, for them that appertained to the throne of the governor beyond the River. Next unto him repaired Uzziel the son of Harhaiah, goldsmiths. And next unto him repaired Hananiah one of the perfumers, and they restored Jerusalem even unto the broad wall.

Nehemiah 3:3–8[91]

"The list is a genre of Biblical literature," explained one of my professors soon after I entered graduate school. I thought to myself, "Oh, this is going to be an interesting class."

Our text is one of those lists for which the Bible is famous—or notorious—right up there with the "begats" and census reports among the texts least frequently studied. It continues in this fashion for several more verses, listing people's names and which part of the Jerusalem city wall they repaired.

[91] Translation JPS.

Admittedly, our text lacks the gripping character development or plot we expect of literary prose. Although it has a certain rhythm, a poetry critic might well ask whether its subject matter stirs the spirit. For our purposes in this book, we will study this text not as literature at all, but as a remarkable piece of evidence that the rebuilding of Jerusalem was a well-managed project.

From the list we glean information about how the wall was built: in addition to stonemasonry, there were beams, doors, bolts, and bars required. If we were to try to replicate the project today, the text would give us a basic idea how to do it. The whole wall being quite large, Nehemiah divided its repair into smaller tasks, with a worker responsible for each subtask. Many of the builders were assigned portions convenient to them, near their own houses.[92] Nehemiah managed the work and created a feeling of camaraderie. Note his use of "we" and his liberal credit to the workers in the same chapter: "So we built the wall, and the wall was joined together unto half the height thereof; for the people had a mind to work."[93]

Nehemiah's efforts to rebuild the Jerusalem wall met many of the criteria by which contemporary managers would recognize a good project. It had a clear, attainable goal, a division of tasks into subtasks small enough for an individual person to accomplish, and a plan of what needed to be done first: they first built segments, then joined them together until they reached half the desired height, then later built the wall up to its full height. There were risks and contingencies: may such a risk never happen to us, but when the project ran into armed opposition, "every one with one of his hands wrought in the work, and with the other held his weapon."[94] Everyone was accountable for their piece, from the builders of each segment to Nehemiah himself, who was accountable to the King of Persia[95] for the whole project.

In this chapter, we will learn a rather strict methodology of planning and executing projects to meet all of these criteria. It would be absurd overkill in a nonprofit to use full-scale industrial project management for every little project. However, a working

---

[92] Nehemiah 3:10, 3:23, and 3:28–30.

[93] Nehemiah 3:38, translation JPS. This is not a matter of the translator's interpretation; the Hebrew *vanivneh* ("we built") is the first-person plural form.

[94] Nehemiah 4:11, translation JPS.

[95] Nehemiah 2:5–6.

familiarity with the several components of a professional project plan has served me very well in accomplishing group projects less formally. Individual formal tools are always available when needed.

Informal project management makes things easier for workers but harder for managers. A working familiarity with formal tools and structures will help us ensure our project teams deliver the goods. I don't think Nehemiah used today's formal tools, but I can tell from the text that he was a skilled manager.

8.2 HIGH HOLIDAY LOGISTICS: AN EXAMPLE PROJECT

Throughout this chapter, we'll consider as an example the logistics of High Holiday services at a synagogue. I don't mean to recommend this as a recipe for every synagogue's High Holidays; nor, for space reasons, do I get anywhere near presenting a complete plan. It's intended as a plausible example. With those caveats, let's dive in.

What needs to be done to pull off the High Holidays? There might be special logistics for parking and traffic. If you're renting a larger space, materials have to be brought back and forth. Clergy need to work with lay leaders and the music director to plan the services. Maybe there's a reception after Rosh Hashanah morning and a Yom Kippur break-the-fast. There are issues of seating and perhaps an RSVP or ticketing system. If there are early and late services, members have to be assigned or choose their services. And we have not even have scratched the surface.

In this chapter, we will learn to plan and manage this project with the same professional methods a business consultant might use. These are available in the *Guide to the Project Management Body of Knowledge* (called the *PMBOK Guide*).[96] Rabbi Mordechai Yosef Leiner, the nineteenth-century Ishbitzer Rebbe, wrote that strict rules assist us in developing the skills needed to accomplish more later, when we will have the base of skills to branch out beyond

[96] Duncan et al. (1996). I've been happily using the 1996 edition since 1996, although it's undergone several updates since then.

that initial strictness.[97] This chapter follows the Ishbitzer's guidance by introducing a very strict approach to project management that is educational and often useful. Once baseline skills are developed, it offers itself as a menu of useful practices that don't all need to be implemented at once.

Most nonprofit managers might very well skim this chapter and conclude that it is entirely overkill. But you'll be glad you studied these methods the next time a project is chronically behind schedule and straining morale. I've often brought out specific parts of the project-planning method I present in this chapter, when those techniques were the right tools to get an ailing project back on track and give participants a much-needed sense of accomplishment.

Major projects, such as construction, require a full project plan, and board members who understand project planning will be well equipped to scrutinize a construction plan.[98] Even in our largest volunteer undertakings, like the High Holidays, a full project plan might be worth the effort if it can serve as a template for many future years. Studying these methods will at least illustrate how to think about your projects as a professional manager would.

As you notice the inevitably many tasks I omitted from the running example, or needs that might be particularly relevant or irrelevant to your community, make a note of them. That's exactly the kind of thinking this chapter is intended to encourage. As we work through this example project plan, I hope that you develop a working comfort with it, which in turn will then enable you to apply its principles and methods as needed within your organization.

What Is a Project?

A *project* is a limited set of related tactical goals, together with the people and relationships required to accomplish those goals, a plan to accomplish those goals within a limited time frame and budget, and ways of assessing the project's success, with a commitment of

---

[97] Leiner (1860), see parashat Vayera and others.

[98] Be aware that many of the techniques we will discuss here, such as three-point estimates, are still new to most practitioners outside major consulting and building firms. A small general manager of construction projects may not have heard of these techniques. That makes it even more important for the board to be informed so as to suggest ways to head off common problems, like budget overruns, or project risks that the vendor may not see coming. It's your building, not the vendor's.

resources to the project and delegation to work. The major goals of a project are called *deliverables*: they are what the project delivers. The definition of a project according to these requirements is called the project's *scope*. Let's break that definition down:

Projects are limited. A project is an effort to accomplish one or more specific, measurable deliverables, after which the project closes. An ongoing activity, like maintenance of a building, is not a project, but it may give rise to many separate projects. If maintenance includes polishing the silver candlesticks every month, then each of those monthly polishings would be a project. Projects can be of any size as long as they are limited in scope.

Project deliverables are tactical. Conversely, a strategic goal like increasing membership is not a project: it cannot be planned because it is not limited. Much of the art of accomplishing strategic goals consists in defining projects that advance the organization toward the strategic goal. So for example, sending out a high-quality newsletter, hosting a new-member picnic, running a capital campaign, and enlarging the building are all projects, although they are of vastly different scope. Any of those projects might advance an organization toward the strategic goal of increasing membership.

Project deliverables are related. If a project has more than one deliverable, the deliverables are related topically or by depending on overlapping work. Otherwise, you have more than one project.

Projects are planned. As we will see in this chapter, a project plan offers reason to believe the project can be accomplished.

Projects are measured. Project plans include ways of knowing whether and to what extent the project has succeeded. These are called *metrics* or *objectives*. Although the latter sounds like a friendlier term, in this book we will use the term *metrics*, because the term *objectives* has too many other meanings in other contexts.

Metrics need not be quantitative, but they could be. In some cases quantitative metrics provide the best window into a project's success, while in other cases numbers may be overkill. If you are hosting a new-member picnic, verbal feedback from attendees might be a good qualitative metric, while the number of new members joining might be a good quantitative metric.

Many practitioners feel that all metrics should define excellent, or minimally acceptable, performance numerically. But I think for synagogue-sized organizations, quantitative targets like "Gain 10 new members" or "Keep High Holiday services within 5 minutes of schedule" are overkill. We already know that we want services to keep close to schedule, so the 5-minute target doesn't help us see anything, and could backfire if it is seen to formally replace an 11:00 end time with 11:05. And while attracting new members is related to our good work, too much depends on chance with numbers this low for any numerical measurement to teach us much.[99]

Quantitative metrics work best when based on experience, and when they shine light on a project that wouldn't otherwise be seen. In large organizations, quantitative metrics proxy for more complex factors, so they help simplify assessment. For example, if you're a chapter-based national advocacy organization coordinating a Day of Action in every state legislature, the number of volunteers involved might be a good indicator to measure: it's simpler than telling every detail of how it went, and it probably correlates with success. But for projects small enough to assess their success directly, there's no need to invent numerical targets just for the sake of having them.

Projects involve people. People make projects go. No project plan is complete without information on who will be doing what, and what their relationships to the rest of the project team will be.

Projects are committed to. An organization's commitment to a project is called the project's *charter*. The charter can take many forms. In a small project, such as the monthly cleaning of those silver candlesticks, the charter could come from an employee's job description, or it could come from management direction. On the higher-level end, a charter for a capital campaign could come from a general membership vote, while a charter for a construction project could come from a contract with a construction company.

Across large differences in scale and size of the project team, what all these charters have in common is a formal commitment of resources—money and time—to the project, and a delegation of responsibility to the project team to do the planned activities. A charter is a "green light" for a project. The charter need not be formally identified for small projects, but everyone involved in a project should always know where their responsibility comes from, and on whose behalf they act.

[99] Mathematically speaking, the sample size is too small to draw conclusions from the dataset.

Producing a year's High Holiday services meets all of the criteria to be a project. As any Ritual Committee member can tell you, it is on the large side of projects usually undertaken in synagogues.

The Scope Statement

A *scope statement* is a short written definition of a project. It has three components: the *justification, deliverables,* and *metrics.*[100] The justification is a short narrative description of why the project needs to happen. It is a good place to include any strategic goals that the project specifically hopes to advance. Next, the deliverables are listed, each with a brief description. Finally, the metrics section briefly explains how the success of the project will be assessed. The whole scope statement will ideally be less than two pages. This might be a plausible scope statement for High Holiday services:

High Holidays: Scope Statement

JUSTIFICATION

The High Holidays occasion a surge in attendance which requires a larger venue, careful management of seating and parking, and precise scheduling with the Rabbis, while also providing unique opportunities for new-member outreach. The Ritual Committee will undertake the logistics of these events, as we have in the past.

DELIVERABLES

- *Tickets:* members will be divided into Early and Late groups for each service.
- *Prospects and new members* will be accommodated and offered information as appropriate.
- *Hall rental* will be finalized and gain board approval.
- *Services* will be planned in consultation with Rabbis and Cantor. Their scheduling will leave time for Early attendees to exit and Late attendees to arrive.

---

[100] For a simpler approach to project planning, see Light (2001), pp. 155ff. Light uses a different terminology, but his "Imperatives," such as "Not enough Little Sisters" (p. 170), are beautiful examples of qualitative metrics presented in a slightly different way. Light then uses numerical data (which he calls "Success Measures") not as targets, but as information to help decide whether there are now enough Little Sisters. I believe we are very well served learning PMBOK project planning, but Light's approach is worth considering in practice.

- *Ushers* will be organized and assigned to shifts.
- *Ritual objects* including Sifrei Torah, books, kippot, tallitot, and bimah items will be brought to and from the rented venue.
- *Receptions* will include honey cake after Rosh Hashanah morning and a break-the-fast after Neilah.

METRICS

- Verbal feedback from the community, clergy, staff, board and committee members (Qualitative)
- Assessment of the flow of people between Early and Late services (Qualitative)
- Services will be timed (Quantitative)

8.3 IDENTIFYING AND ESTIMATING SUBTASKS

To plan the project, we break each deliverable down, specifying the tasks needed to complete it. Then we break each task down into smaller and smaller subtasks, until the subtasks are small enough that we feel confident estimating how long each one will take, and how much each will cost. I will use the word *subtask* for a unit of work small enough for its cost and time to be confidently estimated.

Viewed this way, each major deliverable consists of a hierarchy of tasks needed to complete it, smaller tasks needed to complete those tasks, and so on, down to subtasks small enough to confidently estimate. Such a hierarchy is called a *work breakdown structure*.

I learned[101] to adapt the KJ diagram to identify subtasks. This activity is great for individual as well as group project planning. Everyone involved brainstorms tasks on a stack of sticky notes, one task per note. What needs to be done to accomplish each task? Have you thought of everything? The KJ diagram can also identify topical clusters, which may turn out to be higher-level tasks. Once

[101] I learned the method taught here from my longtime friend Dr. John Hollywood, then a graduate student at MIT while I was an undergraduate, who has been of helpful advice on this book.

brainstorming is complete, we rearrange the notes on a central board in a hierarchy, with higher-level tasks above the lower-level tasks needed to complete them, and the subtasks, which are simple enough for us to estimate, at the bottom. If any tasks are not simple enough to estimate, they are further broken down into subtasks. This activity generates the work breakdown structure.

Offer a few minutes of individual brainstorming time before people place sticky notes on the board. For morale reasons, explain in advance that some duplication is expected. The reason for a little individual time is that as soon as a hierarchy goes up on the board, group members will tend to conform their thinking to it. They will tend to analyze tasks into subtasks, but not add a major forgotten deliverable. The individual brainstorming gives you the benefit of everyone's creativity. Also remind the group to feel free to add, change, or discuss items if they feel something has been missed.

You may find that some subtasks enable more than one task. For example, getting a current list of synagogue members might enable several of our deliverables. It's always okay to duplicate a sticky note in a KJ diagram, and you may choose to duplicate that task or subtask for clarity in the formal work breakdown structure. In the discussion below about the *network flow diagram*, we will make more sense of this situation. For now, just make a note of it to avoid double-counting those repeated subtasks when it comes time to add up the total project time or cost. When you're satisfied with your work breakdown structure, transcribe it into a document.

There is not enough space in this book to present a full work breakdown structure for High Holidays while explaining all of its components. Therefore, for our running example we'll zero in on just one deliverable: organizing the ushers. A work breakdown structure for just the High Holiday ushers might look something like this (with subtasks appearing in italics):

DELIVERABLE: HIGH HOLIDAY USHERS

- Recruitment
    - *Gather list of current and former committee members*
    - *Call or e-mail current and former committee members*
    - *Write ad for synagogue newsletter*
    - *Get rabbis to announce from bimah*
    - *Screen inquiries, discussing importance of role, etc.*

- Assign Ushers to Shifts
  - *Identify shifts needed*
  - Assign ushers, taking their preferences and assigned service times into account (including alternate ushers)
    - *(10 Separate Subtasks, for each service: Rosh Hashanah Evening Early/Late, Rosh Hashanah Day Early/Late, Yom Kippur Evening Early/Late, Yom Kippur Day Early/Late, Yom Kippur Afternoon, Yom Kippur Neilah)*
- *Call or e-mail all ushers on the list 1–2 weeks before to confirm*
- *Buy thank-you gifts for ushers*

Before we move on, a couple notes about that work breakdown structure. First, I am sure there are omissions and mistakes. Do not fear these. Most projects are not so formal or serious that a mistake at this stage can't be easily corrected later. Use the *80-20 rule*: 80% of the work takes 20% of the effort, and the remaining 20% of the work takes 80% of the effort. Get the easy 80% down on paper, and then account for as much of the hard 20% as you can. If your project requires higher accuracy, you can work harder on planning—but for most of our projects, I think we find professional tools intimidating because we are too afraid of mistakes. Just try it. As a rule of thumb, for most of our projects, a reasonable set of deliverables and work breakdown structure can be produced in a two-hour meeting.

Opinions about the work breakdown structure may differ. Is it best to recruit ushers before assigning them to slots, or should we first list all the slots we need and then recruit ushers to fill specific slots? Should we include alternate ushers in case anyone is unable to cover their assigned shift? There is no single right answer.[102] Plan the project in the way your group wants to do it.

Note also the asymmetric hierarchy. For some tasks underneath the Ushers deliverable, like Recruitment, it made sense to go straight to subtasks because the items seemed small enough to estimate easily. For others, like Assign Ushers to Shifts, there was a mix, with one ready subtask and one task that needed to be further divided.

---

[102] For now. Sometimes—not always—there are "right answers" to questions like these, for your situation. But the only way to know is to manage many iterations of similar projects, and base informed opinions on that body of accumulated experience. For more on that topic, see Chapter 10.

Estimating Subtask Cost and Time: The Three-Point Estimate

The next step is to estimate how long each subtask will take, and if applicable, how much it will cost. You might think at first that you can simply add these estimates up to get a total project estimate. But when things go wrong, you end up behind schedule. It's hard to know what will go wrong, so project managers often "pad" their estimates, adding as much time or cost as they think they can get away with, and hoping the padding accounts for overruns. Projects planned this way have little going for them beside guesswork.

Project-management theorists came up with a solution called the *three-point estimate*. The good news is that it works. In my experience, it works extremely well. The bad news (well, I don't think it's bad news, but you might) is that it's based on math. Don't be afraid of the math: a computer will easily do it for you. As with a car, you can use the math to get where you want to go, without worrying about how it works internally. If you want to know how it works, I've explained the derivations on *npgovernance.org*.

It's called a *three-point estimate* because it has three parts:

- A reasonable best-case scenario
- How long you think the subtask will take (called the *most-likely estimate* or, in mathematical terminology, the *mode*)
- A reasonable worst-case scenario

The best and worst cases should be unlikely but not implausible. Think in terms of scenarios that have about a 1-in-100 chance of happening. When everything within reason goes right, you will save time; when everything within reason goes wrong, you will lose time.

To estimate cost, go through all the steps for time estimating, but using dollars and not hours. If you're estimating both time and cost, you'll have *six* numbers for each subtask: a three-point estimate for time, and a three-point estimate for cost.

Cost estimates make sense when you're estimating services at an hourly rate, for instance in supporting material for a bid or grant application. However, cost estimates may not be applicable in volunteer-driven projects, and they may not add new information for projects done by full-time staff. Our synagogue High Holiday example does not require a cost estimate because the relevant costs are primarily fixed: hall rental, additional security, etc. Therefore, in this example we will deal with time estimates only.

As we will see when we get to calculations, three-point estimates give you vastly more accuracy for a little more up-front work. I often bring out three-point estimates to solve problems, like when a project is behind schedule or previous implementations have been problematic. But because three-point estimates do require that up-front work, I don't use them for every project.

Consider the subtask *Call or e-mail all ushers on the list to confirm*. A good strategy might be to try e-mail first. If the usher writes back and confirms they will serve, then they're accounted for. In a best-case scenario (everything within reason goes right) let's say everyone responds to an initial e-mail. So, a best-case estimate might be, say, 30 minutes to write and send the e-mail, a combined hour to read all replies, and perhaps another 30 minutes initially to verify that everyone on the list has an e-mail address on file. We'll put the best-case estimate at 2 hours. It's perfectly fine for this to be an informal estimate, as long as the assumptions are reasonable.

On the other hand, perhaps the worst case includes those same 2 hours plus calling everyone individually, twice. Now if there are 20 ushers (2 each for 10 slots), each of whom we're calling twice, and each call takes 15 minutes (including missed connections), that's already 10 hours for calls. That's a lot of volunteer time to be spending on calls! Let's go with it; we'll add in the original 2 hours we spent on e-mail to arrive at a worst-case estimate of 12 hours. As for how long I think it will take, I'll go with 6 hours.

We often express a three-point estimate as a triplet of numbers from best, to most-likely, to worst case. In this case, we can write our estimate as 2-6-12. When running a sticky-note exercise, after arranging the notes into a work breakdown structure and explaining the three-point estimate, ask participants to estimate time (and cost, if you're including it) right on the sticky note for each subtask. Here are some rules of thumb for three-point estimates.

First, don't worry about precision. The methodology takes into account that estimates are not precise. In big business it might be important to estimate rather carefully, but most nonprofits will see vast benefits in capacity from learning this methodology without worrying about high precision. Also, the more project plans you do, the more accurate your estimates will be, as you gain experience.

Because there is more to lose by things going wrong than to gain by things going right, the difference between the most-likely and worst-case estimates should be greater than the difference between the most-likely and best-case estimates. For example, "1-2-4" (best; most likely; worst) is a more plausible estimate than "1-2-3". An estimate skewed the other way, like a "1-4-5" estimate, could be a red flag that worst-case contingencies have not been considered. Is there really only one hour to be lost if everything goes wrong?

Estimate time in hours, and do not use increments smaller than 0.25 hour. Not only does this avoid wasting time on unhelpful precision, but in practice 15 minutes is a good minimum estimate for tasks, once you count getting started and finishing up. If a task's estimates call for more than about a day of work, ask yourself whether it hadn't better be divided up into still smaller subtasks.

When estimating best- and (especially) worst-case scenarios, consider only possibilities germane to the task. This is not the place to consider risks like natural disasters and people getting sick (may they not happen). If you could imagine it happening 1 in 100 times, consider it in your estimates. Less likely than 1 in 100, skip it.

Sometimes a worst-case estimate means the maximum amount of time you're willing to devote to the task before giving up. In the subtask *Gather list of current and former committee members* (see diagram below) I figured 3 hours was enough time to spend on this, and if after that I still didn't have everyone, I'd just move on.

Note that the subtask *Identify shifts needed* affects the planning of how many "Assign Ushers" subtasks there are. If the stakes were higher, I might insist on figuring out the shifts in advance, as the current project can't be fully planned until that task is complete. But our stakes aren't that high. Maybe looking over the shifts to verify we've thought of everything will take a half-hour, or it's conceivable that nothing will need to be done at all. I threw in a couple hours for the worst-case estimate, thinking any adjustments to the project would take about that amount of time, all-inclusive.

This imprecision is emphatically okay for our purposes. This should be a quick, fun exercise. Hand-wringing precision is not going to be worth it for the type of projects we engage in.

In group planning, members may disagree on the estimate for a subtask. That's okay! They can discuss it until they agree, or you can average the estimates. Remind participants that precision is not very important. We're aiming for generally reasonable numbers.

The Network Flow Diagram

With the work breakdown structure recorded and all subtasks estimated, it's time to move the sticky notes around. Remove all sticky notes except for the subtasks. Now, move the subtasks into *finish-to-start dependencies* from left to right.[103] A *finish-to-start dependency* means one subtask must be finished in order for the next one to start. In the diagram below, we show this with an arrow.

Subtasks that are not finish-to-start dependent should be placed in parallel. If one task is partially dependent on another, but they are not finish-to-start dependent, then the tasks need to be divided into subtasks until finish-to-start dependencies emerge. A white board is great for this because it's easy to draw and erase arrows between the sticky notes as the group zeroes in on agreement. Here's how I organized the subtasks for our "Ushers" deliverable. Note that I filled in three-point estimates for each subtask:.

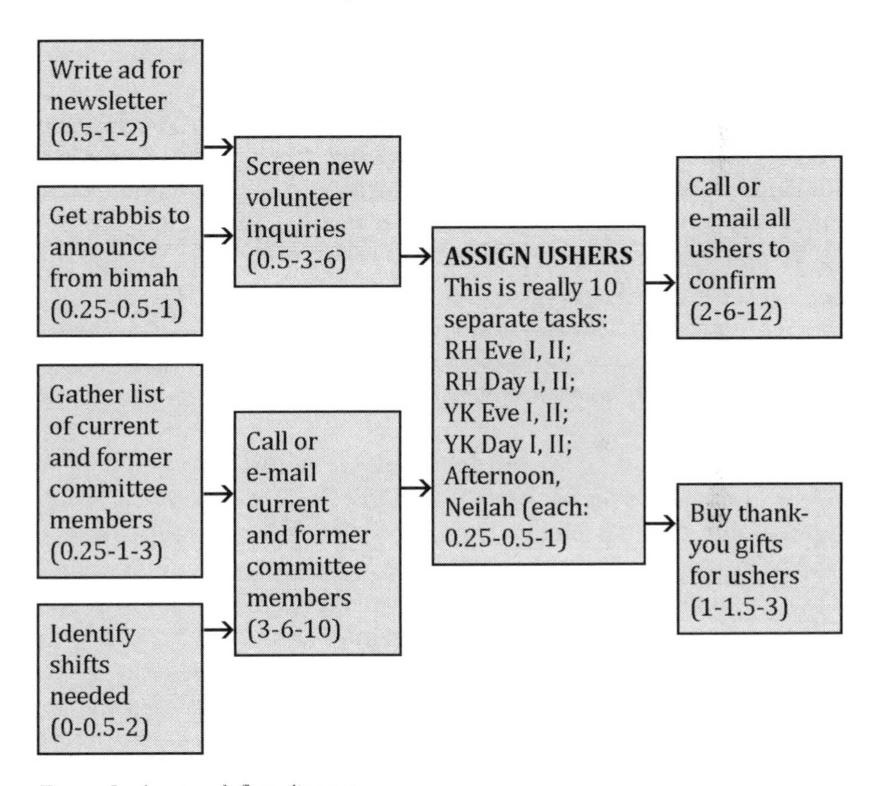

Figure 5. A network flow diagram.

Figure 5 above is called a *network flow diagram*. It's a visual step-by-step guide to completing the project. This example is for

[103] Or, if you're speaking Hebrew, from right to left.

just one deliverable—the ushers—but a real network flow diagram should show the whole project at once.

We're about to see a whole lot of detail on making numerical estimates using the network flow diagram. However, this diagram could be a great management tool in itself, even if you dispense with all the numbers and estimating.

I condensed 10 very similar subtasks into one omnibus note on the assignment of ushers. This kind of shorthand helps avoid the headache of having 10 similar notes that always stay together, but those tasks still need to be estimated separately, not added all together. So, for example, if I put 0.25-0.5-1 for a single usher assignment task, meaning I think it will take a half-hour to get one of the ten services sorted out, but it could be as little as 15 minutes or as much as an hour, I would remember that my abbreviated sticky note contains ten 0.25-0.5-1 tasks. I would *not* write 2.5-5-10 for the set of them. It turns out there's a big difference between ten small subtasks and one big agglomerated one. Remember the individual subtasks, but feel free to abbreviate your list if it helps.

You might be wondering how you total up a project estimate from three-point subtask estimates, if you don't just add them. That's the subject of the next essay. The short answer is: let software do it for you. You're welcome to use my freely available Google Sheet, which is linked on *npgovernance.org*.

Critical Path Analysis: Calendar Time vs. Person-Hours

In addition to a roadmap, the network flow diagram identifies opportunities for parallel work. If there are enough people on the project, someone can gather the list of committee members while someone else makes sure the rabbis make their announcements. One person can screen new volunteer inquiries while another gets in touch with current and former committee members.

Sometimes, it's helpful to take parallel work into account when planning, to estimate how long the project will take *in calendar time*. Other times, you want to know how long the project will take *in person-hours*, to know how much demand you're placing on staff or volunteers. It is possible to make two sets of totals and use both.

To calculate the total person-hours of a project, use all subtasks in making totals. To calculate the calendar time of a project, you don't need all subtasks, because some of the work will be done in parallel. Instead, you'll need the *critical path*: the longest path of finish-to-start dependencies in the network flow diagram, in terms of time estimates for each task. The idea is to add up calendar time using only the subtasks along the critical path; as work proceeds on these subtasks, other parallel subtasks can be done by others.

Calculating the critical path is a hard mathematical problem. Eyeballing it is a fine method.[104] The diagram below shows a critical path I chose by eyeballing, just for the small example we're using.

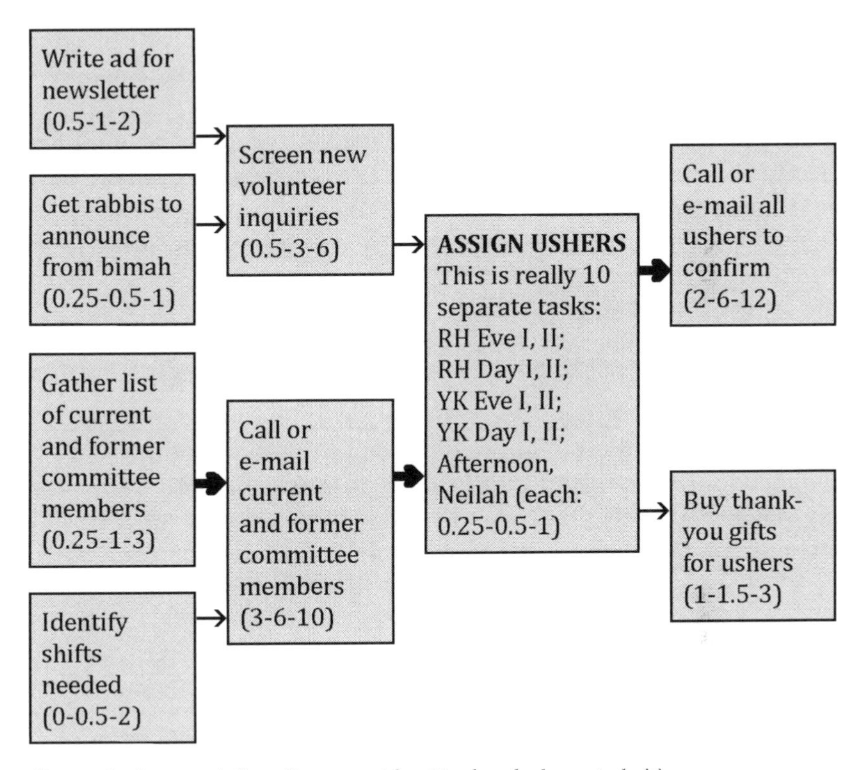

Figure 6. A network flow diagram with critical path shown in bold arrows.

I wanted you to know about critical-path analysis, but it adds complexity that may not be useful. Particularly in volunteer work,

[104] I've simplified our example to just one deliverable, but in the whole project, there will be many more parallel tasks than there are people. If the same person must be assigned to tasks on different paths, then those tasks become finish-to-start dependent due to the person's time. This adds great complexity to critical-path analysis. By the way, when mathematicians say a problem is "hard," we mean that nobody has figured out how to solve that problem.

volunteers do not work at capacity. Someone who's putting in 2 hours a week could double their workload in the event of a problem, although they may not like to, nor is it a good practice. If our project falls behind, someone will do a bit of extra work, or else something will simply not get done, because the stakes are not that high. (We don't have the option, in this case, of delivering the project late: Rosh Hashanah will arrive on schedule.) So you may find it isn't worth the effort to make calendar-time estimates of the duration of volunteer projects such as our example. On the other hand, it's always useful to know the total person-hours of a project, as a gauge of the demand we're placing on volunteers or staff.

In this project, therefore, we'll be using total person-hours for our project estimate. We won't bother with the critical path further. I just wanted you to know about it. I would use critical-path analysis in larger projects that take several weeks for several full-time staff.

Accountability Matrix

Project accountability goes beyond assigning someone to do each subtask. There are up to six possible roles: Participant, Accountable, Review Required, Input Required, Signoff Required, and Notice Required; they are often abbreviated with the mnemonic PARIS-N (which is more glamorous than SPRAIN, less nerdy than SPINAR; use the mnemonic you like).[105] Every subtask needs at least an Accountable member. Use the other roles as needed:

- *Participant:* Someone who will do part of the work of the subtask, but who is not Accountable.
- *Accountable:* Someone whose job it is to make sure the subtask gets done.
- *Review Required:* Someone who must review the work product and provide reactions, but who does not need to approve it.
- *Input Required:* Someone who needs to be consulted for guidance or information. They may or may not be part of the working group.

[105] There are a variety of ways to break down these roles. An alternative is Participant, Accountable, Consulted, Informed. I like PARIS-N because it captures greater variation in roles, and you don't have to use all the roles if you don't need them. I used each of the roles at least once in the example.

- *Signoff Required:* Someone whose approval is needed in order for the task to be considered complete. They may or may not be part of the working group.
- *Notice Required:* Someone who needs to be aware of the work. They may or may not be part of the working group.

An *accountability matrix* is a chart listing each subtask, with columns for each person on the working group, and the letters PARIS-N placed to denote who fills which role for each task. Here is an example accountability matrix just for our High Holiday ushers deliverable. Let's suppose the people involved are Rabbi Adina, Rabbi Ben, Cheryl (the chairperson), David, Ellen, Flo, and George (the office manager).

	Rabbi Adina	*Rabbi Ben*	*Cheryl (chair)*	*David*	*Ellen*	*Flo*	*George (office)*
Write ad for newsletter	R		I	A			I
Announcements from bimah	S	S	R		A		P
List of current and former committee members			P	P		P	A
Identify shifts needed			A				
Screen new volunteer inquiries			A				
Contact current and former committee members			P		P	A	
Assign ushers (note: 10 subtasks)	N	N	A	P	P	P	N
Contact ushers to confirm			P	A			N
Buy thank-you gifts for ushers			A		P		N

Figure 7: An accountability matrix for the High Holiday ushers deliverable.

This accountability matrix provides a handy way to keep track of who's doing what, as well as a visual summary of how the work is divided up. I tried to divide labor among the three committee members, while the chair takes responsibility for the overall project and therefore has some role in everything. Cheryl handles a couple tasks personally; in those she takes the Accountable role.

The assignments of professional staff reflect plausible scenarios: the rabbis approve announcements from the bimah but do not insist on approving the newsletter; the office manager has input for the newsletter because he has to format it. In some tasks the office manager actively helps; in others, he needs to be informed but doesn't otherwise participate. The accountability matrix shows all of these dynamics at a glance, making it clear who's doing what.

8.4 PLANNING AND TRACKING WITH THE TOTAL PROJECT ESTIMATE

Once you've got three-point estimates for all of your subtasks, a little mathematical magic creates an estimate for your full project. We'll gloss over the math here, but I give more detail on *npgovernance.org*. The main intuition is that your three-point estimate contains a lot more information than a traditional one-point estimate, because it contains information about risk. This is very powerful and rather complex. To be sure, the accuracy isn't always worth the complexity, but I've often pulled out three-point estimates to rescue a project that's fallen behind. I call a break, take a few hours with the team in planning, and use the methods of this essay from that point on forward. I've been doing this for 15 years, and I've found the accuracy of three-point estimates to be so good that they have never failed me in predicting a budget or schedule I could meet.

Your three-point estimate carries information about the amount of uncertainty, called *variance*, within the subtask. Variance is an important intuition in project management: it's a measure of how much could go wrong or right. In a subtask like assigning ushers to a service—let's say it's Yom Kippur Morning, Late—you've already got your list of ushers, and you need to find someone who's going to be at that service. Worst case, you might have to call people to fill the slot. Because there isn't much variability either way, this is a low-variance task. It doesn't add a lot of uncertainty to the project.

On the other hand, consider the subtask to contact all the ushers to confirm their slots. In the best case, everyone will respond promptly to a group e-mail. In the worst case, people will be difficult to reach, and some will pull out at the last minute, forcing you to do extra work. Most likely, some will respond to the group e-mail and others will need to be individually chased down. This adds a lot of uncertainty to the project. It is a high-variance task.

It turns out that variances can be calculated numerically from your three-point estimate, and they add up to a total variance. You might have heard of a bell curve: that's the shape all of your three-point estimates add up to. A bell curve comes with a total average estimate (called the *mean*), and a *standard deviation*, which measures the uncertainty.[106]

It is a law of mathematics that, based on the estimates, there is an 84.1% chance of accomplishing the project in less time (or money) than the mean plus one standard deviation, and a 97.7% chance of accomplishing the project in less time (money) than the mean plus two standard deviations. Three-point estimates take advantage of this law to produce estimates with confidence. *It is a best practice to calculate total project estimates as the mean plus two standard deviations*, because you then have a 97.7% chance of accomplishing the project within that time or budget. Adding just one standard deviation doesn't give you enough confidence, and adding three greatly increases the estimates without much of an increase in confidence.

If you are estimating cost both and time, you'll have two parallel sets of total estimates. If you are using a critical path to predict calendar time, include only the subtasks on the critical path for the time estimate. Include all subtasks for a person-hours estimate or for a cost estimate.

Software Options

Not many project-management software products I know support three-point estimates, except for the very expensive ones. The math is not beyond the reach of simple, cheap software, but three-point estimates are still pretty new outside the major contractors that buy those very expensive products. That leaves small organizations with few options right now, but I'm sure the market will fill this gap.

On *npgovernance.org* you'll find a "Project Management Spreadsheet" that I created to handle three-point estimates and

[106] The standard deviation is the square-root of the total project variance.

project tracking. It is freeware; you are welcome to copy and use it; I only ask for proper attribution to be kept intact. Instructions and current copyright information are on the website as well as within the spreadsheet. It's a Google Drive document, and it can also be exported to Microsoft Excel. My spreadsheet may be your best bet for now, if you wish to try three-point project estimates without worrying about the math. I developed the spreadsheet for my own projects, and I've used it for over 15 years.

If you know of a low-cost software product that handles three-point estimates, please let me know and I'll gladly post a link on *npgovernance.org*. We need one.

Results for Our Example

Here's what I came up with for our "Ushers" deliverable. On *npgovernance.org*, in addition to the blank Project Management Spreadsheet, I've prepared a version of the sheet with my estimates for the Ushers deliverable filled in.

Figure 8 at right shows the output from the Project Management Spreadsheet for the "Ushers" deliverable, based on that information.[107] On the next page, Figure 9 shows all of the three-point estimates from the previous essay, as I entered them into the spreadsheet.

Organize Ushers for High Holidays	
-3σ (0.5% chance):	20.38
-2σ (2.3% chance):	23.08
-1σ (15% chance):	25.79
Mean (50% chance):	28.50
+1σ (84.1% chance):	31.21
+2σ (97.7% chance):	**33.92**
+3σ (99.5% chance):	36.62

Figure 8: Estimates for Ushers deliverable, with 97.7% confidence level shown in bold.

These results mean that there's a 97.7% chance of accomplishing the project in less than about 34 hours. That's about how big a project this is. If I ever speak of *the project estimate* in the singular, I always mean this 97.7% confidence number. If I were to make a proposal to manage this project, that's the number I'd use to make my bid.

To develop an intuition for these numbers, load the Project Management Spreadsheet and make a copy for yourself. You can't

[107] The symbol σ means "standard deviation." It's a lowercase Greek letter sigma.

change the numbers on my original spreadsheet, but you can change them if you make your own copy. See what happens to the project estimate when you change the subtask estimates.

	Best Case	**Most Likely**	**Worst Case**
(Totals)	***9.25***	***24***	***48***
Write ad for synagogue newsletter	0.25	0.5	1
Get rabbis to announce from bimah	0.25	0.5	1
Gather list of current/former cmte members	0.25	1	3
Identify shifts needed	0	0.5	2
Screen new volunteer inquiries	0.5	3	6
Contact current/former cmte. members	3	6	10
Assign Ushers RH Eve I	0.25	0.5	1
Assign Ushers RH Eve II	0.25	0.5	1
Assign Ushers RH Day I	0.25	0.5	1
Assign Ushers RH Day II	0.25	0.5	1
Assign Ushers YK Eve I	0.25	0.5	1
Assign Ushers YK Eve II	0.25	0.5	1
Assign Ushers YK Day I	0.25	0.5	1
Assign Ushers YK Day II	0.25	0.5	1
Assign Ushers YK Afternoon	0.25	0.5	1
Assign Ushers YK Neilah	0.25	0.5	1
Contact all ushers to confirm	1.5	6	12
Buy thank-you gifts for ushers	1	1.5	3

Figure 9: Three-point estimates for subtasks in the Ushers deliverable.

The Value of Three-Point Estimates

Now we can see the value of three-point estimates. Looking at Figure 9 above, the sum of all the "most likely" estimates was 24 hours. If that was all the information we'd used in our planning, we'd have vastly underestimated the project. (Sound familiar?)

It may be counterintuitive to think that the sum of "most likely" estimates vastly underestimates a project. But it is a mathematical law. Think of it this way. Each subtask may very well individually be most likely to come out at that middle-of-the-road, "most likely" estimate. But the more tasks you have, the more likely it is that *one* of them will go wrong. To develop the right intuition, imagine rolling a pair of dice. The number you're most likely to get on any roll is 7. You're not very likely to roll snake eyes (a 2) or boxcars (a 12). But if you keep rolling the dice, you're going to get some 11s and 12s in there. If you roll that pair of dice 10 times, the most likely sum you'll get is 70—but if you want to be at least 97.7% likely to come in under your target, then the number to bid actually works out to 86. If your manager, client or funder asks for an estimate, the number to give them is not 70, but 86. That's because the variance of the rolls accounts for risk, and needs to be taken into account.

By accounting for variance, three-point estimates provide a rigorous way to "pad" an estimate. Variance can go wrong or right, but we want to account for reasonable worst cases in our planning. With the variance of our High Holiday ushers deliverable, the job might be done in as little as 23 person-hours—with a 2% likelihood, if you feel like gambling. It's wiser to plan the project for 34 person-hours. And if that principle is true for the High Holiday ushers—only one deliverable chosen as an example here for its manageable size—it's all the more true of the whole project.

I realize this is a rather heavy tool. It is important to learn so that it's available when you need it. And it may inform the way you look at projects even when you don't go through all the steps.

In April 2008, I took over as CEO of a tech company that provided the software for ActBlue.com, a major political fundraising website. I stepped right into an ongoing situation: our company had been promising to upgrade our servers for the presidential election year, but the job was behind schedule. Every week we'd been saying that we'd have the server upgraded in another 2 to 3 weeks.

I told the staff I had a way to plan projects that would take some upfront effort. If they came back next week and said they needed

1 to 2 weeks, we'd do it their way. If they came back and said they needed 2 to 3 weeks again, we'd do it my way. Next week's meeting arrived, and the engineers felt they were still 2 to 3 weeks out.

The next morning, we got together for a half-day retreat to plan the project. We brainstormed tasks with a KJ diagram, and I used my Project Management Spreadsheet. The bad news was, we would not be ready in 2 to 3 weeks, but needed about 5½ weeks. I broke the news to the client. But this time, I had estimated with confidence and could even track progress (see below). We finished the project on the exact day the three-point estimate predicted.

Three-point estimates have been most useful to me when I've needed to make a fixed-price proposal, or to tighten controls when something has fallen behind. I think for projects done repetitively, like those High Holiday services, a template project plan could be a helpful guide, giving members, leaders and future members and leaders a glimpse of what to expect, and making future projects easier to lead. It can be a safety net if things start to go wrong. It requires some up-front effort, but not as much as it might seem.

Tracking Your Progress

As you accomplish tasks, three-point estimates let you see how you're doing with respect to your plan. Let's take a quick example from our Ushers deliverable. Suppose I've finished the first round of phone calls, for volunteer recruitment, and it took me 3 hours longer than I thought it would. It stands to reason that the project is now 3 hours behind, right?

Well, it turns out, not exactly. A three-point project plan has already built in some time for tasks to go slowly. The best way to see where you stand is to enter your progress into an estimation tool such as my Project Management Spreadsheet. The spreadsheet lets you type in how many hours have been spent on a subtask, and your estimate of how complete that subtask is, as a percentage. The readout at the top will show how far ahead or behind you are.

I entered into the spreadsheet that I finished the volunteer recruitment calls (100% complete) and that they took me 9 hours (6 hour for my original most-likely estimate, plus the 3 extra hours the subtask fell behind). The spreadsheet calculated that I'm now 1.93 hours behind on the whole project. I'm less than 3 hours behind because, in accounting for variance, the spreadsheet has already built in some time for things to go wrong. Now suppose I then finish screening new ushers more quickly than expected, in just 2 hours instead of 3. The spreadsheet now says I'm only 0.26 hours behind. You can see these numbers on the filled-in spreadsheet that I linked on *npgovernance.org*. Or, make a copy for yourself and play with it.

If you use the Project Management Spreadsheet's tracking feature, you will see the project's variance get smaller as your project progresses. This is because the tasks you've completed no longer contribute any uncertainty to the estimate: we know exactly how they went because they're in the past. As you approach completion, the best-case and worst-case estimates will get closer together, until finally they all converge on the actual result.

Accuracy in Estimation and Tracking

Until you've completed several estimated and tracked projects, don't treat tracking as a gauge of acceptable performance on the project. Your estimates were educated guesses. If everyone did their best on the project, your performance should measure the quality of your estimates—not the other way around. The goal is to learn how to predict projects accurately, which usually means building in more time in more places than you initially thought. Chapter 10 discusses this process of organizational learning in further detail.

8.5 ASSESSING AND MANAGING RISKS

A *risk* is something that could happen, which would negatively affect your project if it did happen. The *likelihood* of a risk is a measure of how probable it is that the risk will occur. The *severity* of a risk is a measure of how bad things will be if the risk does occur.

Likelihood and severity are totally unrelated variables. It's possible to have a low-likelihood, high-severity risk, and it's possible to have a high-likelihood, low-severity risk. Figure 10 on the next page gives a few examples, still related to our High Holiday ushers deliverable. Right away, we learn that it's not enough to ask how "big" a risk is. We need to get more specific, because likelihood and severity define the profiles of entirely different types of risks.

<table>
<tr><td colspan="2" rowspan="2"></td><td colspan="2">SEVERITY</td></tr>
<tr><td>Low</td><td>High</td></tr>
<tr><td rowspan="2">LIKELIHOOD</td><td>Low</td><td>The rabbi insists on reviewing usher assignments before they're final.</td><td>The board decides to change locations in mid-summer, necessitating reassessment of usher placements.</td></tr>
<tr><td>High</td><td>An usher backs out at the last minute. (That's why we paired them up. Missing one is not ideal but also no big deal.)</td><td>*</td></tr>
<tr><td colspan="4">*Let's hope we don't have any risks in this category. If the risk's likelihood and severity of impact are both that high, the work breakdown structure should probably assume it happens and plan with that expectation.</td></tr>
</table>

Figure 10: A few example risks, categorized by likelihood and severity.

From the chart above, we can get an intuition of the difference between low-likelihood, high-severity risks and high-likelihood, low-severity risks. A low-likelihood, high-severity risk is the kind of roadblock that could cause a serious project delay, but that probably won't happen. With these risks, it's best to plan and execute the project tasks without worrying too much about the risk, and create a plan to manage that risk separately, in case it does occur.

On the other hand, a high-likelihood, low-severity risk is the kind of thing that may be straightforwardly planned for. Suppose we've decided at the outset to assign ushers in pairs. That way if one usher doesn't show up the whole system won't grind to a halt. Perhaps the importance of showing up has been made a part of usher training. Those are good examples of risk management in this case.

There are two major strategies in risk management: *prevention* and *mitigation*. A risk prevention plan works to minimize the likelihood of the risk, while a risk mitigation plan works to minimize its severity. In the risk of the no-show usher, pairing ushers up is a great example of mitigation. What might otherwise have been a high-severity risk has been made into a low-severity risk because of that step. A common mitigation strategy is to find and eliminate *single points of failure*, as was the case here. A lone usher was a single point of failure: a single no-show would cause a crisis. A pair of ushers eliminates the single point of failure. An example of prevention for the same risk would be training that encourages volunteers to take seriously the responsibility to show up.

A risk management plan may include both prevention and mitigation, or just one. Generally, the higher the likelihood of a risk, the more you'll need a prevention plan to lower that likelihood, and the higher a risk's severity, the more you'll need a mitigation plan. But situational needs and realities always prevail. It may not be possible to prevent a risk: if you are building a new sanctuary in an area prone to earthquakes or floods, you can't prevent those risks and will need to focus on mitigation—for example, by investing additional resources in building a physically stronger building.

Qualitative Risk Assessment

Everything in risk assessment is qualitative, for any organization relying on this book. There is no need to put numbers to our assessments. We have nothing to gain by debating whether a no-show usher is 25% or 26% likely to happen. A best practice is to simply use Low, Medium, and High as qualitative assessments of risk likelihood and severity. We can make a grid to give us a language to speak about these risks:

		SEVERITY		
		Low	*Medium*	*High*
LIKELIHOOD	*Low*	1A	2A	3A
	Medium	1B	2B	3B
	High	1C	2C	3C

Figure 11: A qualitative risk assessment grid.

In this grid, I've used the numbers 1, 2, 3 to denote severity, and the letters A, B, C to denote likelihood, both proceeding from low to high. This gives us a language to talk about "a 1C risk" or "a 2A risk." Those nine categories provide plenty of specificity for qualitative risk assessment. There's no need to get any more granular than that.

We've discussed three example risks; now let's place them in the qualitative assessment grid. There's the risk of the no-show usher, and let's say that's a 1B risk: I'll give it a medium rather than high likelihood, out of deference to the personal responsibility of the usher pool, and it's a low-severity risk. There's the risk of the board moving locations: let's agree that's a low-likelihood risk, but it's a high severity because of the amount of rework involved, so we'll call it a 3A risk. And the rabbi insisting on approving the usher list—low likelihood, low severity, just because in the unlikely case the rabbi wants to shuffle someone around, they can always trade places with someone else (that's mitigation right there). That's a 1A risk.

To assess your project's risks, follow these steps:

1. *Brainstorm risks associated with the project.* Include risks related to particular tasks, as well as risks related to the project as a whole. It can be useful to look at the work breakdown structure when brainstorming these risks, but do not forget those last-minute or overarching risks that may not be raised by looking at individual tasks. Place each risk on the qualitative grid, assigning Low, Medium or High values for likelihood and severity.

   This can be a great time for a modified KJ diagram. Draw the grid above on a white board, and give participants as many sticky notes as they can use. As with any KJ diagram, the group can feel free to move the notes around the board. When finished, transcribe the results into a document.
2. Craft a realistic, written risk-management plan for each risk. As a rule of thumb, prevent high-likelihood risks and mitigate high-severity risks, but take each risk situationally. The written plan may not need to be more than a sentence.
3. For each risk-management plan, assess whether it creates tasks that need to be added to the work breakdown structure. Or, perhaps a risk management plan might either worsen or improve a worst-case estimate for a subtask. If so, replan and recalculate your project estimate(s).

Risk Assessment and the Work Breakdown Structure

This risk of the no-show usher shows how risks may not revolve around the project schedule, even if they are potentially severe. Nobody will be behind schedule if an usher fails to show up on Yom Kippur, but it could cause unacceptable project performance. Other risks have everything to do with the project schedule: a decision to move the location of High Holiday services late in the summer would necessitate a lot of time-consuming rework.

Recall that we discussed not letting big, unrelated risks impact our worst-case task estimates. Your task would be delayed if there's a fire, but that would be the least of your problems—and may there not be a fire. Our rule for task estimates was to think only of worst cases that are germane to the task. Risks that are not germane to tasks belong here, in project risk assessment.

Those three risks we considered above are not germane to any one task, but to the whole project. If the venue changed (3A), we would have to add a lot of tasks to the project. Such risks cannot be planned at the subtask level. If that risk were more likely, and if the stakes were higher, it might make sense to have a whole alternative project plan ready to switch over to if the risk occurs. But it doesn't make sense to put all that effort into alternative plans for this case. It's sufficient to write a verbal description of what we'd do if the risk occurs, even if that means we'd have to do some replanning.

Notice that some of these risks have mitigation plans developed on the spot. That's okay! In fact, so much the better. If you can mitigate a risk in 30 seconds, write that idea down and call it a win.

Do we create risk management plans before, during or after assessing the risk? Yes! Qualitative risk assessment is not an exact science. Our goal is to deal with each risk as best we can. In some cases, we might benefit from assessing task-related risks before finalizing our three-point estimates. In other cases, risks and risk-management plans will occur to us after we've seen a whole draft project plan. That's okay too, even if it means giving the three-point estimates a final edit after a project's risk assessment is done.

The rule of germaneness applies at the project level, too. Only plan for risks that are germane to your project. In our High Holiday project, we would not plan for earthquakes or floods: if they were to happen, may they not, we would deal with them according to the existing emergency response plans that are already in place. (If you don't have a general emergency response plan, you need one, but High Holiday planning is not the place to file it.) On the other hand, if you're constructing a building, an earthquake risk may be germane to that project, because the project is all about the physical structure. Such a project could be exactly the right place to ask how the structure could mitigate that risk to this and any future projects.

This essay has been about project risks. However, you may find the qualitative method a useful way to think about nonproject risks, too, such as risks facing the general community. I do not have expertise in emergency response or in risk management outside projects, and I would certainly advise every organization to obtain quality advice in this area. In the context of that advice, you may find Steps 1, 2 and 3 above with the modified KJ diagram helpful.

8.6 PROJECT RESOURCES AND BURNOUT PREVENTION

Resources are what a project needs to move forward. Time and money are tangible, consumable resources that are specifically planned for. Office supplies are a tangible, consumable resource for which we don't typically bother to plan. (But someone pays for them, so they have to be planned for somewhere.) There are also tangible, nonconsumable resources like physical space to meet, or the free use of durable goods like refrigerators and cars. Intangible resources tend to be nonconsumable: community or professional relationships, knowledge and experience, licenses, etc. I consider morale and—especially—legitimacy to be important intangible resources for every project. I can't think of a consumable intangible resource; let me know if you can.

Oy: "human resources." It is the name of a professional field that is not within my area of expertise, so I don't want to be too critical, but I find myself disliking this term. I do worry that the term makes it harder to see the basic dignity of people. I think we were better off calling that area of expertise "personnel." But right now, our problem with the term "human resources" arises not out of moral wordsmithing, but because it is not specific enough for us. People are not project resources, but they may offer a project many resources, such as expertise, a car, morale-building skill, or cash.

What are all the resources you'll need for your project? You may find that you need a place to store the Rosh Hashanah honey cakes, and now you can make sure every venue being considered offers an appropriately sized refrigerator. Otherwise, you might need to add tasks to transport and store the honey cakes.

Succeeding at a Project that Has Fallen Behind

If you don't complete your tasks within the time or money planned for them, then you must either get more resources or reduce the project's scope.

This is not as obvious as it may sound. Project managers everywhere imagine after a setback that they will "make up for lost time" later in the project. It's amazing how popular this idea is, given how consistently wrong it is. Reality doesn't work that way, either in terms of on-the-ground experience or in terms of mathematical theory. If your project falls behind, which is very common, the way to succeed is to get more resources for the project, or to agree to reduce scope to fit within the remaining resources. Don't waste time on blame or embarrassment; it's probably nobody's particular fault.

What does it mean to get more resources? If you've spent more money than planned, then you're going to need more money. If your project has taken more volunteer time than planned, you may need to boost morale and ask for a big push. If you're behind schedule on the calendar, that's a tough one. It may be possible to delay the project deadline; that way the project could at least deliver on a modified agreement. But just as often, that isn't possible. The school year starts on a predetermined date, Jewish holidays have arrived on the same predictable schedule for thousands of years, Election Day (to take an example from my old career) will not wait a week for a faltering campaign to get its act together. These deadlines are fixed. It may be possible to add work resources, volunteers or staff help, to meet the deadline. Or, you may need an agreement to reduce scope, eliminating deliverables or doing some tasks less thoroughly, anything to reduce the resources the remaining work demands.

The key is to face the problem as soon as it becomes known, modify the remaining project plan, and continue by following the modified plan. Avoid blame: almost every project falls behind. Managing projects on time and on budget is a highly valued skill, for which our organizations are excellent laboratories for volunteers and staff alike to develop. You will gain this skill with practice as you participate in and manage properly planned projects. But even the best managers face project risks that impact resources, even if those risks are foreseen, planned for and managed. Just deal with the situation cheerfully, factually, and as soon as possible. Get more resources, whether those be people's time, budget, a deadline adjustment, more fridge space, or any other resource, or reduce scope and agree not to deliver part of what had been planned.

Another reason it's important to get resources or cut scope promptly is that you may not be able to control how your project adapts to the problem later. Have you ever worked most of the night right before a school, volunteer, or work deadline? Some people take pride in that kind of visible effort, but it is a management red flag. Nobody can keep that up, so you will experience burnout and staff turnover if it keeps happening. It seems to me that most burnout in nonprofits is due to mismanaged projects, specifically projects that are forced to get more resources at the very last minute by demanding that everyone work extraordinarily hard. See the next essay for a detailed look at the chaos that predictably follows. But a project plan with some form of tracking enable a manager to catch the problem early enough to deal with it intentionally, before it gets out of control and starts trying everyone's patience.

The same is true for projects that go over budget. If the problem is identified early, the board or applicable budget authority can agree to increase the project's budget in an organized, intentional way. Or, there will be enough time to replan the remainder of the project to cost less. But unexpected, last-minute budget busters wreak havoc on the whole organization's financial plans.

Another last-minute scenario is delivering an incomplete job. This is not the same as agreeing in advance to cut the project's scope in order to be able to deliver a reduced scope by the deadline. The latter scenario manages expectations, allows people to have some input and insight, and gives everyone enough time to plan what to do after your project delivers a reduced scope. Which is better: to say to the rabbi, "Hey, I don't think we're going to be able to get the prayerbooks rebound in time for the High Holidays next month," or to show up on Rosh Hashanah without the prayerbooks?

If you (the manager, the project team, the chartering authority) don't make an intentional decision how to get more resources or reduce scope when a project falls behind, then time will make the decision for you. This rule is familiar to all of us. After 20 years managing and overseeing nonprofit projects, I've had far more projects fall behind than not. Remember, if you're new to planning, your performance measures the accuracy of your estimates, not the other way around. There's nothing to be embarrassed about. Take initiative, take responsibility, and agree to increase resources or reduce scope as soon as you see a project fall behind.

8.7 MANAGING THE UNPLANNED PROJECT —AND WHY YOU'D RATHER NOT

I've noticed a pattern in projects without a plan. Early on, the project lolls along with a slow pace of work. There might be meetings; if so they're snoozers. Nobody is working very hard on the project. Procrastination prevails. There is a distinct feeling that the project has just begun, or that it is early in the project, even if this has been going on for some time. Nobody has any idea how to accomplish the project's deliverables, and that lack of direction becomes an elephant in the room that nobody wants to talk about.

Suddenly, the deadline seems impending. *Uh-oh!* Quickly, frantically, work gets assigned, accomplished, and assessed, not necessarily in that order. Confusion reigns, even panic. People may step on each other's toes and cause social or professional friction in the rush. Sudden decisions are made to cut corners as the project manager "sees the light at the end of the tunnel" and enacts a quickie plan to get out of this cheap. If there is no formal manager, individual project participants may "see the light at the end of the tunnel" individually, coming into conflict with one another's individual quickie plans.

Managers typically rely on top-down authority, forgetting to delegate responsibility, because in their panicked minds there is no time to explain the why and wherefore. Meetings, if they happen at all, may consist of little more than orders being barked out and taken. People may fear to deliver bad news. Everyone works extremely hard, and without a plan, rework and inefficiency are rampant. There may be displays of *heroism*, in which individuals do extraordinary amounts of work. If so, these may be signs that the work culture has turned competitive and sour. There is a feeling that it is late in the project—too late!—with the deadline impending.

It seems to me that unplanned projects undergo a sudden transition from the first mode, which I call the *early phase*, to the second, which I call the *late phase*. This sudden transition is when somebody, usually a manager, all at once experiences the deadline as impending, and sudden decisions are made to cut corners, to "get out of this cheap." They've developed a quickie plan all in their head, which is why the experience feels like "seeing the light at the end of the tunnel." With none of the features we've learned about in this chapter, this "quickie plan" is probably half-baked; it may be totally changed during execution and end up bearing little resemblance to reality. But the experience still feels like "seeing the light at the end of the tunnel," and now the team dives headlong into the work.

Out of desire for a positive-sounding term, I call this transition the *inspiration point*, but it is not a positive phenomenon. I might just as well call it the "panic point." Just recently a cartoon was circulating about graduate students' timeline for thesis writing. The first 80% or so was covered by an unmentionable expression for procrastinating, followed by a brief period labeled "Panic," followed by a short period of staying up all night. I don't think it matters whether you're writing a thesis, planning a gala, or sending out a big mailing: we all recognize this pattern. It arises, I think, because the project was unplanned. I see these three stages—the early phase, the inspiration point, and the late phase—shared by unplanned projects across disparate areas of nonprofit and for-profit work.

The Early Phase	**The Inspiration Point**	**The Late Phase**
• Slow pace of work • Nobody works hard on the project • Feels early in the project • Lack of task direction	• Uh-Oh! • Someone "sees the light at the end of the tunnel" • Sudden decisions are made to cut corners	• Frantic pace of work • Overtime work and displays of heroism • Feels late in the project • Top-down task direction

Figure 12: Work patterns in unplanned projects.

The characteristics of the late phase are all the opposites of those of the early phase, even though the striking reversal takes place suddenly. It's not unheard-of for one frantic e-mail from a responsible party (a committee chair, manager, etc.) to trigger the late phase. What was a slow pace of work on Tuesday can become a frantic pace of work on Thursday.

Some readers may think this is a normal mode of work. My message to you is that it is not a normal mode of work.

Every organization will accomplish better work by using project plans, even if they gloss over most of the formal tools presented in this chapter. If burnout, interpersonal friction, competitiveness, top-down management, inefficiency, rework, and the vertigo of constantly lurching from early phase to late phase have already begun to cause problems for your organization, consider that project planning may help.

Neither the early nor the late phase is efficient. The early phase wastes time and effort through procrastination, while the late phase wastes time and effort through friction, panic, and rework. Panic and procrastination both accomplish exactly the same amount: nothing. Although the early phase is lackadaisical and the late phase is busy, both share the characteristic of not being very productive.

It's important to note, too, that the early phase is lackadaisical only with respect to the current project. Some organizations may experience a slow early phase with nobody working very hard. In others, the early phase of one or more unplanned projects overlaps with the late phase of others, so that staff or volunteers careen from late phase to late phase to late phase without rhyme, reason or respite. That's an instant recipe for burnout.

If you always seem to be putting out fires, does this help explain why? If you're always putting out fires in other people's houses, thank you for your service as a firefighter. If you're always putting out fires in your own house, there's something wrong. You might need to invest in updated wiring, or learn another way of cooking.

I want to emphasize that productivity in the late phase is poor. A lot of hard work goes on in the late phase, but hard work is not the same as productive work. The late phase features a high ratio of friction and rework to task accomplishment going on.

Compared to the vast waste and crimped capacity caused by early-phase procrastination and late-phase chaos, and the corners cut at the inspiration point, we always accomplish more by making the effort to create a project plan, even a very pared-down one. Devote two hours to a planning meeting, bring in a good consultant, and get off the unplanned-project treadmill.

The Inspiration Point

It seems to me that every unplanned project features this "uh-oh!" moment. Suddenly, there is a way forward where there wasn't one before, and that way is found by cutting corners—by "getting out of this cheap." After the early phase's procrastination causes the project to fall behind, the inspiration point represents a decision (typically a haphazard and half-baked decision, but a decision) to get the project back on track by cutting scope.

Unplanned projects follow the rules of resources discussed in the previous essay. But because the decision to cut scope (or, rarely, to get more resources) is rushed, the new scope is never clear enough for people to take responsibility for the new tasks. Instead, a manager keeps the whole crisis plan in their head, which in turn necessitates a top-down management style and brings back the rejection-rework cycle we discussed in Chapter 7. Managers may think sharing their project plan would be a waste of precious time that staff should be spending on execution. In fact, it is the lack of collaborative planning that causes so much time to be wasted.

Before modernity, project management was not often needed. Most projects were simple enough for an individual artisan or manager to know in their head how to complete it. Some projects were more complex, and successful leaders—like Nehemiah in our *shiur*—seemed to have an intuition for dividing a project into written lists of tasks and subtasks. Major projects like rebuilding Jerusalem got done that way.

With the advent of machines, and especially of computers, suddenly everyday work became far too complex to fit in anyone's head. Project management as a professional discipline dates to the mid-twentieth century and flourished with the information age. But as it turns out, some of our activities have always been complex, and it never was a good idea for one person to keep a whole project in their head. Project-management insights from contemporary business help us, even in small nonprofits, by uncovering and illustrating problems we also face.

What does this have to do with the inspiration point? It seems to me that the inspiration point comes when somebody gets a project plan simple enough to store in their head. That's why it feels like "seeing the light at the end of the tunnel," and that's why it involves cutting corners: a more complex project has been replaced with a simpler one, and that way the manager "gets out of it cheap." An unplanned project can never accomplish more than what one person can store in their head. If you want to accomplish more than that, or if you want the management advantages that come with delegating responsibility, then you need a written project plan.

A written project plan moves the inspiration point to the beginning of the project. There is no early phase, procrastinating around the elephant in the room—which is that nobody has any idea how to move forward. There is no need to cut corners, nor for any one person to keep the whole project plan in their head, because it is conveniently written down and can be shared with the entire team.

Managing the Unplanned Project

The first step in managing an unplanned project is to stop and plan it. Then, manage it as a planned project.

Can you create a plan in the middle of a project? Absolutely! If you're still lolling around in the early phase, then nothing's going to be lost by spending a few hours planning instead of lolling. Just get the group together and return to the beginning of this chapter, figure out what you're there to do, and create a work breakdown structure. It doesn't have to be very formal, as long as it's a list of what needs to be done. Do some estimating and get a sense of how much work will be needed to complete the project. If it's too much to fit in the time or budget remaining, it's better to know that now than later. Cut scope or get more resources if needed, then execute your plan.

If you find yourself managing a late-phase unplanned project, it can seem as though there's no time for anything but telling people what to do, or spending long nights doing tasks yourself because it's just easier than involving others. Planning may seem to be a low priority. Let me give you a parable. I've always had great difficulty with swimming. Lord knows my parents tried and tried enough to fulfill their Jewish obligation.[108] I flunked the swim requirement to graduate MIT (yes, there is one) and had to take a remedial class, but I promptly forgot everything after the test. Years later I thought it might be fun to take an adult rowing class. Of course, there was a swim requirement. I got in the pool and it wasn't exactly that I was panicked—I'd done this before—but for all my flailing and flailing, working a lot harder than I needed to, I couldn't figure out how to move forward. Your late-phase project is like my swimming. You're spending an enormous amount of effort, but you're inching forward if actually moving at all.

If you truly are at the last minute—there's less than a week to deliver your project—you might need to do what I did in the pool: just live with it for this time, and take it as a lesson not to be in the same situation again. Next time, try project planning. It might be as difficult as swimming is for me, but I'll tell you: I'd have been a lot

[108] In b. *Kiddushin* 29a, there is a requirement to teach one's children to swim.

better off with just a little preparation, reviewing what I was going to do before getting in the pool. Next time, I'll do that.

If you have more than about a week to go, you might really be better off stopping work and creating a project plan, even that late in the project. It may seem like a sacrifice of time, but you're likely to get a lot more work done with a plan.

8.8 TYING IT ALL TOGETHER

If this chapter were a sermon, it might be a classic American fire-and-brimstone sermon. Otherwise known as a jeremiad, this form was developed by the Puritans and was important to the abolitionist movement. Preachers invoked the Covenant, laid out a bunch of imperatives, and then put the fear of God into people if they didn't follow those imperatives. I don't know many contemporary rabbis who preach jeremiads, but it's fun to switch styles once in a while.

In this chapter I invoked the Covenant, inasmuch as we opened as I always do with a discussion of Torah. I laid out a set of imperatives to follow, which have probably seemed like an awful lot, and then in the previous essay I illustrated the consequences of unplanned projects. When it comes to project management, I seem to be a fire-and-brimstone preacher.

Let's end on a positive note. In place of a Puritan call to repentance, I'll suggest some steps we can take today to develop organizations capable of managing projects well—or to improve if you're already managing projects well. Despite the seemingly heavy requirements of professional planning, it may not take that much work to develop a workable plan on the scale you need.

I model my recommendation for a simplified approach upon a different time-honored literary form: the executive summary.

Professional project plans are accompanied by an executive summary, which is a very short synopsis of the plan. The idea is that an executive responsible for many projects can read the summary quickly, understand the basics, and ask for more information if she needs it. The project's justification might be summarized in a sentence. The deliverables are listed as bullet items. Time and cost estimates, as applicable, will be given in summary form only, at the

97.7% confidence level we discussed above in this chapter. Major risks will be listed in summary; minor ones might be omitted. The executive summary will not include the full accountability matrix, but might mention key accountable people and their responsibility areas. Ideally, an executive summary should fit on one to two pages.

Simplifying Project Planning: The Executive Approach

Think of yourself as an executive, armed with an understanding of project planning. What do you need to know about a project? Take a moment with colleagues to brainstorm things that need to be done, with a broad brush. If all of the tasks are pretty small and clearly fit into the volunteer or staff time available, you might gloss over the time estimates for this project. Take a moment to think about risks: is there anything that could go wrong, and what response would it require? Those thoughts might be all you need to start. Send out an e-mail summarizing your group's decisions to make sure everyone shares an understanding. You've just created an executive summary project plan, even without the full plan itself.

What I like about this approach is that you've covered all the bases at least with a minimal amount of thought. If you find you need more information later, or if something goes wrong, you can do what any executive would do: ask for more information. You'll then need to complete that part of the project plan—if you need it. Your understanding of project planning principles equips you to use this "executive summary" approach, because you know what tools you can fall back on in case of need.

Let's say after sketching out the major deliverables for the High Holidays, you're a little worried about the ushers. You're not quite sure how you're going to get people to agree to those jobs and make sure they show up. You could plan out just that one deliverable, as we've done in this chapter. Or, perhaps you've identified a couple risks that ought to be planned for. Add plans to manage those risks to the "executive summary" you started with.

If confusion starts to form about who's going to do which task, jump in with a cheerfully quick implementation of what, in a more formal context, would be recognized as a work breakdown structure and accountability matrix. Confusion gone! It doesn't have to take 20 minutes if your project is small. Just break the tasks down into subtasks to the extent necessary to assign them to people. Then, the PARIS-N mnemonic can help you remember to ask the right questions about accountability, even if you don't put a formal chart down on paper. Voilà! You're using a work breakdown structure and an accountability matrix, and you don't even need to tell your committee that's what you're doing. This may be a secret worth keeping—until someone asks how you did it.

Using Project Planning Skills without a Full Project Plan

Here are some suggestions for implementing project planning skills on an as-needed basis, as part of your existing projects:

1. After reading this chapter, you'll likely recognize certain elements of formal planning that you're already using. Assess your current techniques, and see which elements of a formal project plan are already addressed in some way by your system—or whether you've thought of something that I haven't accounted for in this chapter. (If so, please tell me on *npgovernance.org*!)
2. If there's anything in this chapter your current system doesn't address, write it down. Then, present such findings to your project group or to whoever charters such projects. Evaluate whether it's worth modifying your system.
3. As your project moves forward, treat your plan as an executive summary, being alert to when you might need more information. Developing some of the plan components if and when you need them is a good compromise between the benefits and the complexity of formal project planning—as long as you know what those components are, how to tell if you need them, and how to use them when you need them.
4. Record your knowledge as you learn by doing. If you needed to add an element to your plan, write a brief explanation of what you added and why, when you get a chance. This way your organization will be better prepared next time. See Chapter 10 for a lot more on organizational learning.

Imagine, for example, that your synagogue's High Holidays are run by an experienced leader who uses an Excel spreadsheet to list all the tasks that need to be done and who's going to do them. That's a fine example of a private method that fulfills most of the functions of a work breakdown structure. It does not offer time estimates, though, and it records only who's assigned to do each task, which would correspond to the *A* (Accountable) role in the PARIS-N mnemonic, without any of the other roles.

After reading this chapter, suppose the group decides not to use time estimates for now, and finds the PARIS-N menu of roles overly complicated. But the *R* (Review Required) and *S* (Signoff Required) roles are helpful, because the rabbi has final say over anything happening on the bimah, while several other decisions need the rabbi's review. The project leader creates new columns on their spreadsheet for Accountable, Review, and Signoff.

Moving to Step 3, suppose (may it not happen) there is a storm warning just before Rosh Hashanah. Don't panic: qualitative risk assessment can help even in a near-crisis. Heavy rain might be a high-likelihood, moderate-severity risk requiring mitigation (replanning traffic patterns in the parking lot; finding a way to safely move the Torah) while hurricane-force winds would be a low-likelihood, high-severity risk (it might be unsafe for people to travel; secure shelter space cannot accommodate a High Holiday crowd). At least we have a language to talk about these risks, as we make the necessary decisions in the moment. Later, an after-action report might help improve those risk responses for next time.

As we will see in Chapter 10, project planning is iterative. Most of our organizations do enough recurring projects that we can gain wisdom about operating better as we go. Some of that wisdom is an art and requires skills that individual people develop over time. But much of it can be written down and shared with everyone.

This chapter has presented a variety of techniques that are used every day to manage million- and billion-dollar projects. I have argued that small and medium-sized organizations will be better off learning and using them, feeling free to pare them down.

Look back now to our *shiur*. Which elements of a modern project plan did Nehemiah use in rebuilding Jerusalem? Which elements are you using today? Which do you think Nehemiah might have benefited from knowing about more formally? (Feel free to read ahead in the Book of Nehemiah.) Which might your organization benefit from learning and using?

Chapter 9
PRODUCTIVITY MANAGEMENT

9.1 SHIUR

> *Rabbi Tarfon said: The day is short, the task is great, the wages are high, the workers are lazy, and the Master of the House is pressing. He would say: You do not have to finish the work, but you are not free to shirk it.*
>
> M. *Pirkei Avot* 2:20–21

On the literal level, this text is a call to industriousness. Rabbi Tarfon appears to be talking simultaneously about spiritual matters and real-time workplace productivity. The Talmudic Rabbis lauded having a worldly trade in addition to Torah study, to occupy oneself with positive pursuits.[109] Today's organizations also require our concern for both the spiritual and the worldly, making sure work gets done in order to achieve the lofty goals we set.

Rabbi Tarfon must have recognized the paradox, familiar to hard workers in every age, that having too much to do leads us to do too little. Overwhelm is among the most consistent complaints of overworked, underpaid nonprofit employees and volunteers. Rabbi Tarfon is at once reassuring and stern: "You do not have to finish the work, but you are not free to shirk it."

Putting that advice to work requires dividing large tasks up into smaller ones, so the advice of Chapter 8 will be helpful. But Rabbi Tarfon is mainly talking about staying on task. Thinkers, inventors and businesspeople have long advised us to be industrious: Thomas Edison's adage that success is "1% inspiration and 99% perspiration" comes to mind. Rabbi Tarfon is certainly teaching these familiar lessons of hard work. But I think he's also saying more than that.

Classical and modern Jewish commentators have focused on the phrase "the wages are high."

[109] M. *Pirkei Avot* 2:2.

Rabbeinu Yonah (1200–1263) compares it to a time-limited spree in a king's treasury: why waste time when you could be carrying out gold? Rabbi Dovid Rosenfeld's commentary on Rabbeinu Yonah's parable is worth reading.[110] There is the idea of having too much work for the time available to do it—and therefore, of an urgency to the work. A women's Passover haggadah connects our text to the haste of the "unfinished bread" of Passover, when the Israelites needed to move as quickly as possible out of Egypt.[111] The Reform movement's prayerbook *Mishkan T'filah*, interestingly, connects it with the weekday Amidah,[112] perhaps to remind us that even as we ask God for many things, we must do our part by also working hard.

But I've always been troubled by the next part: "the workers are lazy." Excuse me? It may be nothing more than emphasis on the advice to work hard. But the text is unchanging, so no matter how hard we work, Rabbi Tarfon will still be calling us lazy. I find it somewhat comforting that the epithet isn't personal: Rabbi Tarfon is speaking about the human condition intrinsically. But the Rabbis take a positive view of humanity, created as we are in God's image. What gives with calling everyone lazy?

Part of the problem may be that I don't think the advice to work as hard as possible is, by itself, actually very good advice. While Rabbeinu Yonah's image of carting off gold at a breakneck pace from the treasury might be instructive as a general call to industry, when it comes to managing an office I don't think that furious pace is where we want to be. We're going to drop the gold in our panic.

Too many nonprofits see themselves as places of frantic work. The day is short, the task is great—and the Master of the House is pressing. Staff and volunteers may feel guilty leaving their work for a moment, lest a needy client go unserved. It is possible to work at this pace for a short time, but month after month, year after year it cannot be done. It eats away at morale. A constant gap between superhuman expectations and human performance is discouraging to everyone. The frantic, harried feeling of too many nonprofits is not what Rabbi Tarfon wanted us to become when he said "the workers are lazy." We have taken industriousness too far. Like all

---

[110] Rosenfeld (2008).

[111] From *Her Seder of the American Jewish Congress, Pennsylvania Region*, reprinted in Anisfeld, Mohr & Spector (2003), p. 189.

[112] Frishman (2007), p. 85.

virtues, industriousness is wholesome when in harmony with other virtues. When maximized at the expense of every, it is bad for us.

Another way to read the first half of Rabbi Tarfon's statement is as five different alarms, which together paint a portrait of a problem we all know: that no amount of our work will ever fulfill limitless expectations. In the second half of the quote, Rabbi Tarfon suggests a solution to the problem. That solution lies in our awareness that it's okay to take the work step by step. In fact, a calm and reasonable step-by-step approach is the only way to get anything done at all.

This suggests a change to performance measurement that is essential to the contemporary workplace. Rabbi Tarfon leads us to measure worker performance not by outcomes—which cannot ever be "enough"—but by the quality and intentionality of work put in. *You do not have to complete the task, but you are not free to shirk it.* The worker is now entrusted with a moral responsibility, namely, not to shirk but to do the best they can. The worker is responsible for bringing their skills and good-faith effort to the job. Good management ensures that the consistent effort of workers results in task achievement according to reasonable expectations.

9.2 EXPECTATIONS MANAGEMENT

Modern ideas about productivity management are based on keeping a consistent, reasonable pace of work, avoiding undirected time as well as unsustainable, breakneck-pace expectations. (They call it a "breakneck" pace for a reason.) After setting frameworks for optimizing the use of time, these ideas define performance expectations around a reasonable pace of work—not the other way around. Productivity management is iterative, recognizing that the definition of good performance depends on the particular work and the particular workers. It takes frequent opportunities for feedback, reflection and self-critique so as to define good performance around times when workers feel they've done their best. Problems are addressed nonjudgmentally, with an eye toward preventing them the next time. As managers get to know their teams, they will come to understand how much can reasonably be accomplished in a given time, and will be able to plan projects accordingly.

Productivity management therefore makes a strong distinction between bad work performance and not meeting expectations. It assumes that bad performance will be obvious to the manager and dealt with elsewhere: a clear deficiency in skills, for example, or a lack of good faith in the work process. Recognizing that managers do not know how long a task "should" take until the task has been completed—iteratively, several times—productivity management assumes that any gap between performance and expectations is a problem with the expectations, not with the performance.

This overall assumption of good performance holds workers accountable to strong, punctual, good-faith effort while freeing them from unrealistic expectations. In turn, by guaranteeing workers they will be judged by realistic human expectations, it requires the worker's full buy-in to those expectations.

A productive work environment is cheerful, even relaxed when possible. People are focused on work, but are never so panicked that they can't be pleasant. Staff socialize to a reasonable extent and take breaks. Approximately the same, predictable amount of work gets accomplished every day, according to reasonable expectations that are informed by successful experience. As successes build, staff gain experience and hone their skills.

Project Management and Productivity Management

In the past half-century, managers have come up with increasingly successful ways to maintain cheerful, effective professional cultures around sensible ways to measure work performance. All of these efforts center on the idea that expectations are guesswork by managers—guesses that can be improved through iteration.

Formal project planning, which we discussed in Chapter 8, is one such idea. Project planning begins with brainstorming and educated guesswork at expectations, accepting in advance that those guesses may be off and using the power of statistics (the three-point estimate) to preempt unexpected delays by factoring variance into estimates. Project planning can also be iterative, learning from past experience and applying that learning to new projects. Chapter 10 discusses that process of organizational learning in more detail.

But formal project planning is a heavy tool. Understanding its principles helps us make good management decisions, yet many of our organizations will never really need a formal project plan. There are other, lighter tools, which might not give us the clear view of formal project planning, but can help us stay on task every day.

The distinction in this book between project management and productivity management is my own. I join most project managers in insisting that a project is a finite, defined scope of work whose goal is completion. Painting your house is a project, but maintaining the paint on your house is not a project. Not all of our activities, therefore, are projects. There are also many small, sometimes repetitive tasks—maintenance jobs that require vigilance and response more than any predetermined to-do list. And there are other one-off tasks that do not fit within a project.[113]

For some of these tasks, partial project plans can help. It's easy to imagine an accountability matrix being of value for non-project tasks; in fact, I'll recommend a way to do that later in this chapter. But a project estimate won't help you maintain the paint on your house. In addition to being a rather heavy instrument, project management does not address all of our organizations' management needs. We need other tools as well. Productivity management will fill in many of those gaps.

9.3 MOTIVATION AND TRACKING: RETHINKING THE STAFF MEETING

In most offices, unproductive work time far outweighs the total of all breaks, tardiness, leave, socializing at the water cooler, and goofing off. Productivity management is about using existing time effectively, which means reducing unproductive work time first.

The biggest offender is the rejection-rework cycle, which we discussed in Chapter 7. In Chapter 8, I suggested this could be remedied by better planning.

The second-biggest offender is often the staff meeting. "But we love staff meetings"—say a majority of managers, perhaps, and a distinct minority of everyone else. Staff meetings give managers the

[113] Those short, one-off tasks are actually tiny projects, but they're far too small for project-planning techniques to help.

comfort of seeing everyone at the table, but they often fail to accomplish anything.

"Isn't it good for all the staff to be together?" one might ask. No, not necessarily, not for no reason. If you want to create a sense of workplace community, have lunch instead. I'm not saying staff meetings are never helpful. I'm saying they are overused.

Most staff meetings violate a cardinal rule of meetings that I presented in Chapter 5: never use meeting time to discuss issues that do not involve every person present. If you have an issue that involves some but not all members of the group, it should be handled in a smaller-group meeting or *offline* (i.e. not in a scheduled meeting). The common technique of hearing a report from each group member round-robin, tempting as it may be to see everyone communicating with each other, wastes a lot of time. The silent audience probably does not need all that information about their colleagues' work in order to do their own work well; when they do, written reports may suffice. Announcements are another common culprit: they could probably be delivered by e-mail.

What staff meetings do offer is accountability. They are a time for staff to come prepared and show what they've accomplished, and to be assigned new tasks. A contemporary technique takes far less time to offer the same benefit.

Adapting Scrum to the Nonprofit Workplace

Scrum is a closely defined set of practices within the discipline of *agile software development*. The name *scrum* comes from the sport of rugby, where it implies close teamwork toward a shared goal.[114]

I don't want people to be intimidated from scrum just because it has its roots in software engineering. By no accident, on the first day of the first computer-science course at MIT, Spring 1996, I was handed a large book[115] with a label in bold letters: "Don't Panic." It was more than a humorous reference to a beloved nerd novel:[116] it was among the best life advice ever given. Much contemporary

---

[114] The idea of scrum was first proposed by Takeuchi Hirotaka and Nonaka Ikujiro in reference to product development, in Takeuchi & Nonaka (1986); we will hear more from these scholars in Chapter 10. It was later adapted to software engineering by multiple authors.

[115] That book was the Spring 1996 edition of Harold Abelson's and Gerald Sussman's classic *Structure and Interpretation of Computer Programs.*

[116] That is, a humorous reference to Adams (1979).

thinking about workplace effectiveness comes from software engineering, perhaps because the novelty and complexity of that field has demanded a lot of intentional thinking about management.

That thinking informs our work. Whether we're stuck in formalistic, Industrial Revolution modes of giving and following orders, or whether we're applying formal project management to set expectations and budgets, we're using management thinking from different eras of engineering. The challenge is the same: our tasks are large and complex, and we don't have enough time to do them. We're not so different from Rabbi Tarfon two millennia ago. But we can create a positive work environment that emphasizes day-by-day, step-by-step progress toward our goals.

Unlike the other methodologies we've seen so far, scrum has yet to be systematically adapted beyond software engineering. It was developed in the 1980s and '90s, and caught on in the 2000s among software companies. Space does not permit a full introduction to scrum here; in any case, we will not be using it. (I offer a number of links offering a fuller introduction to scrum on *npgovernance.org*.) Instead, I will give a quick sketch of how scrum works, and then talk about applying it to our nonprofit offices.

Don't panic.

In scrum, a tight-knit project group works on a shared set of tasks. A fixed period of time[117] functions as the yardstick of accomplishment, usually two weeks or a month. The idea is to accomplish as much as possible within each fixed time period. At the beginning of each cycle, the group leader[118] works with the team to decide what it's reasonable to accomplish, and at the end of the period, the team meets to review accomplishments and challenges, and to prepare for the next cycle.

---

[117] In scrum, this unit is called a *sprint*, which is not my favorite workplace analogy. I will just call it a "cycle."

[118] In scrum, the person accountable for a group goes by the unfortunate title *scrum master*. I suppose more practical and less gendered titles like "scrum manager" or "scrum representative" weren't as well liked. Never mind that: your organization does not need anyone separate from a group manager to play the analogues of this role that we are using. Although *scrum master* is the universally accepted term in the scrum world at present, I will simply refer to the role as *manager* or *group leader* in order to correspond with usage in most of our organizations.

This iterative structure enables scrum to shine just where project management is least helpful: with repetitive or day-to-day tasks that are more like maintaining paint than painting, and with work involving many unexpected tasks and needs. In project management, too much of the unexpected necessitates replanning, but scrum takes the unexpected in stride, accommodating new requests into the work plan within the earliest available cycle. In turn, scrum's weak points are project management's strong points: scrum does not see the big picture, cannot tell you how much to bid on a large project, and focuses more on taking risks in stride than on planning for, preventing or mitigating them. Project management and productivity management play complementary roles.

Perhaps the best single idea from scrum is the *daily stand-up* or *daily scrum*. This meeting involves all staff and occurs in a central, consistent location, every workday at a fixed time. Everyone, regardless of role, reports on what they accomplished yesterday, what they're working on today, and what if anything is preventing them from accomplishing their goals. Here's the catch. The entire meeting takes no more than fifteen minutes. Very often daily stand-ups run much shorter than that. Scrum imposes a fixed maximum speaking time for every participant, which could be a minute or less. Daily stand-up reports are only a few crisp, clear, natural sentences. Because they know they are expected to be crisp and clear, workers know they must come to the meeting prepared.

In scrum, time frames are serious. Both meeting times and cycle times are *timeboxed*, meaning there is never an exception made to the time limit for any reason. If things don't get said, they don't get said. If something doesn't get done within a cycle, it can't be reported as done. It has to be continued in the next cycle—*if* the team decides to devote further time to it. Scrum runs by the clock.

This requires a strict sense of *punctuality*: if anyone is absent, including the manager, meetings start without them. There is never a delay, for any reason. Paradoxically, or perhaps because of this strict discipline where it matters most, offices using scrum can be among the most relaxed workplaces in the world. If you've ever wondered what keeps software engineers in T-shirts and sandals productive, consider how seriously scrum takes meeting time.

As you (re)consider your staff meetings, think about scrum's daily and cyclic (biweekly or monthly) meetings. The daily stand-up is simple and ready for our offices to begin tomorrow. Many people find it highly motivational. The very short duration keeps the focus on the day's work, while creating a sense of teamwork and giving everyone an idea what everyone else is working on. Daily stand-ups can be equalizing: there's no reason a rabbi or executive director can't participate with a receptionist and a custodian in a daily stand-up. In fact, that may lend a greater sense of teamwork and mission to the staff.

The daily stand-up can work across distances and time zones. While it's ideal for a stand-up to be in a consistent location, a videoconference can approximate the benefit. I've experimented with a daily stand-up with a friend in another city, just to provide accountability and motivation every morning. Videoconference technology is still imperfect, but a daily stand-up is so short that the limitations of video felt unimportant. The best part was the need to come prepared. I wouldn't be surprised to see this idea blossom into many novel uses as its simple benefits catch on.

In addition to the daily stand-up, timeboxing and punctuality are other scrum ideas worth considering. Counterintuitively, it is often more important to start and end a meeting on time than to have everyone present. Everyone's time has value. If someone misses a meeting, they can catch the next one, but scrum doesn't permit their tardiness to multiply itself by dragging everyone else into delay.

It can be especially tempting for a manager to think it's okay to have everyone wait for them, but such behavior leads to a haphazard, unaccountable workplace that wastes a lot of everyone's time. As I learned in my "Hot Breakfast Mondays" incident,[119] productivity management starts at the top. It doesn't interfere with management for managers to act at times as a "first among equals," a leader by example who accepts goals and self-evaluates right along with everyone else.

Scrum also reimagines task estimation, replacing the hours and dollars of project planning with qualitative measures of how large a task is. These are usually expressed in abstract numerical *points*, with tasks being assigned a number out of a predetermined menu: scrum groups might use 1, 2, 4 or 8 points to denote respectively small, moderate, large and very large tasks.[120] The intermediate

---

[119] See the essay "Managing and Mentoring" in Chapter 7.

[120] This and the set of values 1, 2, 3, 5, and 8 are among the most common menus of point values used by scrum groups.

numbers are not used, because the goal is not to quantitatively measure the task, just to categorize it roughly by size. Scrum groups can use any point system they wish, or dispense with points entirely. I think numerical point systems are probably too complicated for most of our offices, but they may offer useful food for thought.

As points are added up, the group gains a rough reading of their progress. Further precision is not necessary and would probably be guesswork anyway. It's not important whether you got 10 or 11 points yesterday; what matters is how the team as a whole is doing compared to previous work cycles. Points can give you a rough sense of movement toward task completion—which scrum groups call *velocity*—without bogging you down in the time-consuming quantitative estimation of tasks that could rapidly change anyway.

Note the strong philosophical difference between project-management and productivity-management approaches to task estimation and planning. Project management emphasizes knowing as much information as possible in advance, and gives us tools to estimate large projects with impressive precision. Productivity management accepts tasks and completion milestones as they come, and concerns itself with keeping people productive each day. Don't be confused because these two practices say opposite things about the value of task estimation. They represent a genuine philosophical difference in contemporary management practice.

Fortunately, they are also complementary, as we've mentioned, each providing benefits the other lacks. For most readers of this book, my general advice is to dispense with "points," to use three-point estimates when you feel you need them, and otherwise simply to track productivity toward task completion without worrying too much about quantitative measurement. If you categorize tasks as "big" or "little," that would amount to a simplified point system.

Scrum's emphasis on dealing with unexpected tasks in the moment and within each cycle could add discipline to our organizations' ways of handling these events. Even the discipline of deciding whether a new demand is important enough to divert attention to it that would otherwise have gone to preassigned tasks, or instead to say, "We'll put that right onto next month's docket," adds intentionality to our managing the unexpected. On the other hand, scrum's strong emphasis on insulating the work team from distractions is not appropriate for workplaces where people's job is to interact with people.

Scrum is not as well suited to volunteer committees. Scrum tends to assume a daily work schedule, and its timeboxing and accountability features may not make sense for volunteers. I would tend toward keeping volunteer committee management to the practices described in Chapter 5. I could imagine scrum's end-cycle evaluation and pre-cycle task identification meetings as helpful templates for periodic committee self-management. If you try any practices from scrum with volunteers, I'd love to know how it goes!

If you're running weekly staff meetings, could your goals be accomplished more efficiently? Perhaps a daily stand-up will address your accountability and motivation needs, while e-mail announcements and a monthly staff meeting would suffice for the remainder. Some of us need regular staff meetings; others might do better with different practices. As I mentioned, scrum has not yet been adapted systematically outside its field of origin. So if you try any of these ideas, please engage on *npgovernance.org* and let everyone know how it's working for you. You'll be at the forefront of nonprofit productivity management.

9.4 TASK-BASED MANAGEMENT: THE KANBAN APPROACH

Many innovations in engineering management have followed a similar trajectory: developed by Japanese engineers in the 1980s, 1970s or earlier, and then tested and refined in the world of software engineering in more recent decades, now to be applied to nonprofit management. Japanese thinkers brought a fresh perspective to Western management practices, often emphasizing natural flows of ideas and searching for methodologies less reliant on formalistic control and more trusting of people's natural behavior.[121] The KJ diagram and its related sticky-note exercises, scrum, and now *kanban* have followed this path. Kanban was among the earliest of these innovations in the Japanese business repertory,

---

[121] In particular, management scholars Nonaka Ikujiro and and Takeuchi Hirotaka contributed to many of the ideas in Chapter 9 and Chapter 10 of this book. See the bibliography for references to three of their important works.

originating at Toyota in the 1950s; it was adapted to software engineering in the early 2000s.[122] Kanban is among the most natural approaches imaginable. It is so simple that it may seem obvious, but it can be as central to your office's or committee's productivity management as it is to a software startup's.

Kanban is a practice of listing tasks and who's responsible for them, and assigning to each task a qualitative status. There should be only a few status states; the basic template is *To Do* (equivalents are *Unstarted* or, in scrum, *Backlog*), *In Progress*, and *Completed*. A *kanban board* is a visual list of tasks displaying their status. The kanban board is often a large physical white board located centrally in the office; that has the advantage of catching people's attention every day. It can also (additionally or instead) be online.

A typical kanban board uses sticky notes to represent tasks. Workers move the notes among columns representing the status of each task. Sticky notes of different colors might be used to categorize tasks, or to label who's accountable for the task.

Here is a kanban board representing a typical synagogue newsletter in progress. You can see at a glance how the group is doing on each task, as well as which tasks are done (and might need review) and which are not. Kanban also makes it easy to tell if there's any particular task blocking progress.

To Do	**In Progress**	**Completed**
• Get monthly donor list	• Write main article	• Get e-mail list
• Finalize layout	• Get all committee reports	• Make any special changes to template
• Send e-mail		• Get rabbi's article

Figure 13: Sample kanban board for a monthly synagogue newsletter in progress.

That looks pretty reasonable for a newsletter in progress. But if any one task has been sitting in the "In Progress" column for too long (like getting those committee reports), or if a task was expected to

[122] See Ohno (1988), p. 29, for a historical perspective from Toyota manufacturing, and D. Anderson (2004) for the now-popular adaptation to software engineering.

have been started but hasn't been, those become opportunities for a manager to ask how they can help.

A kanban board shows a profile of the group's work. A key best practice is to limit the number of tasks with "In Progress" status at any one time. Too many "In Progress" tasks becomes a red flag that some of them are not actually being worked on. It is better to follow the discipline of keeping tasks in "To Do" until someone is ready to commit to completing them. Keeping the "In Progress" list narrow helps ensure tasks move expeditiously from "To Do" to "Completed."

While scrum does away with project management's quantitative tracking of hours, kanban takes the qualitative approach even further. Kanban is not interested in how big a task is. Kanban is just focused on keeping workers on task. Remember, productivity management assumes that everyone is working as hard as possible to finish tasks, and that any impediments will be resolved naturally when they come up. Daily stand-ups, offline discussions and management review of things like keeping the "In Progress" column narrow should be enough to diagnose problems. Kanban does away with measuring work speed entirely, encouraging workers just to focus on getting one task done at a time.

Customizing Kanban

Many organizations find it useful to modify the basic set of kanban status categories. Often, tasks completed by staff require review by a manager (even as everyone tries to minimize the rejection-rework cycle from Chapter 7). The "Completed" category is then split into two new categories, called something like *In Review* and *Accepted*. Also very often, organizations wish to distinguish among tasks that haven't been started, according to whether they are actively *To Do* and will be started as soon as there is time, or whether they are in a *Wish List* (also called *Parking Lot* or *Icebox*), not to be forgotten but not timely enough to be assigned to staff right now. Pulling tasks off the "Wish List" and into the "To Do" category then becomes an intentional organizational decision.

The "Wish List" is one of kanban's best ideas. It offers a place to store brilliant brainstorms without the need to distract anyone from their assigned work. Also, the assumption that new demands go into the "Wish List" first, and must be intentionally evaluated to determine if they should displace tasks already assigned, can help us avoid the trap of being reactive, which, again, feels like constantly putting out fires. Maybe they're not fires; maybe they're just new work requests. Calm evaluation against other, previously assigned priorities may be a more appropriate response to new requests than immediate drop-everything attention. Here is one place scrum's places on insulating the work team from interruptions can help. An understanding that not every new request will receive immediate attention (if you can get away with it) helps to manage expectations so that the definition of good work falls within your capacity.

Kanban works particularly well with scrum, although both are useful independently. Kanban and scrum share a similar worldview of incremental, day-to-day progress, as opposed to hierarchical planning. Thus kanban and scrum also share many of the same advantages and disadvantages. Both help us deal with unexpected demands as well as maintenance tasks in stride, and both provide a looser, less formal way to plan and manage projects. They cannot, however, provide detailed insight into a project or estimate large bodies of work in advance. Nor is either particularly helpful in getting projects back on track after they've fallen behind.

One practice in which project management can aid productivity management is the work breakdown structure. The purpose of the work breakdown structure in project management is to ensure subtasks are small enough to be estimated confidently. Productivity management, too, works much better with smaller tasks. Instead of having a whole project-sized load of work ("Send out the monthly newsletter") languishing under the "In Progress" column day after day, it's better to break that project down into subtasks to look more like our sample kanban board above. Smaller subtasks make everything easier to see and manage, and help the kanban board keep a sense of motion. Productivity management is all about taking work in bite-size pieces, so the discipline of a work breakdown structure can translate directly to your kanban board.

Where any of the elements of formal project planning are used, kanban provides a nice complement at the implementation level. Everyone can see at once which tasks are being done, in which order, and can make decisions on the order of work based on the network flow diagram as well as current circumstances, available resources, and new demands.

Kanban and scrum make valid new points about task-based management, which bear consideration even as they sometimes oppose project-management wisdom. A case in point is their philosophical opposition to quantitative estimates. I believe nonprofits underutilize cost and time estimation, and will fare better if we use it more. But sometimes incremental progress is a better model for our work. Sometimes taking change in stride is wiser than replanning. And in any case, God makes sure we don't live completely planned lives.[123]

The great thing about managing today is that productivity management and project management give us a rich choice of tools at our fingertips, and a healthy ongoing *machloket* (debate) over which tools are most useful when. Our experiences managing our organizations right now can add to humanity's knowledge, because we live and work at a time when these questions are new. After you've tried practices from both the productivity-management and the project-management disciplines, join the online conversation at *npgovernance.org* and let everyone know what you think.

9.5 TIME MANAGEMENT

Time management, that universal bugaboo of guilt! Who among us doesn't sometimes rue the ticking seconds, the passing years? The Reform *machzor* (High Holiday prayerbook) of my impressionable childhood memory ruminates on "bitter memories of hours misspent. Now they come back to accuse us, and we tremble to think of them."[124] Time management! Taskmaster of our efficiency, judge of our work ethic, accuser of our guilt!

Our culture teaches us to treat time as a resource to exploit, not to waste any of it. In Rabbeinu Yonah's parable from our *shiur*, it was no accident that time was the unalterable limit of how much we could take from the king's treasury.

Yet in today's context, without some humanizing moderation, this amounts to what my teacher Rabbi Natan Margalit calls mechanical thinking.[125] Natan is on firm ground linking this

[123] The Ishbitzer rebbe (Leiner, 1860) would not agree: he believed in predestination. He was quite alone in that view within Jewish tradition. I have learned to love God's disruptions to my own plans.

[124] Stern (1978), p. 294.

[125] Margalit (2010).

exploitative, maximizing ideology to the excesses of Industrial Revolution thought. We are human beings, not machines. Rabbeinu Yonah would never have agreed his parable was about strip-mining every possible nugget of gold in the shortest possible time, poisoning food and despoiling villages for miles around. He assumed his readers knew that virtues must be balanced with other virtues, that our morality and our mortality place limits on how much we can maximize and control.

I hope this chapter has surprised those who expected tips for forcing lazy workers to work harder. I've never understood why managers with such a low opinion of their workers keep them. There is something passive-aggressive about that complaint. If your workers are really that lazy, fire them and hire better ones. Nobody has time for that kind of negativity. Productivity management recognizes, as I say Rabbi Tarfon did, that the solution lies in a step-by-step approach that structures itself around the assumption that every worker is doing their best.

I keep reading breathless articles declaring that workers are only 50% productive, or 80% productive, or whatever. What does that even mean? If everyone is 50% productive, then who is 100% productive—Superman, the Golem of Prague? As managers, we need complaint restraint. You're managing people, not robots. Not that robots would be better: I'm reminded of a cartoon I saw years ago of a person sitting in front of a computer, with a thought bubble from both human and computer saying, "Wow, this thing is slow!"

Like other areas in productivity management, time management assumes positive engagement and good faith from all. Time management aims to structure the workday around expecting and facilitating everyone's good efforts.

Breaks, Productivity, and Tracking

Of course I let people take breaks. As an attentive manager, I already know whether they're working diligently or not, without the need to account for every second of their time. I'd never think of limiting when people can take a walk to clear their mind. I need people with clear minds. Otherwise, typos, forgotten details and inattention cause problems that are both difficult and expensive to solve later.

I fear that misguided ideas about nonprofit "efficiency" may be part of what leads a maximizing focus on billable hours to run amok. Please don't get me started on the ways in which misguided ideas currently prevailing within the grantmaking community penalize responsible nonprofit management practices and, perversely, both exacerbate and incentivize inefficiency and waste. I've tried very hard to confine my polemics on that topic to the end of Chapter 10.

In time management, breaks are not the problem. As we've discussed, unproductive work time is the problem. Unproductive work time includes undirected time, time spent worrying or feeling overwhelmed, time spent on the rejection-rework cycle, and more. Breaks are a positive good. Breaks help keep people focused: they punctuate the day and, by framing periods of time devoted to task work, they can be used intentionally to structure a day of work.

To that end, some people swear by the *Pomodoro Technique*.[126] I've never been able to get into it personally, but it's worth considering. It illustrates contemporary thinking on personal time management. The extremely simple idea is that you work a set amount of time, and then take a short break. Traditional cycle lengths are 25 minutes on task, and then a 5-minute break, making up a half-hour cycle in total. But Pomodoro aficionados can select cycle lengths that work for them. Pomodoro—Italian for *tomato*—was developed by Francesco Cirillo while he was in college; he named it after the plastic tomato-shaped kitchen timer that he used.

Pomodoro shares with scrum the characteristic of absolutely rigid, non-negotiable timeboxing. On a work cycle (called a *pomodoro* with a lowercase *p*, plural *pomodori*) there are no interruptions and no distractions as a single task takes center stage. Users record their pomodori as an incentive to do more, and so as to develop an intuition for how many pomodori a given task is likely to take. The time limit motivates people to complete their task during the pomodoro—or if the task is too big, to complete a part of it and return for another pomodoro. The Pomodoro Technique website hits me right away with the line "25 Minutes to Get It Done"—and it's easy to see how that can be motivating.

As an adaptation to nonprofit offices, without claiming to be "authentic" Pomodoro, I would relax the traditional insistence on non-interruption to just require that a staff member be working on only one thing for each set interval of time, with the goal of completing it. For most nonprofit staff it isn't practical to hold all interruptions. But there is something to be said for breaking the day

---

[126] See Cirillo (2013).

into manageable blocks, and trying to finish one task within each block. It also helps to acknowledge that when interruption occurs, it can cancel the concentration required for that block—so it might be best to start over after that phone call, assessing where you are now and where you'd like to be after 25 minutes of focused work.

The Pomodoro Technique is one example of contemporary time-management practices that focus on setting aside time dedicated to a specific task. Colleagues are still sending me new methods developing in this rapidly evolving field. I hope *npgovernance.org* will be a place for discussion on how you're applying these ideas or others, and how they're working. It will be through that kind of dialogue that we refine these emerging practices together.

The Productivity Management Approach

Let's conclude by looking at how the practices we've studied in this chapter support time management.

- *Timeboxing* is a key innovation from contemporary productivity management, well worth our study. Timeboxing is to time management what a work breakdown structure is to project management: a way to deal with something too large for us to keep in our heads by breaking it down into manageable pieces. Breaking your day into timeboxed *pomodori* (or less formal pseudo-*pomodori*) is one way to experience throughout the day the motivation we feel at having a very immediate goal. And timeboxing offers an easy, if very strict, way to eliminate delay.
- *Rewards:* When we divide a large workload into small goals, each goal is a chance to create a sense of accomplishment. Rewards for achievement can become the proverbial spoonful of sugar that helps the medicine go down.[127] This is true even if the rewards are private, given by the individual to herself.
- *Structuring the Day:* All of the methods in this chapter structure the workday, so that the individual knows what she plans to do at each point during the day. Scrum insists that every worker be able each day to state their goals for the day. Pomodoro, fully implemented, divides days into half-hour units (counting the break) and asks workers to estimate how many pomodori a job is likely to take. The theme is daily structure and predictability.

[127] Sherman & Sherman (1964).

We've discussed how workers whose jobs make predictability impossible can adopt small parts of the practices we've studied, even if the mainstream versions of those practices are unavailable to them.

- *Reducing Time-Wasting Practices:* Instead of trying to tighten the screws on workers to get them to do more work—a worldview that assumes a basic disrespect for workers, an adversarial relationship between them and management, and a self-defeating preconceived expectation of poor performance—the practices of this chapter target time-wasting organizational practices for replacement with efficient practices that facilitate everyone's best work.

We've seen how productivity management shares the insistence of project management on breaking tasks into subtasks, while productivity management focuses on time units rather than task units. Both support clarity about the work to be done at a given moment, so both assist in avoiding the rejection-rework cycle.

Can productivity management work in tandem with project management? Absolutely! Project management will help you know what you need to get done, and productivity management will help you get it done. Here are a few recommendations:

- Rethink staff meetings. Maybe you do need traditional staff meetings, but perhaps they could be shorter or less frequent.
- Implement a daily stand-up, regardless of what you do with staff meetings.
- Take seriously the idea of spending set periods of time on uninterrupted work for one task.
- Reframe work interruptions by asking whether they can wait for the next work period—whether you're thinking in terms of half-hour *pomodori* or biweekly scrum cycles. If an interruption can't wait, then stop your other work to focus on the emergency. If it can wait, add the non-emergency to the task list to be addressed calmly and intentionally in turn.
- Use a "To Do" list and a "Wish List" to separate good ideas that the organization has decided to implement from good ideas that the organization has not decided to implement.
- Always try to identify and eliminate the rejection-rework cycle.

Chapter 10

PROCESS MANAGEMENT

10.1 SHIUR

> *Even if all of us were wise, all of us discerning, all of us experienced scholars, and all of us knowledgeable in the Torah, it would still be a Commandment upon us to retell the Exodus from Egypt. And whoever expands upon the story is praiseworthy.*
>
> *Haggadah (Passover seder)*[128]

My teacher, Rabbi Natan Margalit, asks: "If I already know the story, what's the point of telling it all over again?"[129] Why do we repeat a story we already know?

The great, controversial twentieth-century Jewish philosopher Yeshayahu Leibowitz defines religion as obedience to God: pure ritual with no further significance.[130] Leibowitz would say that the commandment to retell a story that all or most participants know anyway is a perfect example of ritual in itself, of obedience to law as a paramount value.

But that doesn't quite account for what's going on at our seder tables, does it? Some of us may observe the seder out of obedience, some of us because of tradition and familiarity, a sense of home, pleasing family members, because we connect it with current civil-rights struggles, or for many other reasons. Jews who are otherwise unobservant keep the seder. It

[128] The text of the Haggadah is not completely standardized, even though it is well over 1,000 years old. This text appears in all the Haggadot I've seen, although the version printed in Maimonides' *Mishneh Torah* appearing on *mechon-mamre.org* seems to lack the clause about "experienced scholars." The translation appearing here is original except for the beautiful word "discerning," which I took from Margalit (2014).

[129] Margalit (2014).

[130] See Leibowitz (1953) and Leibowitz (1960).

seems our reasons for retelling the Passover story every year are more complex than Leibowitz makes room for. But is there any reason for the seder that the whole Jewish family has in common?

Natan suggests learning. He quotes cultural anthropologist Mary Katherine Bateson, who distinguishes "classroom learning" from "learning outside the classroom." Regarding the latter, she writes: "Lessons too complex to grasp in a single occurrence spiral past again and again, small examples gradually revealing greater and greater implications."[131]

For Natan, and I think for all of us, "telling the Passover story at the seder is more like this kind of learning than classroom learning: it spirals past every year and we are meant to get new insights as we retell it in different circumstances, at different ages."[132] This makes more sense than Leibowitz's answer. We repeat rituals in Judaism in order to learn something new from them each time. Natan writes:

> The Torah, and Jewish life as a whole, follows a spiral pattern, circling around to the same seasons, holidays, stories, but always moving forward and upward, so that we come back to familiar landmarks but we don't simply walk in circles, we climb upward toward our goal.[133]

It is striking that Natan should talk about spirals of learning in Judaism, because the spiral also figures into the contemporary theory of knowledge management. Organizational theorists Nonaka

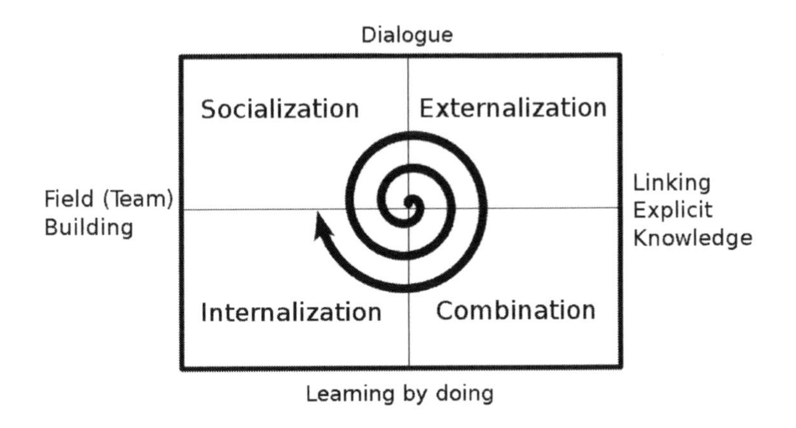

[131] Bateson (1994).
[132] Margalit (2014).
[133] Margalit (May 2012).

Ikujiro and Takeuchi Hirotaka use a spiral to represent the growth of organizational knowledge.[134] The Nonaka-Takeuchi spiral, which appears in Figure 14 above,[135] is by no means the only way to discuss organizational knowledge, but it is a good model and we will return to it often in this chapter—or rather, we will follow its spiraling path "forward and upward."

The idea of organizational learning—that is, an organization coming to have information from its experience available for use—is totally natural to the Torah. The Jewish people are often criticized, not individually but corporately, for inability to learn from experience: "My people are destroyed for lack of knowledge";[136] "My people ask counsel and their staff declares to them"[137] (where the "staff" symbolizes experience); "not a people of understanding";[138] "you are a stiff-necked people";[139] and importantly, "Remember, do not forget, how you angered your Eternal God in the wilderness."[140] That last verse refers to organizational learning explicitly. Those weren't very pleasant verses, but we're also "a holy nation" if we heed God's invitation to "listen indeed to My voice."[141]

I'm not trying to suggest that the Torah explicitly anticipated the contemporary concept of organizational learning. I do suggest that the idea of knowledge belonging to an organization—in this case the Jewish people—is not foreign to the Torah. The concept of a people

---

[134] Nonaka & Takeuchi (1995), pp. 71–2, 89, 284.

[135] Thanks to Wikimedia Commons user JohannesKnopp for permission to use this image.

[136] Hosea 4:6 (JPS)

[137] Hosea 4:12. The Hebrew for "to them" is singular: a more literal translation might be "its staff declares to it." This text refers to the people of Israel corporately as an organization, not severally as individuals. (JPS, adapted).

[138] Isaiah 27:11.

[139] Deuteronomy 9:6 and many other places (JPS, adapted). The "you" here is singular: Moses' speech is explicitly directed to the Jewish people corporately. Actually, the entire passage beginning with the Shema (Deuteronomy 6:4) is addressed to the second person singular, a break from the use of second person plural in 6:1. Although 6:2 suggests the exhortation is directed to each listener individually, 6:3 and 6:4 are directed explicitly to "Israel" in the singular, and 9:6 is addressed unambiguously to a "people," entirely in the singular.

[140] Deuteronomy 9:7. This continues the second-person-singular exhortation of 9:6 (above), which is explicitly made to the Jewish people, corporately, itself.

[141] Exodus 19:6 and Exodus 19:5, respectively.

being exhorted corporately to learn information corporately, which implies that an organization can do so, is seen throughout the Torah.

So we ought to figure out how to learn as a people. In this sense we can gain much from Natan's connecting the duty to retell the Passover story to the Jewish people's learning—to our becoming better at our mission, our vision of ourselves at our best, at being God's witnesses.[142] Every year in the retelling, we improve.

The Nonaka-Takeuchi spiral is unwittingly a very good drash on our Haggadah text and on Natan's teaching on it. Let's understand the terminology, focusing on the example of Deuteronomy 9:7, "Remember, do not forget, how you angered your Eternal God in the wilderness." In Figure 14 above, starting in the lower-left quadrant:

- *Internalization* means an individual or group of individuals learning privately, within their minds. Individual Israelites (hopefully) hear Moses speaking, think about the incident or incidents that Moses is referring to, connecting the references to their life experience. Now those individuals have internalized that the events happened and that God was angry. They have personal, private knowledge, also called *tacit knowledge* in knowledge-management theory.
- *Socialization* in this context means people interacting with one another, exchanging and comparing tacit knowledge, checking their experiences against each other's, resolving discrepancies and agreeing on what to preserve. Moses' speech to the Israelites is a fine, if one-way, example of socialization. If the Israelites then discuss Moses' words among themselves, making sure they share an understanding of what Moses was referring to, that would be a more typical example of socialization.
- *Externalization* means creating documentation and writing information down. The Torah text and the Haggadah text that began this *shiur* are classic examples of externalization. Now the knowledge takes a different form: written, fixed, recorded, and publicly available. It is no longer tacit knowledge but is now called *explicit knowledge*. Writing down Moses' speech was a very good way to ensure it would not be forgotten. Even if whole generations forgot it, which the Prophets tell us they did, the text is waiting there on the scroll for retrieval whenever desired.

---

[142] Isaiah 43:10.

- *Combination* in this context means linking documented explicit knowledge into new juxtapositions and forms, creating links among documents as well as links between already existing documents and new life experience. Jewish text is absolutely full of combination, especially in the Talmud and Midrash, where the Rabbis loved to string texts together to teach new lessons, which were then recorded for new students to learn.[143]

Life experience may seem most applicable to the bottom half of the Nonaka-Takeuchi spiral,[144] where the label "Learning by Doing" suggests that combination and internalization incorporate new experience into the learning process. But experience can shape the socialization and externalization stages too, when it influences what we choose to discuss with others or what we choose to write down.

Above all, as has always been the case for the Jewish people in our stories, the four quadrants of the Nonaka-Takeuchi spiral are not steps to be taken one after the other, but rather continuous processes that happen at different speeds for different people, organizations, and experiences, and that influence each other in complex ways. As Natan's teaching suggests, the spiral shape expresses our continuing growth as we revisit familiar experiences and projects. And the four stages identified by Nonaka and Takeuchi describe contemporary organizational-learning processes just as well as they describe ways of communal learning used for thousands of years by the Jewish people, as recorded in our text.

In this chapter, I will often recommend rehearsing and retelling stories that everyone already knows, searching for ways to learn something new with each retelling. These practices may seem overly ritualistic, almost as if they were the management version of Leibowitz's seder. Just as retelling the Exodus gives us the chance to learn something and improve ourselves at each seder, so retelling what has happened in our organizations creates new opportunities to learn and improve our processes as we consider past experience in light of our changing present.

---

[143] See especially Midrash Rabbah on Song of Songs 1:10. There isn't space here to treat this beautiful and profound topic, but I've placed a few links on *npgovernance.org*.

[144] Often called the SECI model, for the initials of the spiral's quadrants. I prefer acknowledging the researchers by name, which also helps reduce the number of acronyms being used.

10.2 PROCESSES AND KNOWLEDGE

What does your organization know?

This book began by talking about organizational decisions, made by and belonging to the organization itself, and not to any one person. There is also organizational knowledge. Individual people know information, like who the big donors are, or how to send out a blast e-mail, or how to run High Holiday volunteer activities. But organizations can also know and learn information.

What does that mean? It means the ability to accomplish a project or task regardless of who is in charge of it. It means the assurance that anyone taking over in the future will get the benefits of the experience of everyone contributing in the present or in the past, so they will not have to reinvent the wheel. It means the organization is not dependent on any one person, but can accomplish its most important tasks given any group of reasonably intelligent people. And it means still more than that. Organizational knowledge makes it possible not only to replicate projects done in the past, but to improve them each time. This is important for nonprofits relying on volunteers, interns, or short-term staff.

The discipline of which we speak is, like most of the practices in Chapters 8 and 9, less than a generation old.[145] The discipline is now usually called *knowledge management*, and today's scholars are still formulating its basic principles. I shouldn't omit that the distinction between tacit and explicit knowledge has been questioned.[146] I've used the term *process management* in this book for two reasons. First, I admit it: I couldn't bring myself to break my four-chapter alliteration streak. But much more importantly, the idea of process management will help us distill those aspects of knowledge management that are most useful to us right now, glossing over a great deal of other material to focus on a specific model of organizational learning that builds on our work in earlier chapters.

I like terminology to have clear, precise definitions in the context where it is used. We've dealt with some very challenging concepts in this book, and I hope I've done a good job presenting them in plain English as much as possible. The term *process management* now

---

[145] A burgeoning field of research now, there is hardly a mention of it before Nonaka (1991).

[146] Serenko and Bontis (2004).

gives me a bully pulpit to attack one of my buzzword nemeses, the word *process*. Together, you and I will defeat this buzzword by shackling it forever to a clear, useful definition. Here goes:

A process is a recurring set of activities.

Is that it? Is that the stake through the heart of this most annoying of buzzwords, which will prevent it from blurring our view of projects, to-do lists, job descriptions, contracts and strategic initiatives forever? I'm not getting my hopes up: people like buzzwords, and the tendency to call everything a process is not even high on my list of English-language pet peeves. But at least in this book, the word *process* is used precisely and only to denote a recurring set of activities. That has freed us to use more precise terms elsewhere, while devoting attention now to how our organizations can learn from processes.

We will consider processes to contain recurring projects, possibly with more than one recurring project in a process. Remember, a project is a set of related tasks together with a plan for carrying out those tasks.[147] Running High Holiday services in a synagogue is a project each year. Running them in general is a process. Sending out this month's fundraising e-mail is a project. Sending out fundraising e-mails in general is a process, which, in an advocacy organization, might include process goals that are higher-level than any one project, such as being able to respond quickly to news events. Those goals are accomplished by improving the process so as to execute each future project better. In other words, they're accomplished through organizational learning.

Now we can better see the connection between processes and organizational learning. Because processes are recurring sets of activities, we can use knowledge from previous iterations to aid us in future iterations. Some processes are just one recurring project: small projects like sending out those e-mails, or larger projects like High Holiday services, which we get better at executing over time as we learn. Some processes consist of multiple projects that repeat in more complex ways. Some processes have recurring activities that aren't organized into projects.

Recurring projects account for most of our tasks. Jewish holidays like Passover with its seders, seder matching and haggadah supplements, or the High Holidays with their fundraising appeals,

---

[147] See Chapter 8 for a more precise definition.

membership drives, logistical challenges and calls to repentance, come every year. Blast e-mails are sent, curricula are planned, high donors are wined and dined, galas are held, letters are written to politicians. Many of our activities occur on a repeating basis.

Even if the content of your blast e-mail is different this time, or the High Holidays will be at a new location this year, or the school's grade levels have been reconfigured, there is still a lot about each project that repeats. Organizational knowledge enables us to accomplish repeating projects with increasing ease, regardless of which individuals carry them out.

On the other hand, process management is so high-level that it can directly enable advancement toward strategic goals. For an advocacy organization, the desire to respond to current events fast enough to have a say in the news cycle sounds like a strategic goal. In a process-management view, it could be accomplished through many well-managed projects, analyzed after the fact through final reports and dialogue with participants to identify improvements for future projects, and to externalize (write down) that knowledge.[148]

An essential part of that externalization will be summarizing new experience in a periodic brief memo to future projects. Perhaps every year, project experience might be summarized in bullet form over a page or two. This might include tips from experience, risks to remember to plan for, or aspects of the project that did or did not work well. These memos would periodically be *combined* with existing project plans to improve the project template.

You'll know the knowledge spiral has moved forward when those improvements stick.[149] It sounds like a lot of work, but in practice, for a small organization, it might not be much more than jotting down a quick half-page memo of lessons, then integrating those lessons into future project plans. Eventually, at a strategic review you'll say that your response speed is enabling your goal of being responsive to the news cycle.

Complexity in Processes

Painting your house is a project. Maintaining the paint on your house is not a project, because it is not limited in scope. Maintaining

[148] See Light (2001), pp. 189ff for some excellent suggestions.

[149] Rabbi Bunam of Peshischa (1765–1827) said, "How do we know our sins are forgiven? When we no longer commit them."

the paint is a process if you can articulate what needs to be done on a recurring basis.

A process need not recur fully or exactly, with exactly the same project plan being executed in each iteration. There could simply be a few aspects of a situation that recur. It's just that if nothing recurs at all, there's no point learning from past experience. So one way to identify processes is to think about what recurs; another approach is to ask where knowledge of past iterations could be useful.

Take that house-painting example. It isn't immediately clear—at least to me—what recurs about maintaining the paint. I'm not a painter (though I once helped paint my office an unwise choice of colors; within a week my business partners and I decided it looked like an inside-out school bus, and we painted it again). Suppose one aspect of maintenance is to check for rust on the siding, and another is to check the windowsills for chipping, both of which need to be done every so often. Now we've got a process. We can schedule projects every six months to check the paint, and undoubtedly as we do a few of those iterations we'll find ways to do them better and faster. When we write down those improvements and incorporate them into future projects, that's process management.

To add some complexity, suppose we have to check the paint by the gutters after a storm, and we need a thorough check of every square foot after an earthquake. Now we have if-then patterns: *if* there's a storm, *then* we have to check by the gutters. But that's still a recurring activity, even if it doesn't recur on a regular schedule. Processes can incorporate this sort of complexity.

Suppose we're like me—we have no idea at all how to maintain the paint on a house—and we've been tasked with doing so anyway. That's a pretty familiar situation to experienced nonprofit workers. We don't have a clue how to define a process out of that. It would be a waste of effort to write down a bunch of recommendations for future projects when we have no idea how to do the first task.

Instead, we carefully observe, making educated guesses and learning as we go. Part of careful observation is doing as much research as we can in the time available: searching on the Internet or the library, asking more experienced colleagues or friends for help, taking stock of our job and reading any documents left to us by current or previous co-workers. Then, we observe our situation and our job, and take a step in what seems to us the most reasonable direction. Expectations management is essential: we will probably not ace a job we do not know how to do, and our stakeholders need to know that. But as we make educated guesses, we greet experience as a teacher, whether the lessons learned happen to confirm or critique our choices.

We treat our initial guesses what to do as a starting point: not feeling wedded to them, but using them as something to evaluate in light of experience gained. It will take us some time to figure out where to lay the sidewalks.[150] When we've figured out what the recurring, the non-recurring, and the complex parts of the job are, we will have some good experience under our belt. Then we will have a process, and the knowledge we will have gained can be put to use in future iterations.

10.3 DOCUMENTATION

When a new committee chair takes office, hopefully they've had the opportunity to work on the committee for some time, and therefore has some sense how to do things. That personal experience is what the Nonaka-Takeuchi knowledge spiral calls internalization, and their knowledge is tacit knowledge. Their conversations with group members are socialization. Another example: when a new employee joins a team, an informal orientation would be socialization, an exchange of tacit knowledge from one individual to another.

Why not take the opportunity to write that knowledge down—to *externalize* it—transforming it into explicit knowledge that can be *combined* with other explicit knowledge and other people's life experience to move the spiral forward and up? The brilliance of the Nonaka-Takeuchi spiral is identifying externalization as the step after socialization. After socialization happens, we can preserve the wisdom gained by writing that wisdom down. For that reason, *documentation is the central practice of process management.*

To get started with documentation, let every project submit a final report explaining how the project went, and especially what future projects can learn. This can range in length from a paragraph

---

[150] Recall the story about the university that laid sidewalks where people had been walking, from Chapter 4.

to a book. (One to two pages is a good rule of thumb.) If you used a project plan, let it guide the report. Did any of the risks happen? Did any risks happen that you didn't predict? How did the schedule and budget go? Were there bottlenecks? This isn't about judging success or failure; it's about generating knowledge for future similar projects. Committees might also submit reports on an annual basis.

Reports may tend toward advertising accomplishments—which is an important goal—while devoting insufficient attention to recording useful knowledge. Nobody likes to write that they failed, but failures are great teachers. Ideally, reports should advertise accomplishments as well as reporting full results with frankness. If the same report can't do both, then the two functions may need to be separated into independent documents. Advertising the group's accomplishments is not our goal in this chapter, but it is our goal in Chapter 11, and if reports help advance the knowledge spiral while doubling as a treasure trove for communications, social media, new-member outreach or grantwriting, so much the better.

Procedures

Another major way to use documentation is with *procedures*. A procedure, in this context, is a step-by-step written guide to accomplishing a task. The steps are as specific as possible, and are designed to guide staff or volunteers through a task, even though they may be unfamiliar with it.

Procedures are very handy with technology: tasks like sending out a blast e-mail, getting a membership list from the database and merging it to address labels, formatting a newsletter or updating the website can be intimidating, but become much easier when there is a step-by-step guide to follow. Procedures expand the number of staff who can do a task, thus improving your organization's capacity.

Procedures are just as useful outside of computer technology. If I'd had a procedure for checking paint on a house, I'd have been able to write a more convincing example about it before. A procedure for purchasing school supplies will help ensure a school is consistently stocked at the lowest feasible cost. A procedure for emptying and then refilling the High Holiday storage area will prevent a mess. I have some sample procedures from one of my nonprofit roles on *npgovernance.org*.

Procedures figure importantly into the next essay, where we'll discuss measuring a nonprofit organization's capacity.

Heroes and Heroism

American Jewish comic-book authors have contributed much to our culture. But there's a key difference between comic books and process management. In comic books, heroes are good, whereas in process management, heroes are bad.

A *hero*, in the context of process management, is a person on whom the organization is dependent. The only person who knows how to do a mail merge is a hero. If they leave, someone else will have to figure out how to do a mail merge. The only person who knows how the database works is a very dangerous hero. The organization is totally dependent on that person. This is bad. In engineering we call it a *single point of failure*, meaning that the whole organization would be in trouble if something should happen to that person (may it not). Even if you don't wish anyone else do mail merges from the database—or whatever the hero's specialty task is—get them to down a procedure as soon as possible. That way, if your database person has a sick child, or your donor-relations officer quits, the organization will be able to continue.

I have said that heroism may be a red flag for a competitive, frictional workplace culture.[151] A hero who flaunts their overwork is being passive-aggressive about the organization's dependence on them. This attitude can lead to serious ethical problems as well as managerial ones. "In time, they begin to feel and act like martyrs — special because they are deprived, and deprived because they are special,"[152] writes Marilyn Peterson of boundary-violating clergy, but her observation applies to all sorts of heroes. Then, continues Peterson, they "feel entitled to take from whatever or whoever comes their way as compensation for all they have given." The more power such a hero has, the more dangerous they are, but Peterson's warning illustrates how any heroism can lead to ethics problems.

For all of these reasons, managers should be wary of heroes and heroism. An organization can't ask everyone to document all their steps to do each of their tasks. That's why managers must know their heroes, if any, proactively obtaining documentation to transfer knowledge from the hero to the organization. Prioritizing these documentation tasks is a key management decision. Prioritize from the most egregious or unstable instances of heroism on down.

---

[151] See the essay on unplanned projects in Chapter 8.

[152] Peterson (1992), p. 180.

We're back to the Nonaka-Takeuchi knowledge spiral. Heroes are people who have *internalized* a lot of tacit knowledge, for which the organizational knowledge spiral has stalled. They need to share that knowledge (socialization) and write it down (externalization) so that others can make sense of it in the context of their own experience (combination) and ultimately do their own learning (internalization) to move forward and up on the spiral.

10.4 CAPACITY, METRICS, AND PROCESS MANAGEMENT

Nonprofit executives, grantmakers and analysts say a lot about "capacity." Funders want to make "capacity-building grants," which is a concept that theoretically distinguishes day-to-day operations from activities designed to enable the organization to do more. The idea is to teach a person to fish rather than giving them a fish. But what is capacity, and how can we increase it?

In this book, *capacity* means the ability to get things done. It's a simple concept, although it is not simple to identify, measure, or improve. A full treatment of capacity is far beyond our scope. This essay focuses on how organizational knowledge improves capacity with existing resources by enabling more efficient execution. We'll use a model that, like many of the practices I've introduced in the latter half of this book, originated with software engineering.

Readers who have heard of *capability maturity models (CMM)*[153] probably think I'm nuttier than a baklava factory. Admittedly, this is my farthest stretch applying contemporary concepts to nonprofit management. CMM was developed for huge defense contractors, not for tiny nonprofits. But you've stayed with me through three-point estimates, PARIS-N, Scrum and Pomodoro: don't quit now!

I like capability maturity models as a way to think. No small nonprofit will, or should, undergo CMM certification. But CMM gives us analogies and patterns to look for as we assess our capacity. It teaches us how to grow our capacity in situational and incremental ways. And it gives us food for thought about the link between the

[153] CMM is a registered service mark of Carnegie Mellon University (CMU).

organizational learning and capacity. What follows is my own brief interpretation, which I've designed for nonprofit organizations. I've provided links to further resources on *npgovernance.org*.

The first Capability Maturity Model for software engineering appeared in 1995,[154] and I found out about it shortly afterward as an undergraduate at MIT. Impressed, I took its way of thinking into my nonprofit leadership career. CMM has undergone many revisions and has somewhat fallen out of favor, partly because many new versions were published that came to lack focus,[155] and partly because engineers came to see CMM as a paperwork requirement in opposition to looser, leaner techniques like those we discussed in Chapter 9. That's a valid point: documentation is by definition paperwork, and CMM definitely requires documentation. Again, contemporary thinking gives us a wealth of different perspectives and opposing opinions, so it is our job to inform ourselves and decide which tools are most appropriate to which situation.

The 1995 CMM suffices for us. It defines five levels of "capability maturity." That is, an organization's "capability" is seen maturing as the organization gains and applies knowledge. For nonprofits, CMM's definitions are most useful as a way to think about how organizational knowledge enables this process of maturation.

For our purposes here, the "capability" of an organization means exactly the same thing as capacity. They are different words only because they originate from different conversations. The key is that your organization's capacity goes through stages of maturity. So an organization with a more mature capability, or capacity, will be able to do more than an organization with a less mature capability, or capacity, even with exactly the same financial, staff and physical resources. It follows that one of the best capacity-building activities is to try to increase your capability maturity, even slightly.

CMM is the heaviest tool in our management toolkit. Improving your capability maturity is not going to happen, and should not happen, in the kind of rigorously measurable way that would get you

---

[154] Paulk, Weber, Curtis and Chrissis (1995).

[155] Later versions of CMM attempted to apply the CMM concept to particular disciplines, and to cross-disciplinary work; hence we get the People CMM, CMM Integration, etc. There have been many versions since those. My first tech job, in 2000, was an attempt to create a CMM concept for mobile devices, which in retrospect was a cleverly glorified marketing role. The evolution of CMM beyond the simple, original 1995 version is beyond our scope here.

an Air Force contract. But it can and should happen incrementally, in some areas and not others, in ways that are applicable to you. The ambitious goal of this essay is to suggest how. Here are the levels:

Capability Maturity Levels, CMM 1995

Level 1:	Initial (Accomplishing Tasks)
Level 2:	Repeatable
Level 3:	Defined
Level 4:	Managed
Level 5:	Optimizing

Our introduction to the significant wisdom of CMM comes in the observation that accomplishing your tasks is the *first* stage of development. That's humbling. In the critique and refining CMM has undergone, I agree with those who have added a "Level Zero" for organizations that are not yet accomplishing their tasks. Here is my explanation of the levels as they apply to nonprofits:

Level 0: Not Accomplishing Tasks. Level Zero is a catch-all category for organizations that do not yet meet the criteria for Level 1. There is no shame in starting at Level 0. At Level 0, the organization does not consistently succeed at accomplishing tasks. Projects may be over budget, very late, or fail to deliver what was promised. Alternatively, the organization may face stagnation, not taking on projects because of a lack of self-confidence or fear of failure. If you are not yet accomplishing tasks consistently, review chapters 5, 7, 8 and 9 for some helpful tips.

A Level 0 organization should focus organizational-learning activities on recording what has happened. Patterns will suggest themselves eventually, or a consultant may help. The main thing is to record what happened with each project: what worked well, what risks weren't in the plan, etc. Eventually, good people management, project management, productivity management, documentation, and not repeating mistakes will help you reach Level 1.

My fifth-grade math teacher Mr. Taliaferro said that practice doesn't make perfect; it makes permanent. That being so, at Level 0 any procedures should be descriptive, *not* prescriptive. A common but illogical mistake is to issue rigid, detailed instructions without regard to whether they work in practice. Absorb organizational knowledge after—not before—it has proven successful. Treat Level 0 procedures as educated guesses, open to testing and refinement.

Level 1: Accomplishing Tasks. Called the "Initial" phase in the 1995 book, and often called the "chaotic" phase, Level 1 is where most *successful* nonprofits find themselves. A Level 1 organization pulls through, always finding a different way through the thicket. There may be unplanned projects, with the waste discussed in Chapter 8. Or, heroes may hoard knowledge, with the organization dependent on them. Or the organization may lack the consistent experience to be confident in future performance, even if past performance has been good. This latter case may happen because the organization is still too new to have developed that experience, or because the nature of its mission precludes the kind of predictable project work that would enable capability maturity above this level (which, it's important to say, is not wrong for them).

A Level 1 organization can use documentation to recommend the reuse of tactics and practices that have worked, in addition to the purely descriptive reports to which Level 0 documentation should be restricted. At Level 1, the organization's task is to tease apart which aspects of its success are due to haphazard chance, and which were due to high-quality management practices and project plans which could become the basis for templates.

A Level 1 organization can also assess to what extent the knowledge required for successful execution resides with the organization itself. If the organization is dependent on heroes, it can now begin documenting successful processes in order of priority. Where less confidence exists, the descriptive documentation that I recommended for Level 0 may continue, with the hope of finding a way through those experiences toward practices that work.

Level 2: Repeatable. A Level 2 organization accomplishes its tasks, and does so predictably, smoothly, based on its organizational knowledge, with repeatable performance. Task accomplishment is not a haphazard slide into the finish line each time, but is executed with confidence.

Level 2 organizations know enough about themselves and their processes not to be fazed by bad luck. They have accumulated significant knowledge about common risks, and use project planning to account for those risks. It would be unusual for a nonprofit to reach Level 2, although a well-managed nonprofit may show Level-2-like performance in many areas.

There is no way to get from Level 1 to Level 2 without significant experience running similar projects iteratively, with successes *externalized* and *combined* into organizational knowledge, which offers confidence that the organization can repeat those successes. Many of our processes, and many of our organizations, will never approach Level 2 because their work is not predictable enough to offer iterative experience. That's important to know, and it doesn't mean the organization is inefficient or badly managed. For example, an organization doing casework for the homeless probably cannot reach Level 2: their work is just not predictable enough. Maybe they could try for greater capability maturity in a portion of their work.

On the other hand, I could imagine a synagogue's High Holiday process achieving something like Level 2 after years of good project and process management. When the same project happens every year, with kink worked out of the system over time, when risk plans successfully account for what reality throws in, and risk responses work reliably without the need for replanning during the project, when an entirely new project team could sit down and figure out how to do things pretty well just based on the helpfully organized project binder with written procedures and project plans—that's a pretty good portrait of capability maturity at Level 2.

Imagine two organizations in two different cities, both funded by the same grant and delivering successful project performance with identical numerical metrics. But let's say the first organization accomplishes this through required unpaid overtime and frantic late-night deadline sprints, and relies on heroes who would take necessary experience with them if they left. The other organization gets its projects done through careful planning, using template project plans developed through accumulated prior experience; risks are predicted pretty accurately by prior projects' final reports and incorporated into those templates, and risk management plans work effectively. The first organization is Level 1 while the second might be approaching Level 2—even though their bottom-line project results are identical. The second organization has greater capacity than the first, and is a lot more stable.

If you think your organization can achieve something like Level 2, in whole or in part, that might be a good strategic goal. It is a significant feat of high-quality execution to reach Level 2, while CMM's incremental nature implies the right steps to achieve it: first get to Level 1, then increase organizational learning to be able to execute confidently, without needing heroes, in the face of risk. To reach Level 2, you'll need all the tools in this book and more!

On the other hand, if your organization cannot achieve anything like Level 2 due to the nature of your work, you can still make many strides with documentation and the knowledge spiral, not to mention lower-level best practices like project management and productivity management, which will help you accomplish each task or project better. If you take some time to consider which aspects of CMM Level 2 might apply to which aspects of your organization, you'll be on the cutting edge of nonprofit management theory.

Level 3: Defined. A Level 3 organization has what are called *standard processes*: thoroughly documented project plans which have been shown to be repeatable by experience at Level 2. These standard processes give Level 3 organizations a baseline to improve processes that have already been proven in practice.

Standard processes are more than just procedures: they're procedures that have been thoroughly tested, found to be successful at Level 1, repeatable at Level 2, and then selected for formal adoption by the organization. If you try to jump straight to rigid prescriptions without the iterative testing and repeatability of Level 1 and Level 2, what you get will not be a standard process.

In industry, CMM Level 3 certification is a pretty big deal. It requires a lot of documentation and specialized software. Now CMM purists are not going to like the following story, but they've probably long since stopped reading this chapter anyway. I heard about a small service company that used simple procedures for office tasks —let's say tasks like sending out a blast e-mail.[156] The company had worked so well, over so many iterations, that they were able to print procedures that amounted to standard processes on both sides of a laminated 8½×11 sheet. Despite the simplicity of the case and the lack of high-powered corporate CMM software infrastructure, I would join what I'm sure is a minority of CMM aficionados in the opinion that this was a bona fide Level 3 organization.

The rigidity of Level 3 is helpful when you're building airplanes. It is not helpful when you're doing casework. I'd probably set Level 2 as my highest strategic goal. But some of our organizations may have the kind of highly predictable work that makes it worthwhile to strive for a couple of individual processes to reach Level 3.

---

[156] I have forgotten the details of the story, which in any case are not important. Please let me know if you've heard about the case I'm describing. I'd be happy to fill in more detail on *npgovernance.org*.

Level 4: Managed. A Level 4 organization inserts quantitative metrics into Level 3's standard processes, in order to improve performance according to those metrics. I've often said that until you gain experience, your performance reflects the quality of your metrics, not the other way around. Level 4 is the level at which quantitative metrics can be trusted to measure the quality of organizational or individual performance against a known baseline.

That's because at Level 4, those metrics depend on Level 3's standard processes to ensure they're measuring the same thing each time. And Level 3's standard processes presuppose the repeatable results of Level 2, which in turn require baseline task completion before you can even begin to discuss what the organization should be repeating. Attempts at high-level quantitative metrics that shortcut this logic amount to guesswork.

Quantitative project performance measurement is like stepping on a bathroom scale while riding a roller coaster. As the roller coaster goes wildly up and down, so does the scale's readout. The numbers you see tell you nothing about how much you weigh. But if you ride the roller coaster again and again, making careful notes of the outside forces and the numbers you see on the readout, you might eventually learn how to measure your weight that way.

A more mathematically legitimate use of quantitative metrics below Level 4 is to use them purely motivationally. These are like the metrics in a project scope statement that we discussed in Chapter 8. By all means, if you're running a retreat weekend and want a goal of making $5,000 on it and attracting 100 new mailing-list signups, go for it. If you hit the target, record what you did and try for repeatability over the next several iterations. Just don't imagine that such an arbitrary numerical target distinguishes good organizational performance from bad, or offers a basis for comparison between organizations doing totally different work. Distinctions like those require confidence that you're measuring something objective, and are not reading a scale on a roller coaster. The only way to achieve that kind of confidence is to achieve Level 4. And neither you nor I are anywhere near Level 4.[157]

---

[157] One of my reviewers who works professionally with CMM wishes to remind us that Level 4 may not be out of reach for small organizations. The Level 3 organization I mentioned above, with its single-sheet standard processes, might reach Level 4 just by introducing simple metrics into those processes. However,

Let's not forget, therefore, that all of our metrics, goals, targets, estimates and budgets—yours and mine—are guesses, guesses, guesses, guesses, guesses. They can be helpful, illustrative, well-educated guesses. But let's not be too surprised when a project goes over budget. Process management can help you identify where better decisions might be made next time, but from the perspective of process management, the budget was off, not the project. Process management seeks to make expectations fit reality, not the other way around. Process management seeks to identify successes for repetition, and specific mistakes so as not to repeat them, in planning as much as in execution. Process management is not about tightening the screws or adjudicating blame; it is about learning from experience to estimate and execute projects more accurately.

Level 5: Optimizing. A Level 5 organization uses the metrics of Level 4 to implement continuous improvement of its own processes. Some early CMM thinkers saw Level 5 as a purely theoretical state, but more recently organizations have been receiving Level 5 certifications. Level 5 is far beyond our scope in this book.

Lessons from a CMM Way of Thinking

Why, then, did I lead us on this journey into the rarefied air of a few large contractors for the U.S. military? Because even if we're not going to reach the highest CMM levels, there are many useful lessons even in this cursory exploration. Here are a few of those lessons.

Task accomplishment is just the beginning. If you've mastered all the best practices of chapters 5 through 9, congratulations: your organization has probably reached Level 1. This is a significant accomplishment. Yet my favorite thing about the CMM way of thinking is the humility of recognizing task accomplishment as just an initial threshold on a journey toward improving performance. If you find your organization at Level 0, let's get those tasks done. If

---

this remains very rare, especially among nonprofits. Too many nonprofits underinvest in management improvements and overrely on arbitrary numbers (like "overhead") that aren't mathematically able to mean what they claim to mean. Realistically, I think we're best served realizing that our organizations are nowhere close to Level 4, and therefore lack the basis to use quantitative metrics for purposes other than self-improvement and motivating people.

What do you think: should nonprofits use quantitative metrics less or more than they now do? I'd love to hear from you on *npgovernance.org*.

you are already accomplishing tasks, that's not the end of the story: you can improve your operations further by aiming for some aspects of Level 2 where they are applicable to your work.

Documentation enables all progress. In terms of the knowledge spiral, internalization and socialization already happen naturally in the workplace. They might not be as organized as they could be, but co-workers communicate, learn from, and train each other all the time. Organizations, however, don't learn until the information they need to know resides outside people's heads and inside documents. The knowledge spiral tends to bottleneck at externalization (writing) and combination (reading and fitting documents with experience). Knowledge is waiting to be written down. If it is not written down, it is lost. Could there be a more Jewish idea?

There is an ideal cost-benefit to process management. More process management is not always better process management. Process management overarches all of the other tactical practices in this book, with its extremely high-level tools and ways of thinking. These tools are so big and so heavy that they are not appropriate for every organization. For most nonprofits, partial achievement of Level 2 is probably a good long-term strategic goal. A board might legitimately say, "We're happy with our process management as it is. We're going to continue as we are, and not invest in greater capability maturity." But when would I advise a board to say that?

The key is to decide intentionally. You have enough process management when you're gaining organizational knowledge from each project (not just tacit knowledge inside somebody's head), when you're satisfied with how well your work is going, when your organization accomplishes tasks independently of individual heroes, and documents its work to the maximum feasible extent, and when you know your processes well enough to decide when you're happy with your management of them.

Higher-level activities are baseless until an organization reaches their level. Some organizations work well with written procedures. As I said above, procedures are a great way to retain and document organizational knowledge. Just don't get locked into them as the only way to do something: that defeats the purpose of organizational learning. Treat them instead as working drafts. In any organization making use of this book, procedures must be subject to change based on experience and after-action review. That's because you and I are nowhere near the level of capability maturity (Level 3) prerequisite for us to benefit from rigid, formally fixed procedures.

By the same token, high-level quantitative metrics make sense in Level 4, and do not make sense otherwise. Quantitative metrics are often imposed on nonprofits by funders who want to be sure their money is being wisely used, or by agencies that attempt quantitative ratings of charities. But instead of using numbers that compare apples and oranges at best, and are gibberish at worst, it would be wiser to assess the extent to which organizations are doing the best practices that indicate and support organizational capacity, such as those in this book—from strategic vision to healthy board-management relationships, to skillfully managing people, to well-planned projects, to financial security, to transparency and ethics.

Unfortunately, some have become enamored of quantitative "metrics" that are meaningless because they lack the mathematical rigor and relationship to reality that genuine performance metrics presuppose. Worse, some want to talk about entirely fictitious metrics like "administrative overhead." *Overhead* in a for-profit business means activities not directly tied to profit: for example, keeping the lights on in a factory. But nonprofits are not designed to make profit. It is incorrect to call a receptionist overhead, because the concept of overhead does not mean anything in nonprofits.

Compounding that mistake is the insidious misconception that "overhead" is inefficiency. A receptionist might be less glamorous than a rescue worker, but the receptionist is saving the children, too. To call the receptionist "overhead" is a mistake; to say they don't save the children is a calumny. Too often, misguided obsessions with "overhead" cause organizations to warp themselves into mirror images of unreality, devalue the contributions made by nonprofessional staff, and eclipse what should have been everyone's focus all along: good governance and good management.

Measuring charities' financial efficiency is a worthy goal, as is—I think more importantly—weeding out graft. But nonprofit fixed and indirect costs are not, and do not particularly indicate, inefficiency. If one-tenth the effort that now goes into fudging numerical "overhead" metrics were instead put to helping charities learn best practices like those in this book, resulting in improved capacity, a lot more could be accomplished for donors' money.

I'm all for numbers. But I do not like made-up numbers. Nonsense numbers are worse than no numbers, because nonsense numbers actively mislead. Mathematical rigor requires not that we use as much precision as possible, but that numerical precision be limited to what the situation justifies. Unjustified precision is a statistical fib. And claims to measure percentage operational efficiency seem like unjustified precision par excellence to me. I am not about to believe it is possible to distinguish 90% from 91% efficiency in any operating organization. If indeed not, then such numbers ironically cause a great deal of inefficiency and waste. I don't think we ought to be dealing in them.

Process management provides its own assessment tools. How would I assess organizations without the baseless numbers I just criticized? I like qualitative metrics. Remember what I said about risk assessment in Chapter 8, that we use "high," "medium" and "low" to characterize risk likelihood and severity, because finer-grained descriptions are baseless? I suggest the same principle for organizational performance metrics. Instead of asking about an organization's percentage efficiency, a meaningless numerical castle in the air, try describing the organization's efficiency qualitatively.

I've never been enthusiastic about "efficiency" as the gold standard of nonprofit quality assessment, but grantmakers need some way of knowing how far their grants go. The problem is, they certainly delude themselves if they imagine that a $10,000 grant to an organization reporting 7% overhead saves 93 children, while the same grant to an organization reporting 15% overhead saves only 85 children. A lesson for the metrics community is to focus more on qualitative metrics that offer valid, useful information about organizations, and to waste no more of anyone's time on concocted numbers that do not successfully measure anything.

Maybe you want to report whether an organization is "as efficient as reasonably possible," "efficient in most areas," "losing efficiency due to project-management problems," "losing efficiency due to excessive executive compensation and patronage," "beset by unresolved conflicts of interest," "chronically mismanaged," or "unfit to continue." Maybe you want a different set of categories. The challenge is that you and I don't know how or what to assess until we *combine* real-world experience with a specific sense of what we want to measure. If you don't know where to start, don't make up arbitrary numbers. Start with a small list of basic categories—"good," "okay" and "bad" will do as a seed—and get the knowledge spiral going, adding granularity based on the experience you gain.

Chapter 11
COMMUNICATIONS AND ENABLING TECHNOLOGY

11.1 SHIUR

A voice calls: Clear the path of God in the wilderness; make a straight highway for our God in the desert. Every valley shall be exalted, and every hill and mountain made low; the rough places will be made plain, and the crooked places will be made straight.

Isaiah 40:3–4[158]

Rabbi Mira Raz of Yafo, Israel, has an extraordinary teaching connecting this text to the progress of technology. She teaches that the rapid acceleration of technology fulfills the words of Isaiah, making a way through impassable terrain, literally and figuratively, bringing people together where otherwise they would have remained apart.

Isaiah's message is disruptive: "clear a path," he says, "make a straight highway!" Isaiah means for us to change our environment, to engineer solutions to our problems. Facing exile, Isaiah's

[158] Translation for Isaiah 40:3 original; translation for Isaiah 40:4 from Martin Luther King, Jr., speech to the 1963 March on Washington for Jobs and Freedom. Many translators, including the JPS, begin with "Hark!" or similar here, for the Hebrew word *kol*, which otherwise means "a voice." There is much evidence that this word is used as an exclamation in biblical Hebrew, and I do not doubt that the "Hark!" translation is technically more correct than mine. For example, see Song of Songs 5:2, where "Hark! My beloved knocketh" (JPS) makes a lot more sense than "The voice of my beloved is knocking" when the same Hebrew word *kol* appears. However, in Isaiah 40:3 the prophet is in the middle of a speech. Much as *kol* may signify an exclamation, it does mean voice, and there is in fact a voice speaking at the time. For clarity and fluidity, I went with "A voice calls" rather than a modernized version of the JPS's "Hark! one calleth," even given the linguistic evidence in favor of "Hark!" here.

audience needed ways to preserve their identity while apart from each other and from home. Today, as we communicate across much greater distances, we face similar challenges.

Through the generations this text has been read with a social-justice message. I borrowed the translation of Isaiah 40:4 from the Rev. Dr. Martin Luther King, Jr., who used it in his "I Have a Dream" speech to evoke the coming rectification of social inequality, abandonment of sinful social practices, and embrace of the radical equality of people before a God who the Bible says "is coming."[159]

Rabbi Jonathan Sacks, the former Chief Rabbi of the United Hebrew Congregations of the British Commonwealth, finds a similar connection between technology and social justice in his recent essay "On Not Obeying Immoral Orders," a *d'var Torah* (weekly Torah commentary) on the Torah portion *Shemot* (Exodus 1:1 – 6:1).[160] In that essay, Rabbi Sacks recounts the refusal of midwives Shifra and Puah to obey Pharaoh's orders to kill every newborn Jewish boy, Heaven forbid (Ex. 1:16–17). Rabbi Sacks traces the idea of refusal to obey immoral orders through the ages. Frequently, it turns out, authoritarians have felt threatened by the distribution of the Bible, and Rabbi Sacks shows how human rights evolved with the printing press. For Rabbi Sacks, the printing press—and I think it's safe to say, judging by his own skillful use of it, the Internet—is a highway through the wilderness, shining a light on immoral regimes and giving people strength to resist and replace them.

Christian pastor Keith Anderson has a wonderful new book, *The Digital Cathedral*, which he intends "to evoke an expansive and holistic understanding of church—one that extends ministry into both digital and local gathering spaces, recognizes the sacred in everyday life, and embodies a networked, relational, and incarnational approach to ministry leadership for a digital age."[161] Much Jewish debate about the role of technology presupposes that technology is secular and Jewish spaces are holy, proceeding then to ask to what extent technology should be permitted in Jewish spaces. We do need to consider our Shabbat practices, but other than that, Anderson invites us to reconsider the presuppositions underlying those debates. He retells the history of Christian cathedrals as

---

[159] Psalm 96:13, Psalm 98:9.
[160] Sacks (2015).
[161] K. Anderson (2015), p. 5.

spaces of the people, always open, where people came to visit, pray and work, and which were the center of communities where people's lives were lived. In conceptualizing a "digital cathedral," Anderson imagines a way of living in community not just one hour a week but every hour of the week, meeting people where they are, celebrating and embracing the gratitude and the grit of their lives.

Liberal Jewish audiences may have even more to gain from Anderson's thinking than Christian congregations, because as a minority religion physical distance is always a challenge for us. We may not live in the same neighborhood or even in the same city as our synagogue. We would do well to ask how technology can help "clear a path" to connect people separated by miles or by continents.

To be sure, technology gives rise to new and serious risks. Our planet is at risk from mismanagement of technology; our spiritual well-being is at risk from addiction to it. Technology has made us so powerful that our human decisions now determine whether we will survive on this earth (and whether we deserve to). That being the case, it is no exaggeration to say that we live in the end times, insofar as our technologically empowered selves are now able to determine whether we continue or extinguish the line of Adam.

We cannot run from technology. We have no other choice but to harness it for social justice, for the remediation of wrong, and for the limitation of our demands on natural systems that give us life and that we cannot recreate. We must identify and resist its misuse. Rabbi Raz reminds us that the name *Eden* comes from the Hebrew for gentleness, *edna*. We cannot go back to the garden of gentleness, to our former innocence. We must create our own gentleness in the world, a gentleness held and guarded by the technological power we have—but gently, gently, not to lose its gentleness in the guarding.

We live in the age of technology. We can't avoid it, we must not fear it, for it is before us to learn and use. Our Jewish responsibility is to do good with it. Technology empowers us, and every decent person finds power frightening.

We might start where Isaiah started: creating connections between people, across barriers of distance, time, language and opinion. With technology we are capable of harm, but we can also hear the voices of Isaiah and our ancestors guiding us toward a new world of gentleness. The whole world and future generations can also finally hear our voices. We can make communications and enabling technology into our highway through the wilderness, our voice against injustice, our strong tool to use gently. It is our job now—*aleinu*, it is on us—not just to understand contemporary technology but to excel at its use.

11.2 COMMUNICATIONS

A treatment of nonprofit communication strategies would require a large book in itself. This essay is intended as a very brief introduction to a few selected concepts that especially need discussion. I've compiled many suggestions for further reading on *npgovernance.org*.

Frowny Faces and Smiley Faces

There are two types of messaging, whether you're recruiting volunteers, raising money, or advertising your organization. I call them *smiley-face messaging* and *frowny-face messaging.*

People like to be in places where they feel good. Smiley-face messaging attracts people. Frowny-face messaging, on the other hand—"help us, we're understaffed and overwhelmed, and if you don't donate right now, all will be lost!"—is a bona fide part of Jewish tradition. It sometimes works in the short term, but it undermines your supporters' and employees' morale by appealing to a negative organizational self-image. I recommend smiley-face messaging, which builds morale by presenting your organization as a positive, successful, pleasant place to be. That in turn lays the groundwork for stable growth.

To the observation that frowny-face messaging works, I'll offer two counterarguments. First, you often see frowny-face messaging (alarm! alert! help!) in national fundraising or minor volunteer drives where you are asked to do something specific that doesn't take long: to sign a petition, make a donation, etc. And you might just do it while it has your attention, before emotional fatigue from all those alarms sets in. But our organizations need to build lasting structures of people based on friendship and caring, and endless alarm bells aren't the right background music for that. Moreover, to the point of the past four chapters of this book, we want to create structures based on a positive self-image of practical, principled, competent management and visionary, ethical governance. Smiley-face messaging shows the world a positive self-image of our values.

Second, speaking of emotional fatigue, I think the era of urgent frowny-face appeals is on its way out. Our culture is saturated with advertising. When not one but a thousand organizations all need your urgent help immediately, human beings naturally disengage from all that clamor. Relatedly, the alarms have exceeded their shelf life: I'd like to see a demographic study of the performance of those red-alert messages, but it seems to me that after several decades of nonstop alerts, all such messages begin to sound like crying wolf, regardless of whether (or not) a given organization really is in peril. Most of all, with the evolution of nonprofit marketing strategy over the past few decades, there are better messaging options available now, which compete against those same-old, same-old urgent alerts.

People do what they feel wonderful about doing. They give to organizations they see as successful and effective. Success breeds success. Organizations across the nonprofit scene are finding success from getting donors, volunteers, anyone to "join" them, which makes supporters feel like they are part of a success. "Laugh, and the world laughs with you; weep, and you weep alone."[162]

Smiley-face messaging is always available. A good exercise would be to find examples of frowny-face messaging in the nonprofit sector and see if you can reframe them into smiley-face messaging.

Brand and Marketing

If the nonprofit community were a town in the Wild West, the words "brand" and "marketing" would have been run out of town long ago. I understand why these words are viewed suspiciously, fraught as they are with images of for-profit excess and hucksterism. But they've been framed. As we continue to smoke out the real culprits —for-profit excess and hucksterism—we need to rehabilitate brand and marketing. Not only are they not the real culprits, but we now need them back at work on our posse.

Your *brand* is the sum total of everything you want people to think and feel about your organization. It involves a lot of the strategic-identity questions in Chapter 2. It includes your purpose

---

[162] Ella Wheeler Wilcox's short, wise 1883 poem "Solitude" is no longer as frequently quoted as its opening line, but it's well worth reading in its brief entirety. A link can be found on *npgovernance.org*.

and mission: what kind of an organization are you, and what are you here to do? It touches on questions of value proposition, which in nonprofit work should not mean what the donor gets in exchange for a donation, but rather how your organization improves the world on a daily basis, which is to say, why a donor should invest. It may include your members and their activities. It involves high-level decisions about your presentation, including visual decisions like logos, color schemes, fonts, as well as the presentation of your physical plant if applicable, and intangibles like the member or client experience, or interacting with your staff. All that is unique about your mission, all that is special about your community, all that is intentional in your self-presentation, is part of your brand.

The point of having a brand is to stick to consistent ways of presenting, in order to reinforce the messages you intend to communicate about who you are and why people ought to be interested in your organization. In politics, we talk about staying "on message," which is an advocacy spin on the same idea. What is your message, and how can you ensure that you're "on" it?

If you're a synagogue, your message might have to do with warm community, adherence to tradition, openness and inclusivity, etc. If you're an advocacy nonprofit, your message might relate to your top project this year, or your central issue. If you're a service nonprofit, your message might be about the people you're helping, or about a new initiative. Keep "on message" long enough for that message to sink in with the public; that's a judgment to be made in individual cases. Make your message simple, understandable, memorable and intentional, reflecting what you want people to think about you.

Management gurus frequently tout the *elevator pitch*: if you're in an elevator with a wealthy donor who's just asked what you do, what would you say about your organization before the door opens? It's a good exercise in framing your message, and it's no coincidence that it's often used as an impromptu speaking exercise.

Direct all communications to serve your overarching message. For example, if your message is welcoming people, see what happens when you ask how every e-mail, every phone call, every print piece and every public statement furthers the message of welcoming people. How does an action alert welcome people? How does a solicitation welcome people? How does answering the phone welcome people? How do synagogue ushers welcome people? That's what it means to be "on message."

Is it possible to have more than one message at a time? I say no. You don't have enough of your audience's attention to communicate anything that complex. Try aiming higher. Go back to your strategy and be reminded of what you're here to do. Create a message at a high enough level that all of your communications can serve it.

All of this is part of the discipline of *marketing*. Even a cursory introduction to marketing would fill a textbook, nor do I know enough to write that book. But I can speak in favor of marketing not being a bad word. Marketing means connecting what you offer to the people you offer it to. That's as valid a concept in nonprofits as it is in business. It's more complex in nonprofits, because nonprofits need to attract two potentially overlapping groups of people: those who benefit from the organization's work, and those who donate, volunteer, or otherwise support the organization and its work.

So far we've spoken about marketing in terms of getting your message out, but it's just as important to identify the people you want to reach as it is to know what you want to say to them. In fact, the best messages are products of constant interplay, feedback, and testing between the organization, its clients, and its supporters. Contemporary technology makes that interplay cheaper and easier.

New Opportunities from New Technologies

Since the 1990s, new technologies have enjoyed unprecedented acceptance in society. With this acceptance came applications to fundraising and communications. Galas, phone-a-thons and print newsletters remain useful, but new options are now available too.

Websites. Your website is your home on the Internet, a place to offer resources and accept incoming requests for contact. A key online strategy is to use other technologies to send viewers to your website. In all of the technologies considered below, a goal of any initiative is to attract "clickthroughs": people who click a link through to your website. It is possible to measure clickthrough rates as a quantitative metric of how those initiatives perform.

I'm not a gambler, but I once went to a casino to eat at the cheap buffet. Casinos are carpeted with very intentional carpet patterns, designed to get you lost in the casino, increasing the time you spend there. Casinos have a lot of money to spend on research like this. In any case, the same principle applies to websites. You certainly want to make it easy for people to find the information they want. But you also want to put options on their screen that they find interesting, so that they click through and remain on your website. The more time they spend on your website, the more likely they are to donate, because your donation button appears on every page. (Doesn't it?)

I've tried to make *npgovernance.org* a model of best practices. I say that with some trepidation because it is will always be growing. You and I may share some opportunities and limitations with our websites. On *npgovernance.org*, you can comment on any post, ask questions, and start a conversation going. We can talk not just about the content, but also about why I put it there, and if you like, whether I wouldn't be better advised to do it some other way. I look forward to learning and sharing website successes and challenges with you.

Websites and e-mail pieces should have a donation button on every screen. Many donation buttons seem to be placed toward the upper right, because viewers' eyes seem to be drawn there. (Look at some websites you like and see if they follow this pattern.) With donations and anything else you want viewers to do, it's essential to minimize the number of clicks required for them to do it.

E-Mail. E-mail allows you great creativity in your presentation, compared to print. E-mail shares none of the expense and size limits of print, and it is easy to include links to more information. Many new e-mail editors try to make their pieces look as much as possible like a good print piece, but e-mail is its own powerful medium.

E-mail designs should be a notch calmer than print pieces. In print, you need something eye-catching so the piece stands out. But in e-mail, we're finding that simple, clean lines without too many images perform best. E-mails need to look good on mobile devices, too, with their small screens. In choosing a design, you might have a *charrette* (design workshop) by having people choose 3 e-mail pieces they like, and 3 from highly successful organizations (these may or may not be the same). That should provide food for thought.

The purpose of an e-mail is to capture the viewer's attention and get them to click through. That might mean donating, or clicking any of the links you may put in your e-mail. Blast e-mail programs allow you to measure these clickthroughs. Don't include too many links lest you overwhelm the viewer; just focus them on where you want them to go. For example, on the *OrganicTorah.org* e-mail list, our goal is to get readers to read the blog posts on our website. So we place several links to our website in each of our e-mails.

Subject lines are your first impression. Using nothing but the subject line, viewers decide whether to open your e-mail within a few seconds. Writing good subject lines is both a skill and a matter of getting to know your audience. Test different ideas and see how they perform. Don't do practices just because you see others doing them. Trends change so rapidly that you will be behind if you attempt to follow them. Just be yourself.

I'm going to call out my mother as an example of great subject lines. She has a blog called The Did Ya Notice?™ Project ("noticing is mindfulness with a smile"). She started it a few years ago without any experience blogging, and she writes striking subject lines that get great open rates (I've seen her stats). Visit *DidYaNotice.com* to see what I mean.

E-mail lists are for announcements, gathering viewers to your website, and fundraising. There is an emerging field of research on blast e-mail fundraising. My general recommendations are to have a donation button on every blast e-mail, but just to let it be there without pushing too hard. Then, send out periodic fundraising appeals, starting with about a 1:4 ratio of appeal e-mails to non-appeal e-mails. You can certainly, and I would, have non-appeal content within an appeal e-mail. Remind me about it when your organization has me in to speak, and I'll tell you a story about a much more aggressive high-profile e-mail fundraising campaign that, to my surprise, worked. I still recommend starting with the 1:4 ratio.

Facebook and Twitter. People seem to consider Facebook and Twitter as a unit. We are guilty of the same offense here. They are very different technologies, but they share certain similarities that motivate their consideration together. Once you get the hang of them, these technologies are not terribly difficult. Both are harder to set up than to maintain. Both, however, really should be regularly maintained by staff or by a social-media vendor in order to be most useful. That mainly means making sure you're posting consistently.

Some organizations thrive on lively comment threads, while others ignore their social-media comments. It depends what you're up to. If you deal with current events, expect that comment threads may turn ugly. Unfortunately, the ease and anonymity of online commenting can attract incivility. On websites and especially on Facebook, you may need to *moderate* (approve) comments. This can add a lot of work, but it may be necessary for your organization.

The burden of maintenance is certainly worth it in organizations whose members or supporters display at least an average level of technology utilization. However, that burden is real. Because these accounts are easy for trained staff to maintain, small organizations may wish to pool resources and contract with a person who could split their time. Better yet, if umbrella groups hired a local staff person or two, they might be able to provide Facebook and Twitter maintenance for Jewish organizations in a whole metropolitan area.

Twitter works by attracting "followers" who read short, 140-character posts, or *tweets*. Your Twitter presence will get lost if you are not posting frequently. I recommend compiling a large list of pithy quotations, "today in history" factoids and wise teachings, and tweeting these anywhere from 2–3 times a week to 2–3 times a day. Software can handle this automatically. Consistently sending out these interesting or heartwarming tweets tends to get followers on Twitter. Then, when the organization has an announcement to make, tweeting it will reach all those followers. It may even bring new people from the ether into the door of your next event.

Compiling such a list would be a good project for an intern, and it could serve many organizations at once. It would be easy to make sure that not everyone is tweeting the same thing on the same day.

Facebook allows you to keep in touch with people easily. Go ahead and create a "page" or "group" on Facebook if you have not already done so, and post events and announcements periodically to it. Facebook groups can be closed (members-only) or open to the public; you can have both. Facebook enables members to share content with friends in the course of their normal social interaction. Therefore, the more sermons, thoughts of the day, etc., you post to Facebook, the more people will share it. Nevertheless, Facebook can get overwhelmed with the sheer volume of quotable quotes that are par for the course on Twitter, so I would keep Facebook posts to announcements, articles in the newsletter, sermons, etc.

New Technology Adoption. Jewish organizations' offices may not be the first things that come to mind when most people think of technology utilization. But there's no reason why not. Our *shiur* infuses with spiritual urgency what might otherwise be just a matter of sensible consulting advice. Because technology evaluation and adoption is not a core competency of most Jewish organizations, I wonder if umbrella organizations or third-party initiatives might centralize these processes with pooled resources, providing the results of their investigations, recommendations and enabling technologies to local Jewish organizations at economies of scale.

11.3 TECHNOLOGY MANAGEMENT

My entrepreneur friend Benjamin Rahn co-founded ActBlue.com, a major social-network fundraising site for U.S. politics. He's given talks around the country about the way we manage technology in organizations. Although his example referred to political campaign organizations, his message applies directly to our organizations.

Imagine a house without electricity—let's say, a house from the eighteenth century. Then, imagine a shed on the side of the house, and in that shed, imagine placing everything that could possibly have anything to do with electricity: the toaster-oven, the hot-water heater, headphones, the fridge, three laptops, eight jump drives, two humidifiers, everybody's cell phone, the washing machine and dryer, a whole lot of light bulbs and a whole lot of wires. Nobody builds a house that way. So why do we manage technology that way?

Sometimes fear of technology causes us to isolate it, putting high-tech tasks aside for assignment to a particular individual (a "tech person") or volunteer group (a "tech committee"). This model can work in the short term. But in the twenty-first century, job descriptions ought to be determined by organizational function, with enabling technology integrated into each job. In a climate of support and mutual learning, we can invest in skill building to enable our professionals and volunteers to do their jobs well.

We don't keep an electrician in the technology shed to be on call every time we turn on a light. Most staffers don't need to be able to build a computer, but most of us now need to be able to use one.

I don't want to give short shrift to the challenge. Some of our organizations may be ready to implement the recommendations in this section now, some already may have done so. For others, it will be a long-term strategic goal. That's okay—as long as it remains the goal for every worker to be able to use the technology they need to work. Achieving that goal will save a lot of trouble and expense.

Remember "desktop publishing"? Back in the mid-1980s, when we had just graduated from typewriters to Wangs to that 9-pin dot-matrix font now reserved for receipts, it was a big deal to be able to produce a passable magazine or brochure on the desktop. People would say things like, "My friend Dave is really into desktop publishing." It was cutting-edge, cool, transformative, reserved for early adopters with new computers with huge 20-megabyte hard disks (that's thousands of times less space than today's USB thumb drives). It was hard to imagine that in 20 years everyone would be expected to do their own "desktop publishing" at work. But computers improved, software got easier to use, and we evolved.

Another reason for skepticism about having a "tech person" who does tech tasks stems from the disparate nature of jobs that happen to use technology. For example, the person you want running your website is a dynamic, extroverted communicator, someone who is bubbly and creative, loves to get people involved, and can take direction and work within design preferences and messaging priorities set by others. That may not be the first person you meet who happens to know what HTML and CSS are.

On the other hand, to manage your database you want someone who is organized and methodical, quantitative, detail-oriented, and cautious about making changes that could create serious problems. You want someone who can patiently explain complex issues to supervisors while also being able to take direction.

Although websites and databases both require comfort with computers, there are few pairs of jobs less suited to being done by the same person. You're best advised to place your website in the care of a communications person, and your database with a specific database role. In a pinch, if you can't afford a database professional, managing a small database has more in common with bookkeeping than with website management.

Nor is technology skill level the most important consideration for a technology hire. This may be counterintuitive, but when identifying people for tech roles, I focus much more on personality than on particular technical skills. Skills can be learned; personality cannot. Ideally, of course, a candidate would offer both. But I'd much rather take a chance on a demonstrated good learner who's new to a particular skill than someone with solid skills but the wrong personality for the role.

I recommend giving even less weight to prior experience using your particular software, be it database software, website, blast e-mail, or any other software you use. Nonprofit office database products all do pretty much the same thing; the same is true of website, e-mail, word processing, and other functions. Someone who understands databases can figure out the menus on a database product that's new to them, while someone whose understanding is limited to memorizing the menu maze on a particular product will falter in an unexpected or troubleshooting situation.

For these reasons, I counsel against the "tech person" model. Instead, look for people who fit the roles you need them for. Plan to train all staff to use the technology their responsibilities require.

Every rule has exceptions. Here's what I'd recommend if you really feel you need the specific role of a "tech person."

If your organization is so small that the same person must perform technology functions as disparate as the website and the database, awareness of those differences and intentional choices of hire and work priorities would be essential to managing that person. I would try to divide the workplace roles in a different way.

Could the same person who formats the newsletter (perhaps an office manager?) be trained to operate the website? Contemporary website platforms have become a lot easier to use. Could an office manager perform small or routine tasks (data entry, minor database corrections like changes of address, minor website updates like posting a new article), allowing you to compile more demanding tasks into projects and hire a vendor as needed? Could we pool resources under local umbrella organizations to offer those more complicated tech services that are beyond the reach of small-office staff, at cost-effective rates?

Many large organizations need a director of technology, or chief technology officer (CTO), but that is an entirely different job from the "tech person" we're talking about. A director of technology is an executive focused on large technology and data decisions to advance the organization's strategy, not someone to edit the website, clean out the database, and print mailing labels. If you don't have staff engineers or proprietary big data, you don't need a CTO.

Another phenomenon is that of the *technology committee*, a group of volunteers—often, the organization's tech buffs—who come together to handle technology tasks or to make decisions. I advise boards to think twice before commissioning tech committees. If tech buffs want to volunteer, that's great, but is "technology" really the right circle to draw around a governance committee's oversight responsibility? If the tech committee is mainly handling office-type tasks, would it perhaps be more appropriate for those very helpful tech buffs to volunteer in the office, directed by staff?

Technology committees develop because computer utilization requires certain skills that are scarce in the organization, so it becomes tempting to recruit volunteers. But in addition to the conceptual problems with the "tech person" role discussed above, tech committees tend to create structural hurdles to getting tasks done, because other committee and staff needs become inbox work for that group of volunteers. When your Social Action Committee has to go through your Technology Committee to post something on the website, that tends to create unnecessary friction and delay. I've seen tech committees start out as a group of helpful volunteers and end up as a control and approval bottleneck, even though nobody intended it that way at first. Tech committees can also lead to and attract "Uncle Moe" situations (see below).

For these reasons, I recommend against tech committees in most cases. Instead, let each committee use shared technology resources as they need to and as shared rules allow. That's exactly the same advice I offer for staff. "Technology" is not a job; it's part of all of our jobs. The technology wiring runs through every room of the house. All of us need to be trained and empowered to use the technology we need to do our jobs.

If your organization is large enough to need a CTO, it *might* make sense to have a "tech committee" assist the board in providing oversight and strategic advice to that executive. If not, I would try to get enthusiastic tech-savvy volunteers involved in other ways.

Beware of Uncle Moe

Someone on the board has an Uncle Moe. Or, Uncle Moe is on the board. Or, Uncle Moe has started a tech company by himself and is a member of the organization or is friends with members. Uncle Moe's very own technology has all the best features you need. Often, Uncle Moe's features are written specifically for your organization, thereby preventing anyone other than Uncle Moe from ever supporting or updating them.

Eventually, the relationship sours. Uncle Moe's preferences, rather than the organization's corporate preferences, become the issue in decisions about the database or website. Uncle Moe may exert an undue amount of control over access to data. After a while, Uncle Moe loses interest, Uncle Moe's company goes out of business, or Uncle Moe is too busy to serve the organization's growing needs. Because Uncle Moe is a volunteer, or because of Uncle Moe's social connections to the organization, the organization has no leverage over him and no enforceable contract.

Danger. Be on the lookout for Uncle Moe. Do not do business with Uncle Moe.

Look, I have a lot of sympathy for Uncle Moe. I've been an Uncle Moe myself: I'm thinking of at least five separate occasions in my own life. Did I ever want that business from the nonprofits I loved and cared about! I offered them a better database or website, better tailored to their needs, which I knew so well because I was already so involved with them. It felt so right. It was not right. Three out of five organizations were right not to hire me. One was wrong to hire me, for the same reason. (One was an exception which I still should have extricated myself from sooner.) It can be painful to say no to Uncle Moe, but it's going to be a lot more painful to sit down with Uncle Moe in a couple years, a day late and a dollar short, to say the relationship isn't working.

Sure, there are exceptions. With one-time tasks Uncle Moe is harmless, often indeed helpful. By all means, let Uncle Moe fix the plumbing in the sink, or cull former members out of the database. Just make sure Uncle Moe is safely extricated from all control over the organization's assets once the task is done. Uncle Moe can also create useful things that are not mission-critical (i.e. you'd be okay if Uncle Moe disappeared midtask)—as long as someone else can take over when Uncle Moe's involvement ends. And by all means, go ahead and hire qualified men named Moe whose siblings have kids.

There are corporate versions of Uncle Moe, without the personal connection to your organization. A vendor who touts their support of your mission but is weak on fundamentals, or someone who's been doing this forever but has not really grown the business in proportion to that longevity could be (but is not necessarily) an Uncle Moe. If the sales pitch is partly emotional and the company doesn't seem very stable, that's a red flag for Uncle Moe.

The specific problem with Uncle Moe is that he is in a conflict of interest. Uncle Moe's volunteer and/or social relationship to the organization's members or leaders is in conflict with his business role. He can't be managed because his volunteer or donated service and/or his ties of emotion, friendship or membership make it impossible to exercise legitimate authority over him. Uncle Moe relationships are hunky-dory until the first time the organization's preferences differ from Uncle Moe's preferences. Then, suddenly, the organization finds itself out of control in the relationship.

This isn't a diatribe against small businesses. Small businesses may provide superior service, and everyone has to have a first client. The problem with Uncle Moe is the conflict of interest that makes it impossible to manage him, and creates incentives to ignore red flags or weak fundamentals that would otherwise disqualify him. Here are some indicators when it's perfectly fine to hire a vendor:

If contractual mechanisms exist to manage them. Disclosure, mitigation and arm's-length dealing, as discussed in Chapter 3, could help if Uncle Moe is uncomfortably close to the organization. A good contract can go a long way, as long as leaders have the stomach to enforce the contract. If you want to give someone a chance who you're worried might be an Uncle Moe, and you have confidence in your ability to manage and if necessary close the relationship, it might be okay. However, this does not cover volunteers. Never use volunteers for irreplaceable, critical technical work.

If the task is relatively short-term or the work could be done by others, you have less to worry about. The danger with Uncle Moe is getting into situations you can't get out of. Using open technology can greatly mitigate the risk. For example, it might be okay for even a full-fledged Uncle Moe to design a website in WordPress or Wix. When the project is over, a staff member could maintain the site.

Uncle Moe is a siren song: a tantalizing offer of free or reduced-cost service at mysterious technical tasks that need doing—but once you get involved with Uncle Moe it becomes very difficult to leave his island. It's okay to proceed when there's a clear end to the task and the involvement, when a contract gives you confidence you can handle the dangers, or when a borderline case turns out not actually to be an Uncle Moe. Otherwise, just say no to Uncle Moe.

Managing Technical Staff

Again, in lieu of a full treatment of managing technology, which would take a whole book, here are just a few thoughts most likely to help those who manage technology in Jewish nonprofits. You don't have to understand the technology to manage it. But it's important to understand something about how technical people work.

The more technical the job—the more it requires specialized skills like programming or databases—the more likely it is that your staff member will need to work with a minimum of interruptions. Technical staff are always in the middle of complex tasks demanding a high degree of mental focus, so even brief interruptions can cause them to lose their place and set their productivity significantly back. Try to insulate technical staff by placing them in a back office, and don't make them cover the phones. Whenever possible, schedule meetings with them in advance, and give them maximum control over their workday.

Technical staff and vendors need precise, written definitions of what to accomplish. They may not have the strategic intuition to make a work product out of your general sense of what you'd like. Be as precise as possible, and take the initiative to ask your technical staff or vendor if they understand what you're requesting. Don't assume that your terminology means what you expect it to mean to them, nor that you understand the terminology they use.

Failure to communicate clearly in advance leads to the rejection-rework cycle (see Chapter 7), and is a classic failure mode in technology management. This is especially damaging when you pay a vendor by the hour. There's no panacea to avoid it, but if you take care to check your staff's or vendor's understanding of your requests and they do the same, you'll be as protected as possible.

A good database administrator, social-media professional, or website and blast e-mail editor will make everything look easy to their bosses. Don't be fooled. If you don't know what a staff member is doing, it can be hard to praise them for their skill, but your efforts at it will be appreciated. My former boss Paul Berendt would come into my office a few times a year and say, "Jeremy, I don't understand what you're doing back here, but keep it up." Paul is a political guy: he didn't understand my technology but he understood people's feelings, and his simple gesture is worth taking a cue from.

By the same token, don't take technical work for granted just because the worker makes it look easy. It's not easy. Tech workers spend their day putting all their mental energy into making magic, to the exacting specifications of people who don't know how to do the magic themselves. You'll do wonders managing tech workers if you take a moment for wonder at the magic they do. If you don't know how something works but you use it every day, take a moment just to say, "wow." The magician will know you appreciate them.

On the other hand, it can be challenging to offer constructive criticism for a staffer doing work you yourself cannot do. Most tech workers I know are familiar with this problem and are willing to take valid critical feedback from managers. Don't ask them to work faster and harder while not understanding their tasks. On the other hand, done well, feedback can be a chance for the worker to explain what they do while receiving guidance about that ongoing work.

If you are managing work in a field you don't understand, you can succeed brilliantly with two principles: vision and listening. A visionary executive knows that vision is strategic, and separates her vision from the need to give out orders. Share your vision with your tech staff and talk through what you want to accomplish. Dream big: don't be afraid to ask for what you imagine. You may not know what is easy and what is hard, so let your tech staff give you ideas.

That brings us to listening. It isn't easy to manage work you don't know how to do. Always be listening. Let your staff inform you of the facts they're dealing with. Most of the tech workers I know would be happy to explain the basics of their work to a manager over lunch. Admit that you don't know how to do their job (don't worry, they already know that!) and ask them what they'd like you to know about their work. That goes far beyond creating a positive management relationship, because I find that listening and vision make a positive loop. The most common error I've seen in technology management is not knowing what is possible. Your tech staff may open your eyes to new visionary possibilities.

11.4 DATA MANAGEMENT

Database utilization is to the first half of the twenty-first century what word processing was to the second half of the twentieth: a new technology that quickly became a basic daily need for all office personnel. In 2016, database utilization is still treated as a specialized skill—as had been the case with "desktop publishing"—because we're making a bigger deal out of it then it needs to be. Databases may seem unfamiliar at first, but they make common tasks much easier. I've included this section in my book, at the cost of having to cut words elsewhere, because I strongly believe that database literacy is the single best, most cost-effective investment in operational skills development—for executives, policymaking leaders, staff and volunteers alike—to increase our organizations' capacity. In today's world, we are best equipped to do the work of our organizations, to ask the right questions on a board, and to make the decisions that advance our organizations, when we know what databases do.

What Databases Do

I've got an ice-cream cone. It's a scoop of chocolate ice cream, in a sugar cone, topped with fudge and rainbow sprinkles. My friend has another ice-cream cone, and hers is vanilla, in a cake cone, topped with butterscotch and chocolate sprinkles. My other friend has yet a third ice-cream cone, and his is strawberry, in a waffle cone, topped with whipped cream and no sprinkles.

Notice a pattern? Instead of a paragraph of text, I can represent all that information in a structured way, like this:

ID	Owner	Flavor	Cone Type	Gooey Topping	Sprinkly Topping
1	Jeremy	Chocolate	Sugar	Fudge	Rainbow
2	Irene	Vanilla	Cake	Butterscotch	Chocolate
3	Harry	Strawberry	Waffle	Whipped Cream	

Figure 15: Three ice-cream cones represented as records.

The data table in Figure 15 is very different from a spreadsheet. You might be familiar with spreadsheets because they are often used to store data like this, but spreadsheets are built for calculations, and are actually very clunky and user-unfriendly when used for data. A spreadsheet is just a bunch of cells you can multiply and subtract, format into graphs and move around every which way. A *data table*, which is what this is, has a structure.

A few years ago, I was invited to speak at a national conference on fundraising ethics. I was the president of my company. I arrived to find my nametag, which read: "Jeremy D. Sher, Senior Research Associate." I immediately knew what had happened. Undoubtedly someone had a bunch of data in Microsoft Excel ready for a mail-merge to print nametags. They sorted the records, but they forgot to highlight the correct fields before sorting, and as a result, the names got sorted without the titles. It's a very common error in Excel. It wouldn't have happened if they'd been using a database product. Databases are designed to keep records together, so you never have to worry about getting names and titles mixed up. You can sort records by any criteria you want, but the records will always stay intact—because the software is designed for that.

Databases support multiple tables. Let's say I have a table of ice-cream cones along with a table of people. Here is a table listing with information about some of my friends:

ID	Name	Title	Phone
1	Jeremy	President	(617) 398-SHER
2	Irene	Chairperson	(415) 555-0179
3	Harry	Chancellor	(206) 555-0158
4	Galit	Chief Executive Officer	(860) 555-0137
5	Fred	Senior Research Associate	(202) 555-0116

Figure 16: A table containing records of people.

Now, if you look at the table of ice-cream cones in Figure 15, you'll see that some of my friends (records 1, 2, and 3, to be exact, in Figure 16) have ice-cream cones. Galit and Fred do not have ice-cream cones. Perhaps they are still in line at the creamery. A database program lets you *join* the tables by specifying that there's more information available about the *Owner* of an ice-cream cone by looking up the record with the same *Name* in the People table.[163] Could be useful if the ice cream melted and you needed to notify the owner by phone. Or, you could look at the ice-cream-cones table to see if a given person has an ice-cream cone, and if so, what kind of ice-cream cone they have. A database with tables related in this way is called a *relational database.*

That's it!

That's what a database does.

If you've followed me so far, congratulations! That is all the technical knowledge you need to make responsible decisions about when and how to use a database. Your database professional can explain more complicated issues, and you now know enough to ask them the questions that will help you understand your database.

Databases are for dealing with records: information about people or things in which the fields always need to be kept together. Databases are for tasks like sorting records by one or more fields, asking for a set of records based on criteria, and joining one table to another to look up information like whose ice cream is whose, whose donation is whose, the total amount somebody has donated, which zip codes have the highest or most frequent donors, how your recent blast e-mail did among women, and so on.

If you find yourself sorting and scrolling through spreadsheets to find records that meet certain criteria, try a database. If you find

[163] In practice we use ID numbers to join tables, not text fields like names, because ID numbers are less vulnerable to typos, and there's no reason for users to ever want to change them.

yourself using pivot tables in a spreadsheet, you definitely need a database. It will take some time for database utilization to go the way of "desktop publishing"—from an advanced, specialized skill to a standard office expectation. When we get there, I am convinced our organizations will be significantly more productive.

Choosing a Database Technology

There are many database products available, some specifically for synagogues and many for nonprofits. If I compared specific vendors here, I'd greatly reduce the useful life of my book. I will offer some general tips from my experience as a data professional.

Back in 2000, when I worked in a synagogue office to see if I wanted to be a rabbi, I was not impressed by the database products then available for synagogues. I took another look at them while researching this book, and they've come a long way. There are some great Jewish options out there. The following suggestions apply across the board, to synagogues and to all nonprofits.

Software as a Service (SaaS). An emerging category of software is called *Software as a Service*, abbreviated SaaS. SaaS uses the Internet rather than local computers to store software and data. Every organization has different needs, but I'm comfortable saying with a broad brush that SaaS is simply a better way to do software. If you have a rickety old data server overheating in your closet and you live in fear of power outages, or if you've got mission-critical software installed on an aging desktop computer that you can't upgrade from Windows XP because you'd have to reinstall that software, whose installation diskettes a long-gone office manager misplaced back in 1998—there's no longer any need for any of that.

The idea of SaaS is to charge a relatively low monthly fee for an online system. SaaS products are easily accessible, inexpensive, usually with clean user interfaces, and robustly backed up. They *should* be frequently improved and updated, and stable because their large customer base will catch bugs so that the vendor can fix them. Best of all, there's nothing to reinstall when you upgrade computers: all you need is a web browser to access the system.

Early SaaS pioneers had lean business models dependent on keeping central costs low, so technical support and customer service, which are huge cost centers for web business, lagged behind desktop software vendors. As a result, a consulting industry sprung up around SaaS products. With brand-name vendors now getting into SaaS, you may be able to enjoy the advantages of SaaS with the high-quality customer service provided by larger firms.

Does that mean your data will be stored "in the cloud" if you use SaaS? Yes, and I know some people worry about that, so let's talk about data security. Today's secure servers, accessed through secure Internet connections,[164] are much better suited to prevent unauthorized data access than your nonprofit office, which probably has no expertise in cybersecurity and may suffer viruses now and then. It may be counterintuitive, but your data is much more secure on a SaaS vendor's computer than on your own.

Microsoft Access. I wasn't going to mention specific vendors, but Microsoft Access is a useful everyday office tool. I don't consider or recommend it as a central database solution in most cases. It can seem intimidating at first, and sometimes it isn't the world's most user-friendly product.[165] Having said that, it makes many common office tasks a lot easier once you learn it. For example, if you've ever done the sort-and-scroll dance to retrieve records meeting certain criteria from a spreadsheet (like e-mail addresses of people living in three zip codes), that's quite a headache in Excel but it's a snap in Access, which was built to answer exactly that kind of question.

Nonprofits may be able to buy Access at greatly reduced cost as part of Microsoft Office. Database professionals pooh-pooh it and office professionals ignore it, but I constantly see office managers, accountants, executive directors, fundraisers and all sorts of people trying to wring information out of Excel when Access was built to do what they're trying to do, and does it a lot more easily.

Consider Mission-Specific as Well as Bare-Bones Standard SaaS Products. There are some fantastic SaaS database products out there for synagogues and Jewish organizations. There are also some very bare-bones SaaS products that offer basic lists of people with contact information. The general name for software that deals with information about people, contact lists, contact histories, groupings of people and the like is *customer* or *client relations management*

---

[164] If you see *https://* instead of *http://* in your browser, then you're on a secure connection.

[165] Dear Microsoft: "Reserved error (–1104): There is no message for this error" is not the world's most articulate communications messaging to customers. Please purchase my book and review Chapter 11. A discount is available if you purchase a copy for all Microsoft staff. Yours truly, Rabbi Jeremy Sher.

(CRM). Small organizations may not need much more than a very basic CRM system. In choosing a product, I recommend considering mission-specific vendors (synagogue, political, etc.) alongside bare-bones SaaS CRM systems to compare costs and features.

To go along with those recommendations, here are some common software-vendor pitfalls to watch out for:

Bad Romances. There's a certain business model for small-organization software that I do not care for. These vendors are always there for you when you have no one else—in fact, they're always there for you *because* you have no one else. The products are clunky and buggy, but clients stick with them because the clients lack the operational capacity to switch vendors, or may not know that their experience should be better for the money they're paying.

To find out whether a product is likely to be a bad romance, ask about a vendor's three most recent upgrades and the three features they are working on now. Make sure your data is easily exportable. If you sense displeasure from the salesperson, keep on walking.

If you are unhappy with your database product, it is time to evaluate new options. The field is evolving so rapidly that there are now excellent choices that weren't feasible even five years ago.

Unfavorable Contract Terms. Aside from high prices, vendors have several tricks up their contractual sleeves. The first two items below don't apply to vendors who did large amounts of custom work for you. But I don't think most people reading this book are going to need custom database development.

- *Long Contract Durations.* Don't sign a contract for more than a couple years if you're unfamiliar with the product. You're not hiring a rabbi. Long contract terms are a red flag for a bad-romance vendor. You want to be staying with a product because you like the product, not because you're locked in. As someone who's run three for-profit software companies, I don't see any reason for a vendor to lock you in beyond a couple years, if at all. Again, this is a fast-changing field.
- *Charging Money for Updates.* No. The customer bought the product and they're entitled to updates if the vendor thinks something needs to be updated. It's OK to charge a *reduced* price for a substantially new product, like upgrading from Windows XP to Windows 10, but software companies are

constantly finding and fixing bugs in existing products. There should never be a charge for those fixes, nor for minor feature additions. The vendor should always be maintaining and updating the software they've sold.

- *Charging Money for User Licenses.* Vendors need ways to charge large organizations higher prices than small organizations. That's perfectly legitimate. An early way of doing that was to assess software prices by the number of user accounts, but that was an ill-conceived idea from the beginning. To get around limitations on the number of user accounts, staff just share accounts, which makes everything clunkier and introduces errors. You're better off with a vendor who no longer insists on this silly game. It's a lot more sensible to set price points based on database size.
- *Vendors with a History of Suing their Customers.* I know a few, not specifically within the Jewish community. Do some research, *caveat emptor*.

Extremely Expensive Products. These are marketed mainly to large organizations, but as with so much else in our aspirational economy, they are often marketed to organizations a couple notches too small to need them. These products do everything imaginable, for stratospheric fees. I've worked with organizations with eight-digit budgets who pay more than $200,000 for fundraising software. For most organizations using this book, I think a heavy, intense, way-way-way-over-the-top database contract using today's most powerful technology might cost a quarter of that amount, give or take. But sometimes high-dollar thinking is entrenched at large organizations, so vendors who sell extremely high-priced products make money.

A related peeve is vendors who don't publish their prices. Use the steakhouse rule: if you have to ask, you can't afford it.

Uncle Moe. We met Uncle Moe in the previous essay. The database version of Uncle Moe creates an inordinate number of special features just for you, which look great but, wouldn't you know it, nobody but Uncle Moe will ever be able to maintain, secure, or explain them. I've seen nonprofits paint themselves into Uncle Moe's corner by demanding special features that they think they need. Most nonprofits do not need custom features, as opposed to finding ways to work with standard features.

Data Strategy and Tactics

Our organizations need to be in two-way communication with the world. We talk about getting a message out, but it is two-way conversation that establishes and maintains our relationship with the world, according to our organization's strategy. We speak to the world through mailings, e-mail, websites, social-media postings, advertising and the like. We listen to the world through data.

Listening to data is a strategic matter that goes far beyond your organization's database. It's professional wisdom I gained from my experience in politics. An ideal database would have all sorts of information coded into it, but if you're leading an organization, you'd probably be surprised how much data you know in your head about your database that isn't in your database. There's information about people, particularly socioeconomic and geographical; there's information about the performance of your messages, even if it is anecdotal and not recorded in your database; I'll bet there's a lot more. The following principles will help you listen to your data:

Ask questions. The most common data management mistake I've seen is managers and board members not knowing that they can ask questions, or which questions they can ask. Be curious. Read data-driven reports such as the recent Pew study of American Jews[166] or political data blogs[167] to gain an intuition for the types of questions you can ask. A consultant with data experience may be able to help you find questions relevant to your strategy and communications.

Test, test, test. In terms of data strategy mistakes I've seen, a close second is leaders being extremely persnickety about exactly how their organization's communications have to look and feel. Communications have everything to do with your strategic image, so taking them seriously is wise. But communication is a two-way street. You don't know what works for your audience until you try a number of different ideas. And your audience keeps changing.

---

[166] Lugo et al. (2013).

[167] I don't agree with everything Nate Silver has to say, either on politics or on data science, but his *fivethirtyeight.com* blog provides excellent examples of the kinds of questions data can help us ask and answer. Never mind the politics right now. Just look at the way data characterizes communities, their needs, their hopes, and their likely reactions to messages and policies. I'm also an avid reader of Reid Wilson, Philip Bump and Chris Cillizza at *The Washington Post*, all of whom often use data in their columns.

So be a little looser and branch out a bit. If you're debating two different marketing tactics, divide your audience in half, try both tactics, and see how they do on your metrics. That's a basic version of what is now called *A/B testing*. Political message professionals would tell you they'd be flying blind without A/B testing. You try message *A* and you try message *B*, and see which one does better.

This implies that you need to measure how messages perform. Blast e-mail gives you ready statistics to use as quantitative metrics, such as open rates and clickthrough rates. There are general guidelines about what a "good" open rate is, but I won't repeat them because I've found that membership nonprofits are all over the map. Remember our discussion of quantitative metrics in Chapter 10: we don't have a legitimate basis to compare one organization's open rates against another's, but we can get a sense of your organization's usual baseline open rates and then watch for messages that seem to perform over or under that baseline. Other online media such as websites, Facebook, Twitter, etc., also provide a wealth of useful quantitative metrics. It's a little more complicated, but also possible, to measure the impact of direct mail, print advertising, telephone or other media.

This also implies that data should be part of every strategic decision. Making decisions without data is like talking without listening. If you don't have enough data to know how a message or even a strategic decision is likely to resonate with your members, supporters, opponents, stakeholders or community, do some testing to answer those questions. If you don't have the time or capacity to do that, at least be aware that you're making a decision without data. You can then be open to the decision itself becoming a test.

Intentionally tolerate a rate of data error. Databases obey the principle of decreasing returns to scale: the fewer errors there are in your data, the more expensive it is to find and fix those errors, and to maintain a database without them. In database trainings I used to ask people, "What is your ideal error rate?" Invariably they'd answer zero. They were surprised when I explained that it's an enormous waste of time and money to maintain a database closer than necessary to zero error.

That ideal error rate varies with every organization and is a high-level decision. I was running a political database, and so I was unconcerned, given the expense, about people's names being misspelled as long as mail was going to reach them. A synagogue would want members' names spelled correctly. But every database faces the problem of constantly changing phone numbers and addresses, and of some people leaving and new ones coming in (which is called *churn*). I recommend letting errors come up and be corrected in process. If you don't already do so, send a mail piece with return service requested once a year to change any addresses that come back. It might be nice to do that in conjunction with a more exciting message. For example, a membership organization might use its annual contact-information check as an occasion to reach out personally to each member.

Personalize communications using data. We've heard a lot about "microtargeting" in politics, advertising and solicitations—in which different messages are presented to different people based on information about them. Google ads are a prime example of microtargeting. Current technology enables you to do that if you wish. I recommend hiring a consultant if you want to go in that direction, lest the effort come off as heavy-handed and creepy.

But there's a lot more you can do to genuinely personalize communications. Knowing your audience will help you choose outreach, action, fundraising, community-building and spiritual messages that will resonate with them. Knowing your audience will help challenge assumptions about their lifestyles, preferences, demographics or socioeconomics that may no longer be correct. Knowing your audience keeps you in relationship with them.

Data and the Jewish Community

The Jewish community is at a crossroads. The Pew study slices and dices data to give us a picture of where we are. Few things could be more important to the future of Jewry than understanding this kind of data. Through such data, affiliated and unaffiliated Jews alike are talking to us. They've taken the time to tell us all about their dreams, their disappointments, their values, their needs. Urban Jews, female Jews, Orthodox Jews, Jews of color, Jews in middle-class zip codes who attend synagogue only on the High Holidays, non-Jews living in homes where Judaism is practiced, all are talking to us. They want us to know what's on their minds, how we can help, what they think of us, whether they'd like to be with us, or not, and why. We don't have any lack of information. We just need to know how to listen.

11.5 CONCLUSION

We started this book at the highest level. Before we even got into strategy we discussed what a decision is in the first place, from the very first decision to the cosmic and ethical role of every decision. We worked our way down, through governance structures, leadership, money and management, until we got so deep into details that we found ourselves discussing how databases work.

Now that path has led us right back to strategy. The more we look into the details of our data, the very last section of the very last chapter of a book arranged from high-level to low-level issues, the more we hear those details speaking to us about our highest-level decisions, about our identity, audience, mission and community. When we view high-level decisions through a magnifying glass, we see low-level details. And when we view low-level details through a magnifying glass, we see high-level decisions. Strategy and tactics are not a dichotomy but a cycle—or maybe a spiral.

This book has also been a search for meaning in the Jewish texts we've studied, as we've applied that meaning to issues facing our organizations. Has the Torah offered commentary on our journey into organizational governance, or has our whole journey really been a commentary on the Torah?

Turn it and turn it again.

BIBLIOGRAPHY

Adams, Douglas (1979). *The Hitchhiker's Guide to the Galaxy.* London: Pan Books.

Anderson, David J. (2004). *Agile Management for Software Engineering: Applying the Theory of Constraints for Business Results.* Upper Saddle River, NJ: Prentice Hall.

Anderson, Keith (2015). *The Digital Cathedral: Networked Ministry in a Wireless World.* New York: Morehouse.

Anisfeld, Sharon, Tara Mohr, and Catherine Spector (2003). *The Women's Seder Sourcebook: Rituals and Readings for Use at the Passover Seder.* Woodstock, VT: Jewish Lights.

Bateson, Mary Katherine (1994). *Peripheral Visions: Learning along the Way.* New York: HarperCollins.

Brohaugh, William (1993). *Write Tight: How to Keep Your Prose Sharp, Focused and Concise.* Cincinnati, OH: Writer's Digest Books.

Cirillo, Francesco (2013). *The Pomodoro Technique (Third Edition).* Berlin: FC Garage.

Cohn, Werner (2005). "When the Constitution Fails on Church and State: Two Case Studies." **6** *Rutgers Journal of Law and Religion* 1.2. Available online as pdf: *http://lawandreligion.com/sites/lawandreligion.com/files/Cohn.pdf*, accessed August 4, 2015. Pagination cited in the text is from the pdf.

Duncan, William R., et al. (1996). *A Guide to the Project Management Body of Knowledge.* Newtown Square, PA: Project Management Institute. Note: The first edition is cited; later editions were published in 2000, 2004, 2009 and 2013.

Epstein, Isidore, et al. (1935–1952). *The Babylonian Talmud.* London: Soncino Press.

Fogel, Joshua, and Hershey H. Friedman (2008). "Conflict of Interest and the Talmud." *Journal of Business Ethics* **78** (Issue 1–2, March 2008), pp. 237–246.

Frishman, Elyse D., ed. (2007). *Mishkan Tefilah.* New York: CCAR Press.

Gamoran, Hillel (2001). *Talmud for Everyday Living, Book 1: Employer-Employee Relations.* New York: URJ Press.

Gordis, Robert (1968). *Koheleth, The Man and His World: A Study of Ecclesiastes* (3rd edition). New York: Schocken.

King, Martin Luther. "Where Do We Go from Here?" Atlanta, GA: Speech to the 11th Annual Southern Christian Leadership Conference Convention. Text available online, *http://kingencyclopedia.stanford.edu/encyclopedia/documentsentry/where_do_we_go_from_here_delivered_at_the_11th_annual_sclc_convention/*, accessed August 17, 2015.

Kushner, Lawrence (2006). *Kabbalah: A Love Story.* New York: Morgan Road Books.

Leibowitz, Yeshayahu (1953). "Religious Praxis: The Meaning of Halakhah." Appears in English in Leibowitz, ed. Goldman (1992), pp. 3–29.

Leibowitz, Yeshayahu (1960). "Of Prayer." Appears in English in Leibowitz, ed. Goldman (1992), pp. 30–36.

Leibowitz, Yeshayahu; Eliezer Goldman, ed. (1992). *Judaism, Human Values, and the Jewish State.* Cambridge, MA: Harvard University Press.

Leiner, Mordecai Yosef (1860). *Mei Hashiloach.* (Compiled by students and published posthumously.) Isbitza: Gershon Hanoch. Other editions followed, including the translation into English by Edwards (2001) in this bibliography.

Leiner, Mordecai Yosef, trans. Betsalel Philip Edwards (2001). *Living Waters: The Mei Hashiloach.* Lanham, MD: Jason Aronson, Inc.

Levenson, Jon D. (1994). *Creation and the Persistence of Evil: The Jewish Drama of Divine Omnipotence.* Princeton, NJ: Princeton University Press.

Light, Mark (2001). *The Strategic Board: The Step-by-Step Guide to High-Impact Governance.* New York: John Wiley & Sons.

Lugo, Luis, et al. *A Portrait of Jewish Americans.* Washington, DC: Pew Research Center, 2013.

Mailer, Norman (1955). *The Deer Park.* New York: G. P. Putnam's Sons.

Margalit, Natan (2010). "The God Delusion: Mechanical Thinking and Organic Thinking." Blog post, *OrganicTorah.org, http://organictorah.org/rosh-hashanah-sermon-the-god-delusion-mechanical-thinking-and-organic-thinking/*, accessed August 24, 2015.

Margalit, Natan (May 2012). "The Spiral of Jewish Learning." Blog post, *OrganicTorah.org, http://organictorah.org/the-spiral-of-jewish-learning/*, accessed August 24, 2015.

Margalit, Natan (July 2012). "Truth Sprouts from the Earth." Blog post, *OrganicTorah.org, http://organictorah.org/truth-sprouts-from-the-earth/*, accessed August 18, 2015.

Margalit, Natan (2014). "The Many Stories of Passover." Blog post, *OrganicTorah.org, http://organictorah.org/the-many-stories-of-passover/*, accessed August 24, 2015.

Margolis, Max, et al. (1917). *The Holy Scriptures According to the Masoretic Text.* Philadelphia: Jewish Publication Society of America.

Matt, Daniel (2004–2014). *The Zohar* (Pritzker edition, 9 volumes to date, out of a planned 12). Redwood City, CA: Stanford University Press.

Michaelson, Jay (2009). *Everything Is God: The Radical Path of Nondual Judaism.* Boston: Shambhala-Trumpeter.

Mieder, Wolfgang. *"Making a Way Out of No Way": Martin Luther King's Sermonic Proverbial Rhetoric.* New York: Peter Lang Publishing.

Mueller, Jon (2014). "The Ugli Orange Exercise." Adapted from George Mason University Institute for Conflict Analysis and Resolution. Available online at *http://jfmueller.faculty.noctrl.edu/crow/ugliorangesactivity.pdf*;

part of *Resources for the Teaching of Social Psychology*, website, *http://jfmueller.faculty.noctrl.edu/crow/*, both sites accessed August 20, 2015.

Nonaka Ikujiro (1991). "The Knowledge Creating Company." *Harvard Business Review* **69**:6, pp. 96–104.

Nonaka Ikujiro and Takeuchi Hirotaka (1995). *The Knowledge Creating Company: How Japanese Companies Create the Dynamics of Innovation.* New York: Oxford University Press.

Ohno, Taiichi (1988). *Toyota Production System: Beyond Large-Scale Production.* New York: Productivity Press.

Olitzky, Kerry M., and Avi S. Olitzky (2015). *New Membership & Financial Alternatives for the American Synagogue.* Woodstock, VT: Jewish Lights.

Paulk, Mark C., Charles V. Weber, Bill Curtis, and Mary Beth Chrissis (1995). *The Capability Maturity Model: Guidelines for Improving the Software Process.* Reading, MA: Addison-Wesley.

Peterson, Marilyn (1992). *At Personal Risk: Boundary Violations in Professional-Client Relationships.* New York: W. W. Norton.

Pinker, Aron (2011). "Qohelet 10:10," in *Old Testament Essays* **24**:1, pp. 173–191.

Rosenfeld, Dovid (2008). "The Urgency of Life." Torah commentary, available online at *http://www.torah.org/learning/pirkei-avos/chapter2-20.html*, accessed August 24, 2015.

Rubenstein, Jeffrey L. (2003). *The Culture of the Babylonian Talmud.* Baltimore: The Johns Hopkins University Press.

Sacks, Jonathan (2015). "On Not Obeying Immoral Orders (Shemot 5775)." Blog post, *rabbisacks.org*, *http://www.rabbisacks.org/obeying-immoral-orders-shemot-5775/*, accessed August 27, 2015.

Serenko, A., and Nick Bontis (2004). "Meta-Review of Knowledge Management and Intellectual Capital Literature: Citation Impact and Research Productivity Rankings." *Knowledge and Process Management* **11** (3), pp. 185–198.

Sherman, Robert, and Richard Sherman (1964). "A Spoonful of Sugar." Song, in *Mary Poppins* (film). Directed by Robert Stevenson. Burbank, CA: Walt Disney.

Steinsaltz, Adin (2012). *Koren Talmud Bavli. Volume 1: Tractate Berakhot.* New Milford, CT: Koren Publishers Jerusalem.

Stern, Chaim, ed. (1975). *Gates of Prayer.* New York: CCAR Press.

Stern, Chaim, ed. (1978). *Gates of Repentance.* New York: CCAR Press.

Takeuchi Hirotaka and Nonaka Ikujiro (1986). "The new new product development game." *Harvard Business Review* **64**:1, pp. 137–146.

Tuckman, Bruce W. (1965). "Developmental Sequence in Small Groups." *Psychological Bulletin* **63**, pp. 384–399.

INDEX

In this index, page numbers appearing in **boldface** indicate the page or pages on which the given term is defined in the text.

Made in the USA
San Bernardino, CA
06 March 2017